Dalit Short Story
A Study of three writers in India

Dalit Short Story

A Study of three writers in India

Swati Deepak Chandorkar

KALPAZ

Published by

Kalpaz Publications
C-30, Satyawati Nagar,
Delhi – 110052
Ph.: 011-47034999, 9811692060
www.kalpazpublications.com
E-mail: kalpaz@hotmail.com

Distribution Network

www.gyanbooks.com

India, USA, Canada, UK, Australia, France

ISBN: 978-93-5722-577-9 (HB)
First Published, 2024

Printed at: Gyan Press, Delhi.

DALIT SHORT STORY: A Study of three writers in India
AUTHOR. Swati Deepak Chandorkar

Content

Preface

The present study focuses upon the writers in Indian languages, namely Indian English, Hindi and Marathi. The writers chosen for the purpose are B. Rangrao in Indian English, Ratan Kumar Sambharia in Hindi and Baburao Bagul in Marathi.

This study aims at bringing out salient features of Dalit short stories as literary form and its effectiveness in giving expression to Dalit sensibility. It is an attempt to define Dalit sensibility in literary works of three major writers. Efforts are also made to bring out its relevance to contemporary social situations in India. The study is bound to be an important contribution to understanding literary endeavours of the writers who come from a community which once was oppressed and lived in dehumanised social conditions.

Dalit literature in India is a phenomenon which has caught everybody's attention. It is a literary work of a marginalised class which was once "untouchable". The depressed class was a term used to describe the age-old existence of oppression and despair. The latest term however is "The Scheduled Caste" which states the lowest rank of the caste system in India.

Dalit literature was inspired by the teaching of Dr B. R. Ambedkar who struggled throughout his life to uplift the lives of the untouchables. Dr Ambedkar had insisted upon education to empower the untouchables so that they can rise on a par with others in our social system marked by "Graded Inequality". The movement of Dalit literature began in Maharashtra in the late 1960's and spread throughout the nation within a short span of time. Dalit creative writers are found in all major languages in India including Indian English. Poems and short stories were used as a powerful medium to vent their agony, sufferings and frustration to express creative urges and feelings.

The availability of Dalit literature in Indian English is very less because these were the writers who came from poor uneducated families. Therefore, they did not have access to English education. That is the reason why a large portion of Dalit literature is written in regional languages. Nevertheless, this literature in regional languages is available in English translation. The writers writing in original Indian English are few indeed. B. Rangrao is one of them. His collection of shorts stories ***"Desperate Men and Women : Ten Dalit Short Stories from India"*** is representative of Dalit creativity in Indian English. Baburao Bagul is a major Marathi Dalit writer. He is well known specifically for short stories collected in two volumes. The present study focuses upon ten representative short stories of the writer from the book ***"When I Hid my Caste" (Javha Mi Jaat Chorli Hoti)*** translated by Jerry Pinto. Ratan Kumar sambharia is a well-known writer in Hindi. He has published books on social aspects of the Dalits in Haryana and Rajasthan. His collection of short stories ***"Thunder Storm" (Dalit Samaj Ki Kahaniya)*** translated by Mridul Bhasin, reveals his creativity and is an asset to the movement of Dalit Literature in India. Ten representative short stories of Ratan Kumar Sambharia are taken up for detailed study.

The purpose of this book is as follows :

To comprehend and analyse Dalit short stories which are an expression of anguish and desperation of a community which has been oppressed socially and economically for centuries.

To understand deep and honest confessions of the depressed classes and their vulnerable conditions in the society.

It is also intended to know how these short story writers express their feelings to highlight issues and grievances of the marginalised community and how they utilise these issues as a source of their creativity.

It is hoped that the book will be useful to scholars as well as to the common readers of Dalit sensibility across the world.

Swati Deepak Chandorkar

Acknowledgement

The book is, in fact, a revised version of my Ph.D.Thesis submitted to Shri. Jagdish Prasad Jhabarmal Tibrewala University, Jhunjhunu, Rajasthan. I have received help and assistance from several persons in building up the thesis. First and foremost among them is my guide Dr Anshu Sharma, Professor and Head, Dept. of English, JJT University. Other persons from the university, particularly, Dr Madhu Gupta, Dr Anju Singh deserve special mention. Chancellor of the university, Dr Vinodji Tibrewala, has always been a sources of inspiration. He will remain so always also in future for me and for all students.

I am thankful to my family members, especially to my husband Deepak Chandorkar for his unconditional support and encouragement and to my mother-in-law for her genial love and affection. Arush and Dhruv, my two sons, extended delightful co-operation during my study. I thank them both whole-heartedly.

15th August, 2023

Swati Deepak Chandorkar

Mumbai

Chapter - I

Introduction

A Brief Survey of Dalit Literary Movement

It is believed that Literature is mirror of the society, but in the context of Indian literature, this adage did not take on a concrete form, till the rise of Dalit literature. Dalit society and literature have continually fought for their existence and identity. Dalit literature is committed to preserving these qualities. Dalit literature seeks to establish a more humane and equal society. It focuses on the lowest element of Indian society, the working class, the proletariat, and countless human beings, who have been physically and mentally enslaved for ages due to the *Varna*-system and untouchability. History attests to the reality that from ancient times to the present, the *Shudra* and *Ati-shudras* have been exploited and oppressed. Indian civilisation was enslaved by the *Varna* system, whose corrupt mentality divided people into four *varnas — Brahmins, Kshatriyas, Vaishyas, and Shudras*. The lowest caste was deprived of basic necessities like proper shelter, food and education. Their participation in religious rites and functions was outlawed, and they were forced to serve the higher castes. As a result, they were stripped of all rights and their life were made a living hell. Literature is a reflection of life. Therefore, it was expected that Indian literature should reflect life in general. From antiquity to the present, various manifestations of Dalit consciousness have existed. Dalit society is continuously battling against atrocities and demanding its rights, trying to give rise to its prominence. This was never reflected in Indian literature.

The voice of protest and bitterness in Dalit society is continually shown by Dalit writers through their writings. Many other social and political movements have also sharpened their edges. The Dalit movement's aim is to abolish the *Varna* system and replace it with a social structure that emphasises individual's social, economic, religious, and political liberation and allows society to be judged on the basis of equality. It was through Dalit literature that the Dalits became conscious of their rights and lay the groundwork for a new society to be built upon. The key inspiration to Dalit writing is Dr Bhimrao Ambedkar, who served as an idol to Dalit literature. His foresight and philosophy steered Dalit literature onto a new path, resulting in a new identity. Dr B. R. Ambedkar's ideology is a major source of inspiration for Dalit writers. Contemporary Dalit writing is flourishing as a result of his efforts, and it can be found in a wide range of genres, including poetry, fiction, drama, and autobiography among others. He has paved the way for Dalit literary movement.

To fully understand Dalit literature, one must first understand the meaning of the word "Dalit."

All of those people who were not Aryans were referred to as *Dasa,Dasyu, Shudra, Ati-Shudra*, the Fifth Varna, and the Untouchables in the texts of the Aryans, which are known as the Vedas, the Upanishads, and the Puranas. These were the people who were forced to perform menial labour; they were denied the right to live a life of dignity and were the ones who were perpetually oppressed. It has bean rightly pointed out.

When the Aryans entered India; they had outgrown the stage of tribal endogamy. Among them there were only three divisions of priest, warrior and artisan. 'Varna' in this trivarnic society indicated a particular social function and a distinct level of culture and way of life. The clash between Aryan invaders and the aboriginal inhabitants of India accentuated not only the cultural but even the occupational and functional divisions. A fourth caste, the 'Shudras' came into being. Thus, the society became 'Chaturarnic'.[1] (Tila Kumar)

Dalits were considered as "Outcaste" because they did not have a place in the fourfold caste structure which included Brahmans, Kshatriyas, Vaishyas, and Shudras. The term "Dalit" refers to a person's caste rather than their class. This word first appears in the Rigveda (Purusuha Sukta), and is derived from the Neo-Sanskrit word 'Dalita' and root word 'dal' which means to break, burst, split.

The verse borne out by Taittiriya Brahmana, describes as follows:

Brahmana is a receiver of gifts, a drinker of Soma, Kshatriya a seeker of food and liable to removal at will; a Vaishya is tributary

to another to be lived on by another and to be expressed at will and Shudra is a servant of all others above him to be expelled at will and be slain at will ....[2] (Tila Kumar)

It all appears heinous even at reading. But this is what the so-called 'sacred' scriptures prescribe for a 'harmonious' coexistence of many social groups. The devotion with which the Indo-Aryan community holds this ideal, four-varna structure, is beyond words. They most likely desired to be the undisputed ruler for all time, and in order to do so, religious divinity was linked to *Vedic* and *Upanishadic* literature, legitimising its power. In contrast, when Manu (the author of *Manu Smriti*) was on the scene, he finally released society from the divine constraints, declaring that the "*Vedas* are the single and ultimate sanction of Dharma." The Vedas and the literature based on the *Vedas* did not look back as they filled their pages with deceitful schemes and prejudices, erasing all mention of man-to-man interactions in the process. In the name of *Shudras, Panchamas, Antyajas, Untouchables, Chandalas,* and *Harijans*, and now their modern derivation - the *'Dalits'* the lowest of the wretched creatures on the earth were created and institutionalised.

According to the laws of Manu *(Manusmriti)*, which he had derived from the Vedas-

"From his (Brahma's) mouth he created the priest (Brahmin), from his arms the ruler (Kshatriyas), from his thighs the commoner (Vaishyas) and from the feet the servant (Shudras).[3] (Tila Kumar)

People who have been subjected to centuries of oppression, crushing, and exploitation at the hands of Brahmins and other so-called "upper caste" are referred to by the name Dalit. 'Dalit' describes those people who have been subjected to caste discrimination. A Marathi rebel of the nineteenth century, Jyotirao Phule, upheld the term "Dalit" to refer to the oppressed and shattered members of Indian society who were considered outcastes and untouchables. However, it was only in the 1970s that Maharashtra's Dalit Panthers gave the phrase currency as a reminder of their long history of tyranny and hardship. The term "*Dalit*" in Marathi, much like the term "Black," was selected by the community itself and is proudly used by members of that group. Such a meaning by Dalits themselves replaces names like Untouchables, *Harijans* (named by Narsi Mehta and used by Mahatma Gandhi), Exterior Castes (by J. H. Hutton), Depressed Classes (used by British officials), and Scheduled Castes (used by the independent Indian government).

The word 'Dalit' has been defined by several dictionaries, philosophers, and researchers as follows:

According to Macmillan Dictionary it means "someone who belongs to the lowest caste (= social class) in the traditional Hindu system.[4]

According to the Oxford Dictionary it means "(in traditional Indian caste system) a person who does not belong to one of the four castes in the varna system, in particular a member of the Scheduled Caste.[5]

Molesworth's Marathi-English dictionary states the term 'Dalit' as 'ground, broken or reduced to pieces generally' suggesting all kinds of disabilities - be it social, economic, political or cultural (qtd. in Zelliot 267).[6]

According to Free Dictionary By Farlex, Dalit means "A member of the lowest class in traditional Indian society, falling altogether outside the Hindu caste categories and subjects to extensive restrictions.[7]

According to Dictionary.com Dalit is "a member of the Scheduled Castes in India, sometimes also considered to include a member of any India's Scheduled Tribes.[8]

According to Collins Dictionary the term Dalit refers to "a member of the lowest class in India, whom those of the four main castes were formerly forbidden to touch."[9]

According to Wikipedia, Dalit is "also known as untouchable, is a name for the people belonging to the lowest stratum castes in India."[10]

According to Dr M. N. Wankhede - "the noun Dalit, not only Buddhist or backward peoples are included but also exploited workers. All these different identities are clubbed together in the word 'Dalit' (Gupta, 1988, 15)[11]

Narayan Surve says, "This (Dalit) doesn't mean only Buddhist or backward castes but also whoever suffers in society due to his identity or is being submitted to structural torture" (Gupta, 1998, 3)[12]

Keshave Meshram defines Dalit as "The people who have been tortured for thousands of years, these we have been calling untouchables, only they are Dalits." (Gupta, 1998, 5)[13]

According to A. P. Nirmal, a pioneer of Dalit theology in India, 'the Dalits are (1) the broken, the torn, the rent, the burst, the split; (2) the opened, the expanded; (3) the bisected; (4) the driven asunder, the dispelled, the scattered; (5) the downtrodden, the crushed, the destroyed; and (6) the manifested, the displayed' (139).[14]

Caste is such an important factor that it virtually completely dominates society. The hierarchy may be seen everywhere; but, with the passage of time, it has shown itself in the form of protests leading to movements.

Dr B. R. Ambedkar, a pivotal figure in the Dalit movement, was a trailblazer who spoke out against the inequalities of the existing caste system and was a pioneer in the fight against caste discrimination. Following Jyotiba Phule, he formed a political organisation that advocated for the rights of Dalits. It was the first of its sort to gain widespread acclaim. Writings by the Dalits, who had been neglected by the mainstream literary canon, began to appear in Marathi language during the 1960s. As a result, it started to develop into a symbol of resistance. The term "Dalit" in modern times refers to more than what it did in the past when it was used to describe a certain group of people. Gangadhar Pantwane, a Marathi scholar and the founding editor of the magazine *Asmitadash,* provided the most succinct description of the term Dalit in modern usage. He says —

"To me, Dalit is not a caste. He is a man exploited by the social and economical traditions of this country. He does not believe in God, rebirth, soul, holy books teaching separatism, fate and heaven because they have made him a slave. He does believe in 'humanism'. Dalit is a symbol of change and revolution".[15]

Though the term 'Dalit literature' has contemporary relevance, its origin goes back to medieval time. Madara Chenniah, a cobbler saint in the eleventh century, is thought to have been one of the earliest Dalit authors in history. He lived during the reign of the Western Chalukya and was dubbed as the ***Father of Vachana Poetry*** by certain researchers. Dohara Kakkaiah is another poet who was born as a Dalit, but only six of his confessional poems have made it to the present day.

Impact of Bhakti Movement

The Bhakti movement was largely a socio-religious movement aiming to reform Hinduism. During eighth century BC, two groups in South India started this movement. The Nayanar are Lord Shiva worshippers, whereas the Alvaras are Lord Vishnu devotees. Anti-Brahminical attitudes may be seen throughout the movement. One of the movement's main assets was its use of indigenous languages, which was a slap in the face to the Brahmans, who held a monopoly in Sanskrit. They wrote poetry in regional languages and abandoned Sanskrit, which was solely available to Brahmans. As a result, the campaign was successful in gaining respect for regional languages. Another feature of the movement was the participation of Sufi Muslims. In Hinduism, only Brahmins or members of the higher caste are said to receive *Moksha* or salvation. With the advent of the Bhakti movement, Dalits were welcomed to salvation. This broke down the barriers erected by the upper castes. The saint-poets saw poetry and music as the finest forms of devotion. The Bhakti movement has become a huge phenomenon in the Indian subcontinent because it has given birth to the voices of the masses, as many of the saints were from the non-brahmin castes. Chokhamela, a Mahar saint and poet from Maharashtra, was the most notable. He composed songs that extolled Lord Vittobha's grandeur. *Abhangs* a specific meter, was used by the saint poets in Maharashtra. They employed *abhangs* to convey their opposition to untouchability.

The following is one of the Chokhamela's *abhangs:*

"O Lord, why you put me

In this predicament?

Solve this riddle

For me, please

The Mighty should be

True to reputation

You ought to realise this

On Your own

Out caste that we are

What rights we have

Everyone shoos us

Far away

Chokha says such

Demeaning existence

I am in a dilemma

What should I do?......."

(Translated by Chandrakant Kaluram Mhatre)[16]

In this *abhang* Chokhamela asks Lord Vitthal why he has assigned him such a task, he begs Lord to explain the mystery for him, and he urges him to put himself in the shoes of an outcaste and learn for himself how they are treated and what rights they have. He claims that this is a poor human body that everyone drives away from. He expresses uncertainty about what he can do in such a circumstance. Many saint poets utilised *abhangs* and poetry to convey their dislike for untouchability in this manner. Other bhakti poets like Ravidas, Tukaram, Kabir, etc, composed poems. In contrast to dominant ritualism and intellectualism, they gave expressions to love and devotion. It is both a manifestation of indigenous knowledge and a popular movement. The Bhakti movement is an indigenous people's aggressive, and affirmative approach to their own existence. The Bhakti movement was unable to have influence on a national scale because regional writings were available only in the respective region's native language. However, it casts deep impact on the minds of the people of those regions.

Colonial influence on Dalit education

A major shift took place for the Dalits during British rule in India. According to Anand Teltumbde, the arrival of the British in India aided the advancement and enlightenment of the Dalits, also tore apart the so-called caste system. He says -

"The British colonial rule, which lasted for more than two centuries, had great impact on the caste system mainly in two ways: one, it brought in a Western institutional framework of governance with its army, police, rule of law, judiciary, modern education and new ideals of human rights, democracy and human dignity, and two, capitalism with new technologies and scientific knowledge. It had for the first time impacted the sphere of ideas as well as social production, thereby directly denting the caste system. Although prompted by its own colonial logic and so unintended, it tremendously helped the lower castes in rising against their oppression."[17]

With the arrival of the Britishers job prospects for the Dalits brightened. They joined the British army and showed their military valour by winning several battles for the British. This job helped them financially. It also offered Dalit youngsters with educational opportunities at military schools. This offered the oppressed class hope and opened up new possibilities for advancement and deliverance from repressive life.

"At the start of their reign over India until the Mutiny, the British army was the enthusiastic employer of large numbers of the lowest castes and untouchables. Military service brought not only a steady paycheck to these classes of Indians, but also long-term prospects of advancement. Recruits generally learned English, and the East India Company ensured both soldiers and their families had free access to education. By 1856, a full third of the Bombay army was made up of Mahars, Ambedkar's untouchable caste." (R. K. Kshirsagar.)[18]

British officials had to make up their minds on whether or not to tamper with the Hindu religion and breach the caste system by providing education to Dalits before they could take initiatives. Christian missionaries used Western concepts to criticise the caste system and were instrumental in expanding English education across the nation. This aided Dalits in their educational pursuits and made them more aware of the injustice of the caste system. This also prompted many individuals from the lower castes to abandon Hinduism and embrace Christianity. By the end of 1830, several Christian missionary schools were established in various regions of the nation, but it took about a half-century for education to reach the Dalits and establish itself as a new ethnic asset. Missionary education influenced the mindset of several early reformers. As a result, the colonial authority had a significant impact on the history of Dalits' educational advancements. Education gave them a new perspective on the world, taught them to recognise their place in it, and provided them with the mental fortitude to fight against injustice.

Contribution of Jyotirao Phule for the enrichment of Dalit Consciousness

Modern education was a tool for advancement of human beings and human society in nineteenth century. This occurred to social reformers such as Jyotirao Phule, who understood that if the untouchables were to be raised, they needed to be educated. In the modern era, Jyotirao Phule was the first Shudra educated individual. A product of Christian missionary schooling, he was also one of the first to spearhead the anti-caste movement in India. Christian preachers influenced him. Christian missionaries were lauded by Jyotirao Phule for their efforts, and he considered them as liberators of the lower castes. As an example, he used the imagery of Bali Raja in one of his literary pieces. He wrote:

'Missionaries, followers of Bali raja in the West, that is Jesus Christ, came to this country... preached the true teachings of Jesus among the Shudras (low-caste) and freed them from the deceit and slavery of (caste).'[19]

'God did not create the caste system; it is the result of the upper class's selfishness.' This was the opinion of Phule, who vehemently opposed the Brahmins' cultural monopoly and was the first to educate Dalits about their rights. As a result, He formed the *Satyashodhak Samaj* in 1873, and since the Dalits were being mistreated as untouchables, he authored an incendiary book *'Gulamgiri'* against the caste system and its standards. It wasn't only social slavery that Jyotirao Phule fought against. He envisioned a society founded on liberty and justice for everyone and he strived for the formation of that society. Jyotirao Phule is credited of being the first social reformer to take a radical stance against caste, creed, and the *varna* system. The major goal of his protests was the emancipation and advancement of the Dalit community. He also made his home's water tank available to the Dalits. In Pune, Jyotiba Phule and his wife Savitribai Phule established a school for both Dalit girls and boys. In 1851, he established the first school for the untouchables in Pune.

They believed that education could only raise awareness and thereby improve the lives of the downtrodden classes. Muktabai, a Dalit girl, attended one of the schools established by Phule in Pune. She authored a Marathi article on Mangs and Mahars' pain. *Dnyanodaya* magazine published this piece in 1855. Mukta's essay is the first Dalit women's essay written in India. Muktabai's article criticises the so-called hegemony of Vedic culture while simultaneously encouraging her fellow Dalit youngsters and students to study hard since education alone would be able to end caste-based oppression and empower them. She writes —

"Oh, the Mahars and Mangs, you are poor and sick, only the medicine of knowledge will cure and heal you. It will take away from wild beliefs and superstitions. You will become righteous and moral. It will stop your exploitation. People who treat you like animals will not dare to treat like that anymore. So please work hard and study. Get educated and become good human beings." (Raj Kumar, 105)[20]

Jyotiba Phule's role in the Dalit liberation struggle is priceless. He is also an inspiration to the majority of Dalit authors and Dalit literature as a whole.

Dr B. R. Ambedkar as the paragon of Dalit literature

Buddhism and Jyotirao Phule's intellectual foundation have influenced Dalit writing. However, Dr Babasaheb Ambedkar was the one who developed the fundamental concept of Dalit existence. So it is essential to introduce Dr Ambedkar's work.

Dr B. R. Ambedkar returned to India in 1923, having completed higher education in the United States and in England. After returning to India, he served as secretary to the state of Baroda. He became professor at Sydenham College in Mumbai. Based on his social experiences during this time, he realised that in Indian culture, caste is innate. Furthermore, this caste cannot be altered by education, knowledge, etc. Caste remains with a person till death. In order to elevate the oppressed and disadvantaged

Dalits in the established society, this class must be educated. This class must be compelled to be educated, organised, and equipped for the fight, the battle for self-determination. He established an organisation named 'Bahishkrit Hitkarini Sabha' to raise awareness among the untouchables. He also founded a periodical called 'Bahishkrit Bharat' to support this cause and spread the word via meetings, conventions, etc. He initiated *Satyagraha* in Mahad, Nashik, and Pune in order to provide untouchables access to public places. This gave momentum to the movement against untouchability. By public burning of the *Manusmriti*, he cast off the shackles of *Dharmashastra* and honoured rational thinking. Dr Ambedkar's primary function within Hinduism was that of a social rebel.

The British government hosted the Round Table Conference in 1930. Dr Ambedkar attended this conference as the representative of the untouchables. His work appears to have shifted somewhat as a result of this conference. He advocated for the rights of the Indian untouchables and requested a separate constituency to preserve these rights for the first time at this convention. He was successful in gaining separate constituencies for the untouchables. However, Mahatma Gandhi opposed this cause and protested at Yerawada Jail in 1932. Dr Ambedkar eventually gave up his desire for separate constituency for Dalits, and saved life of the Mahatma. This was the 'Poona Pact' that Mahatma Gandhi and Dr B.R. Ambedkar had signed.

Dr Ambedkar thought that religion should be the cornerstone of human existence. However, staying a Hindu appeared to make it hard to achieve social equality. Therefore, he proclaimed conversion in Yeola in the month of October 1935. At this time, signs of independence started to emerge. In these circumstances, an autonomous organisation was necessary to safeguard the interests of the untouchables. He established the 'All India Labour Party' in August 1936, which was later renamed as 'All India Scheduled Caste Federation'. At the time of independence, an interim government was created. Dr Ambedkar was appointed as the law minister in this ministry. The Indian Constitution was drafted under the chairmanship of Dr Ambedkar. As all other members remained away from the actual work for some reason or the other, the entire responsibility of drafting the constitution fell upon Dr Ambedkar which he carried out with hard work and determination. Therefore, Dr Ambedkar is regarded as the architect of the Indian Constitution. Untouchability was outlawed in India, according to the Constitution. In addition, a legislation prohibiting untouchability in public places was passed. Parliament approved it in

1955. Pandit Nehru entrusted Dr Ambedkar with authoring the "Hindu Code Bill" while he was in the government. The 'Hindu Code Bill' was presented in the parliament by Dr Ambedkar. However, several members of the Congress rose up in opposition to it. As a result, Dr Ambedkar resigned from the government in 1951. In the Lok Sabha elections that took place in 1952, he contested from a reserved constituency in Mumbai. His campaign was unsuccessful. In this election, he had to face defeat. His predilection towards Buddhism became stronger after this loss. He earlier had declared that **"Though I was born a Hindu, I solemnly assure you that I will not die a Hindu".** In 1956, he fulfilled his pledge by becoming a Buddhist initiate. Thousands of his supporters turned to Buddhism along with him, and reconstructed Buddhism as they desired. Conversion, on the other hand, did not resolve the issues of social equality and integration faced by the untouchables. Also, conversion did not solve economic problems of the erstwhile untouchables. However, the conversion brought about thorough change in their attitude towards life in general. They became rebel against Hinduism and discriminatory traditions practiced by it. Today, they are the only community in India who look forward to total social change that will offer liberty, equality and fraternity to every Indian citizen. For democracy to be robust and stable. Dr Babasaheb Ambedkar's thoughts and strong opposition is required. Therefore, he formed the Republican Party of India and instructed his supporters to join a 'Republican Party' since the *All India Scheduled Caste Federation* had lost its relevance. As fate would have it, Dr Ambedkar passed away immediately after this party came into existence.

When we look at Dr Ambedkar's work, we can see that freedom, fundamental rights, and personal growth were crucial in the Dalit liberation movement that he founded. It was through his labour that the Dalit community became more confident and ambitious. He was the first to instil in the Dalit class the notion that they have the same rights as the higher castes have, and that fighting for those rights is their legitimate and moral responsibility. Dalits should employ means such as organisation, educational institutions, revolutionary ideology, power, law and order, politics, social democratic ideals, conversion, and so on to achieve this. He taught them to educate, organise and agitate, also to acquire political power to bring about social change. As for Dalit writers he said —

Through your literary creations cleanse the prescribed values of life and culture. Do not limit your objectives. Remove the darkness in villages by the light of your pen. Do not forget that in our country

the world of the Dalits and the ignored classes is vast. Get to know intimately their pain and sorrow, and try through your literature to bring progress to their lives. True humanity resides there. — Dr B. R. Ambedkar[21]

Dr Ambedkar's life and mission is dedicated not only to upliftment of the erstwhile untouchables in India. A proper understanding of his work reveals that his aim was to steer the nation out of age-old superstition and harmful social customs. His efforts were aimed at improving the social status of every individual, including women. If Indian women today are well-educated and socially free, the credit goes to Dr Ambedkar's broad vision and understanding. His contribution to the making of Indian Constitution is mammoth, — the Constitution which dispels the notion of "graded inequality", and envisions India as a socially and economically free nation where everybody is equal, free and well-educated capable to see "truth as truth and untruth as untruth". Working in a position of authority in British India, Dr Ambedkar initiated several projects and administrative reforms on which India today is firmly standing. It was he whose modern outlook resulted in construction of several dams and water reservoirs which provide drinking water to the Indian population in the midst of the burning heat of summer. It was he whose suggestions on Indian currency resulted in the formation of Imperial Bank of those days renamed as Reserve Bank of India after Independence. It was he, again, whose ceaseless efforts towards modernisation placed India among respectable nations of the world. India will always be indebted to the legacy of Dr B. R. Ambedkar.

In the words of Rangrao Bhongle —

"Dr Ambedkar saved India from being lost into the dreary land of dead habits and customs. His relentless struggle against untouchability and the entire social system placed India among the newly emerging rational community capable of facing challenges of the new world. Working in a position of authority in British India, he initiated the process of modernisation in the various walks of life, and, at the same time, demonstrated the ugly face of tradition when followed blindly. He aspired for democracy with its inherent principles of liberty, equality, social justice and brotherhood, and incorporated them into the constitution, which he believed, is the safest means to run the nation...... His position in India today is like that of a lighthouse offering guidelines to the nation to follow a right course of action......"[22]

Although Buddha and Jyotirao Phule are the driving forces behind Dalit literature, Dr Ambedkar is the actual inspiration behind it. The Dalit literary movement is one of the outcomes of Dr Ambedkar's efforts. His quest for 'Samyak Kranti' gave birth to Dalit literature. As a result, the fundamental influence for Dr Ambedkar's worldview resides at the heart of this literature. Also, Jyotirao Phule, Rajarshi Shahu Maharaj, the Marxist ideology, and other figures have had some effect on the literary movement. The Dalit communities, which were unfortunate enough to experience deprivation on all levels, was given identity for the first time. As a result of Ambedkar's ideas and the battle for human freedom that he began, Dalit philosophers and authors were inspired and began to highlight their place in society. Dr Ambedkar's ideas were a significant source of inspiration for Dalit writers, and Dalit literary movement as a whole.

Dr Ambedkar's views on literature can be summarised thus: Literature that promotes social life and national life is needed today. Our country is in dire need of unity and brotherhood. Unity and brotherhood should be the core of our nation. Without it, a strong team will not be formed. Therefore, it is essential for humanistic literary art to be born. For this, a wave of nation-friendly revolution should rise in the field of literature. Lately, the edges of literature have turned black. The crop is plentiful but it is useless. Therefore, writers should be cautious and cultivate the values of life and culture through literature. So I want to tell the writers: discover your noble life value, cultural value through your literary creativity. Don't limit your goals. Make it huge. Don't keep your voice to the four walls. Struggle to uplift the life of the neglected and miserable community in the country. That is true humanity.

This influenced Dalit writing. The personality of Dr Ambedkar was as fiery as the sun. He fought against injustice and inhumanity towards Dalits to the very end. At the same time, he emphasised the need for identity. In this manner, he demonstrated the path to Dalit upliftment. While describing Dr Ambedkar's efforts towards humanity, Namdeo Dhasal, the renowned Dalit poet, has written in one of his poems—

Turning their backs to the sun, they journeyed through centuries;

Now, now we must refuse to be pilgrims of darkness.

That one, our father is bent from carrying,

Now we must lift that burden from his back.

Our blood was spilled for this glorious city

And what we got to eat was stones.

Now, now, we must explode that building which kisses the sky!

After a thousand years we are blessed with a sunflower- giving fakir;

Now, now, we must, like sunflowers, turn our faces to the sun.[23]

(Tyanchi Sanatan Daya)

In this poem, Namdeo Dhasal refers to the Dalit communities as "pilgrims of darkness," an allusion to the Dalit communities' long history of caste inequality in society. Dr Babasaheb Ambedkar is referred to as their liberator, and he is called "The Sunflower Giving Fakir."

Dr Babasaheb Ambedkar demonstrated to the Dalits how to break free from the awful, unfair cycle of tradition. Human dignity was important to him and it was of ultimate value. Dalits' sense of self-identity as 'Human beings' was reawakened. All of his life, he aspired for liberty, and he worked hard to achieve it. As a result, his personality became role model for Dalits. He became the Dalit community's identity and dignity. In a nutshell, the whole 'Ambedkarism' or Dr Ambedkar's ideology can be claimed to be the only source of Dalit Literary Movement others being less important.

Influence of Dalit Panther upon the Dalit writings

The Dalit Panther Movement began in the early 1970s by a group of Mumbai's slum youths who were inspired by Dr Ambedkar, Raja Dhale and Namdeo Dhasal, two of India's most prominent writers and poets initiated the movement. They were later joined by J V Pawar, Arun Kamble, Ramdas Athavale, and others. This movement was in response to the Black Panthers' civil rights and anti-racism campaigns in the United States of America. Anger was stoked by recent atrocities committed against Dalits, such as an incident in Pune district where a Dalit woman was stripped and paraded. In Akola district, two Dalit men had their eyes gouged out. The Ilaya Perumal Committee had documented the atrocities faced by the Dalits. It was in reaction to these atrocities against Dalits in Maharashtra that the Dalit Panther movement came into being spontaneously and with great power. It changed the political landscape of the state and had a significant impact on Indian Dalit politics.

The fearlessness of the leaders, as well as the incendiary revolution, had drawn a huge number of young Dalits to Dalit Panther. Unemployed youngsters in the slums and members of the educated middle class lent their support to the movement. As a result, the Dalit Panthers had become a belligerent and persistent group. The Dalit Panther movement had its beginnings in Maharashtra's urban areas. Eventually, this movement expanded to rural regions as well. Furthermore, the Dalit Panther movement extended to states including Gujarat, Karnataka, Andhra Pradesh, and Uttar Pradesh. Panther played a significant part in resolving the issue of landless Dalits and also opposed the prevalent feudal and caste systems in the villages.

The Dalit Panther united the Scheduled Castes and Scheduled Tribes, the Buddhists, the working masses, the workers, the impoverished peasants, and the agricultural labourers to bring about an all-encompassing economic, political, and social revolution. They desired to establish a class of workers' groups for the economic advancement of the oppressed.

Dalit Panthers' contributed significantly to the drive to rename Marathwada University. They battled to address the Dalits' fundamental necessities and get justice for them. They vigorously protested against the atrocities on Dalits. They organised and raised awareness among Dalits. However, the collapse of the Dalit Panther hindered the Dalit movement's momentum. Dalit Panther imbued the Dalits with confidence and motivated them to fight without fear. In light of this, the role of Dalit Panther is crucial to the Dalit struggle.

The rise of Dalit literature was one of the effects of the Dalit Panther movement. Several Panther leaders were writers themselves. They argued that Marathi writing should depict the suffering, rebellion, and ambitions of the Dalit class, in contrast to traditionalist, caste-egoistic, anti-socialist tendencies. Thus, the development of Marathi Dalit Literature was facilitated. When the movement expanded, it led to rise in Dalit writing in places where it took root. To provide one example, the Dalit Panther campaign in Gujarat has led to Gujarati Dalit literary works. The Dalit Panther movement in Gujarat produced revolutionary Gujarati poets like Neerav Patel, Harish Manglam, Madukant Kalpit, Joseph Makwana, Raman Waghela and others. The Dalit Panther movement had a direct impact on an increasing number of writers throughout India, and these authors eventually formed a part of Dalit literary group. So, they began to express their sentiments in poems, short tales, novels, and memoirs. A alternative narrative in Indian literature was thus created by the Dalit Panther. As a result, the field of Dalit literature has established itself as a distinct entity in Indian culture.

Motivation of Dalit writing

Self-awareness and self-realisation

The movement of Dalit literature focuses on self-discovery via self-respect which is indicated by a Marathi term - *"Asmita"*. The Dalit literary movement sprang from Dr Ambedkar's Dalit liberation campaign. The Dalit movement's principal goal was to give dignity to man as a man. For many years, established religious rules and the traditional philosophy had denied the *Shudra* and *Ati-shudras*. The Dalit castes were deprived of self-respect due to the diverse social structure at all levels. Babasaheb Ambedkar and his movement taught them to live with self-respect. His thought was guided by the ethos of education. They questioned their very existence. Financial concessions were less significant to Dalits than self-esteem. Poverty is no longer an issue. Economic success does not always imply self-respect. Understanding what self-esteem is to open the doors to eradicate poverty. That is why Dalit literature expresses this consciousness of self-respect. Thus, the major goal of the Dalit liberation movement is to give an individual self-respect and dignity, *'asmita'* as it is called in Indian languages.

Refusal to Canonical Norms and Thinking

Untouchability is a stigma and the Dalit class should wipe it off with its own blood. At the core of Dr Ambedkar's idea is the creation of self-awareness among the Dalits, and removal of any barriers to self-respect. Religious conventions, customs, and social systems should be rejected in Dalit writing. Dalit literature rejects anything that stands in the way of denying slavery, exploitation, imposed by tradition. Any rebel movement's credo is to reject a deeply ingrained, unfairly formed order in society. Dalit literary moment rejects all that is canonical and unjust.

Revolt Against Tradition and the System

In Dalit literature, rejection and revolt are two aspects of 'self-esteem.' Dalit literature has adopted a defiant stand against Indian bourgeois values. It's a revolt against its own people. Dr Ambedkar's Satyagraha of 'Chavdar Lake' in Mahad or the Satyagraha of 'Kalaram Temple Entrance' in Nashik are the examples. Despite such satyagrahas, the Dalits were denied equal rights. In such circumstances, there was no option except to pursue punitive measures. In ***Dalit Sahitya: Vedana and Vidroh*** (Dalit Literature: Pain and Revolt) by Dr Bhalchandra Phadke offers elaborate justification to the Dalit revolt –

"Our strategy is to climb. We don't ask for anything out of humility. The objection is against us that it makes even those who are in favour of untouchability unfavourable. But I think those who make such objections should be ashamed, even if they are not of the people. Who in the world is as humble and helpless as the untouchables? Have we not remained humble for centuries? Didn't we stay humble in the miserable and poorest conditions of our life? Please do not teach us the lesson of humility and modesty. Teach it to the upper castes now. With the help of requests, petitions, delegations, it would be possible to get the lost liberties and oppressed rights, then the people of the oppressed class would have become the kings of Hindustan by now and Hindu Dharmasatta would have been seen working in the houses of untouchables! We don't have a habit of arrogance, or we don't have a tendency to be arrogant? How to get two morsels for your stomach by working hard all day is our daily motive. But we fell into this trap as humanity is superior to bread. Because the door does not open without knocking and even the basic rights of humanity do not get to your hands without being snatched."[24] (self.trans.) (p. 64)

Aforementioned ideas led to self-awareness and self-discovery through literature, also their rejection of the existing system and creation of new a one.

The development of Dalit literature may be seen in the two-tier battle that today's educated Dalit youth confront. The conventional Indian system has dimmed the brains of the higher castes, just as it has dimmed the minds of the Dalits. On the one hand, they must fight with their kin, on the other, they must fight with the established society. As a result, the character of the revolution becomes two faceted. Shankarrao Kharat's article ***Ek Sangharsh***, for example, is a narrative based on the life of Gopal Khandu Nandiwala. In the story ***Chindhya*** by Madhav Kondwilkar, Ragho's son Dajihas to fight against his father, which says that he is superior to Buddha. He also has to fight against the unfair untouchability placed on the Chamar community by Hindu culture. Paru has to battle against caste prejudice in the untouchable circle itself in Datta Bhagat's one-act play 'Ekti,' just as she has to fight against all the students with rowdy inclinations. The play emphasises the contentious truth that the caste against whom the Dalits are fighting is still enslaved by itself. It never goes.

The revolt depicted in Dalit literature is mostly against the system that strives to keep Dalits enslaved by declaring religion, norms, traditions, and culture, among other things, to be holy and superior. The revolution is directed against the system, against those who accept it and indirectly contribute to preserve it. It also attacks the newly educated Dalit's white middle-class aspirations which seem to have appeared in some section of the Dalit community. If the attitudes of the white middle class infiltrate the newly educated Dalit community, the Dalit movement's basic character would be crushed. The insurrection in Dalit writing is something to bear in mind. It is not directed against a specific individual caste, religion or tribe; rather, it is directed at the system as a whole. This uprising is not meant to be against a class or caste, but rather to defend the necessity for humanity and self-respect of every individual.

Human Suffering and Its Reflection Today

The Dalit is not considered as 'man' in Indian society even today. He is, in fact, treated worse than animals. The Indians developed the exploitative *Chaturvarnya* system at many levels of life, such as social, political, religious, economic, etc. This system constituted the fourth caste as Shudra. They were compelled to live outside the community. The existing system denied them education, status, identity, and so on. As a result, Dalit writers campaigned against the existing system for social change, claiming that 'humanity' is of the utmost importance. They voiced their anguish at the old religious system's rejection of humanity to the oppressed class. Shankarrao Kharat's short story ***Daundi*** depicts the hardship of Dalits, who are not acknowledged as human beings.

I have no one here, brother! I'm not here to call anyone's guts. I have no choice but to live in this village. I've zipped my lips and fastened shackles to my hands and feet, and I'm labouring like a slave day and night for the sake of my wife and children.[25] (self.trans) (p.71)

Ideological Support of Buddha, Phule and Ambedkar

Dalit Movement and Dalit Literature display respect for ideologies formulated by the Buddha, Phule, and Ambedkar. They are the ones who have fought against the exploitative system and for the dignity of man. Their activities have also targeted the mindset of the higher castes, which sustains the caste system. They were the ones who proposed the concept of an egalitarian society. According to Buddha, 'man' is of the essential value, and he denounced caste and untouchability as forms of social inequity. The societal virtues of equality, liberty, justice, and morality form the foundation of the Buddha's thought. Dalit literature has similar ideals. The Dalit community has embraced Dr Ambedkar's reintroduction of Buddhism. Thus, Buddha and his ideas are at the foundation of Dalit literature. In Dalit literature, the etymology of revolt, denial, and mythology seems to have originated in the works of Jyotiba Phule. Phule seems to have influenced both the Ambedkarite and pre-Ambedkarite communities. Poets and artists who wrote plays, tamashas, ballads, shayari, poetry-songs, etc., based on this inspiration. Among them are Baba Valangkar, Shivram J.V. Kamble, Pandit *Kondiram*, Kisan Phagu Bansode, and others.

Although Dalit life and writing have been influenced by the work of Buddha and Jyotiba Phule, Dr Babasaheb Ambedkar's ideas and actions are the true source of inspiration for them. Dr Ambedkar arrived as 'Revolutionary Sun' in the dismal lives of the Dalits. He is like 'Koti Surya', 'Hirva Surya', 'Vidrohi Surya', 'Krantisurya' etc. Dr Ambedkar rebelled against diverse, casteist social systems and the fourfold social structure, caste discrimination, and untouchability, which deny humanity to the Dalits. His battle for Dalit emancipation spawned and influenced the development of Dalit literature. He thereby became the father of Dalit literature. He became the first rebel author and a significant source of inspiration for Dalit writings.

In a nutshell, Jyotirao Phule influenced Dalit literature through advocacy of individual freedom, anti-untouchability and anti-caste thinking. He gave a new vision of life, a feeling of self-respect and self-discovery. Dr Ambedkar influenced the writing of Dalits and his lifetime journey has become a source of inspiration of Dalit literature as a whole. Thus, Lord Buddha, Jyotirao Phule, and Dr Ambedkar are the three inspiring stalwarts to Dalit writings.

Expression of Collective Sensibility

Every piece of art is the product of individual sensibility. The sensation represented through art is a subjective one. The experience of a person at the level of production in Dalit literature, on the other hand, is both subjective and social, because he is a representative of the society which has been tormented by unfair, varied manners. Exclusion of religion, customs, traditions, and so on is a part of this society's experience. As a result, when a Dalit writer writes about his experiences, he is writing about the experiences of his community as well as his personal experience. Thus, every Dalit literary work expresses collective consciousness of the Dalit community.

Literature of Commitment

The term "commitment" literally means "dedication to a certain task." One of the definitions of commitment is the willingness to communicate one's sentiments openly and honestly towards a goal. This commitment is linked to the author's creative consciousness. Dalit autobiographies, particularly, show the innovation of self-realisation and devotion to the social cause.

The commitment shown in Dalit literature is also in the backdrop of the suffering and misery experienced by the oppressed classes, such as religious and social inequity, living a life worse than that of an animal, and it also shows the way of light offered in the shape of Dr Ambedkar and others. In the context of Dalit literary culture, for example, the term "commitment" must be read differently. Dr Bhalchandra Phadke says —

'Today Dalit literature is rejecting something because it has embraced something important, Man of utmost importance, according to Dalit literature, and his reputation is the most valuable asset. So, rather than proclaiming man's greatness, Dalit literature is compelled to criticise a society that continues to tolerate high-low, racial pride, and religious supremacy among the people.'[26] (self.trans) (p.73)

Dalit literature, stands for social equality. As a result, it condemns discrimination based on birth, religion, or other factors. The expectation that man should be treated equally is prominent. No one should be treated unjustly because of his religion, caste or social position. That is, it opposes slavery and promotes liberty. The goal of Dalit literature is to promote man's freedom, equality, fraternity, and justice. The conventional system needs to be abolished in order to achieve this. Only then can the individual's dignity be preserved. As a result, Dalit literature exposes the Dalit community's struggle and pains while expressing the hope for peaceful co-existence among all human beings.

Scientific Outlook

The Dalit literary movement examines the idea of 'religious' intellectually. God is a concept that Dalit literature rejects and adopts a scientific perspective as a goal. Ambedkarism is a form of humanism that emphasises human values. It is a staunch believer in rationality. Science is a component of Buddhism since that is where it all began. Ambedkarism, like Lord Buddha, denied the concept of God, soul, and so on. Worshipping God, jurisprudence, and its doctrinal teaching have been rejected by Dalit Literature. According to Raosaheb Kasbe :

> **"Wisdom, humility, compassion, and friendship**
> **are all characteristics of Ambedkarism.**
> **Impermanence, modesty, atheism,**
> **and scientific attitude is Ambedkarism**
> **Acceptance of rationalism, compassion, speed, logic,**
> **and intellectualism is Ambedkarism"[27] (self.trans) (p. 75)**

Dalit literature was motivated by Dr Ambedkar's campaign against untouchability. It is seen as literature associated with the Dalit struggle. Untouchability was a kind of exploitation against humanity. Such exploitation always exists in some form or another. Therefore, relevance of Dalit literature remains intact. In the history of Marathi literature, Dalit literature has a significant role. Marathi Dalit literature has had an effect outside of Maharashtra as well. Bhalchandra Nemade explains how Dalit literature has spread throughout the nation:

'Maharashtra's leaders have influenced individuals from other Indian states since Mahatma Gandhi's time. We may also claim that Dalit writing has revitalised it. In the history of Marathi literature, Dalit literature is a significant event. Taking Marathi Dalits authors as role models, Gujarati, Kannada, and Northern Dalits began writing confidently in their regional languages. Maharashtra's Dalit movement, which has extended throughout the nation, is genuinely astonishing. In Maharashtra, no other caste has accomplished such a wonderful performance in the twentieth century.'[28] (self.trans) (p. 75)

Thus, Bhalchandra Nemade has critically examined Dalit movement and literature in exact terms. He has also illustrated Dalit literature's contribution to the history of Marathi literature.

Forms of Dalit literature

The purpose of Dalit writing was to express sorrow, agony, suffering, and outrage. Kisan Faguji Bansode, Shivram Janba Kamble, Gopal Baba Valangar, Pandit Kondiram, Kerubuwa Gaikwad, etc. were among those who vehemently attacked the rituals, norms, and traditions of Hinduism. Dr Ambedkar had awakened the Dalit community later on. Consequently, the literary works were more successful and produced the desired effects. Dalit writing became more successful after Babsaheb's death, as his followers had become more combative and sincere in their ideology after his *mahaparinirvan*.

Dalit literature is written in various genres. Several forms of literary expression were successfully handled by these writers. The most prominent form, however, is poetry. Other forms like drama, fiction (including story) were also written. Annabhau Sathe, Shankarrao Kharat, and N.R. Shende have written skillful short stories. Later, Baburao Bagul's short story collections ***When I Hid My Caste*** and ***Death is Getting Cheaper*** sparked a literary revolution in Marathi language.

Authors like Bhimsen Dethe, Yogiraj Waghmare, Vaman Howal, Amitabh, Yogendra Meshram, Arjun Dangle, Ravindra Hadsankar and Bhaskar Chandanshiv have added to the richness of Dalit stories. B. Rangrao's collection of short stories in Indian English was a later development and is equally important.

Autobiography in Dalit literature has been regarded as a significant genre that conveys the actual, rich experiences of Dalits. Autobiographies by Dalit authors depict plight of the lower castes as inhumane treatment was meted out to them by the higher castes. There are remarakable Dalit autobiographies like ***Balut*** by Daya Pawar, ***Mukkam Post Devache Gothane*** by Madhav Kondvilkar, ***Athvaniche Pakshi*** by P.E. Sonkamble, ***Taral Antarai*** by Shankarrao Kharat, ***Fanjar*** by Nanasaheb Zodge, ***Gavki*** by Rustum Achalkhamb etc. These were followed by a series of autobiographies by Dalit women writers,***The Picturesque Story of Life*** by Shantabi Kamble ***The Way We Live*** by Baby Kamble, ***Antsphot*** by Kumud Pawade, ***Aidan*** by Urmila Pawar, ***Closed Doors*** by Mukta Sarvgode, Malika Amar Sheikh's ***I Want To Destroy Myself*** had created sensations during those days because it exposed the inner working of the Dalit Panther, headed by her husband Namdeo Dhasal.

Novel is yet another rich literary genre of Dalit writings. There are remarkable novels by such writers like Annabhau Sathe's ***Warnecha Wagh, Fakira, and Makadicha Mal***, Shankarrao Kharat's ***Hatbhatti, Mi Mukth! Mi Mukth!, Gavacha Tinopol Guruji,*** Keshav Meshram's ***Hakikat Ani Jatayu*** and ***Pokharan,*** N.R. Shende's ***ShrungarlelaPret***, Namdev Whatkar's ***Apradhi Ani Solah Shringar,*** Namdev Dhasal's ***Hadki Hadavla***, Baburao Bagul's ***Sud,*** Ashok Whatkar's ***Melela Pani*** and Bhimsen Dehte's ***Iskot.*** B. Rangrao has also contributed significantly to Dalit novel by writing three remarkable novels, namely ***Soma,Timirangan*** and ***Eka Amurtachi Gost***.

Writing drama has proven to be a rewarding experience for Dalit authors. There was, in fact, a movement of Dalit theatre for sometimes. Preman and Gajvi and Datta Bhagat are two prominent Dalit playwrights. Gajvi's ***Ghotbhar Pani*** and Bhagat's ***Wata Palwata*** are considered as classics in Dalit theater. Kerubuwa Gaikwad's ***Yugayatra,*** Prabhakar, Ganveer's ***Naukarichya Jalat***, Gangadhar Pantawane's ***Manuskiche Band***, Prakash Tribhuwan's ***Thamba Ramrajya Yetay***, Ramnath Chavan's ***Bamanwada*** N.V. Wagh's ***"Mrigaj," "Sharan Mi Buddhala,"*** and ***Bundalbaaz,*** as well as ***Aga Je Ghadalechi Nahi*** by Yogiraj Waghmare are some other plays. Recently, ***Dhadant Khairlanji*** by Pradnya Pawar and ***Underground via Bhimnagar Mohalla*** by Rajkumar Tagade had created sensations among the theatre goers. A serious study demonstrates that Dalit theatre is expanding in terms of literature and theatre.

Dalit literature moved beyond Maharashtra as new social awareness spread across the nation. Mohandas Nemish Rai, Omprakash Valmiki, Shoraj Singh Bechain, Ratankumar Shambhariya, and other Hindi Dalit authors have made significant contributions to Hindi Dalit literature. Dalit writers in Gujarati include Nirav Patel, Joseph Macwan, Mohan Parmar, Harish Mangalam, Mangal Rathod, and others. Dalit works became well-known in languages like Punjabi, Tamil, Telugu, Kannada, Malayalam, and Bangla. As the Dalit awareness grows, the Dalit literary movement gets stronger in all major Indian languages. Today, it occupies the centre stage and is a popular topic of study both in India and abroad.

In Dalit literature, poetry is seen as a significant literary form. It emerged with encompassing sufferings, rebellions, denials, etc. This genre has a unique position in literature due to grandeur of expression. It plays a significant part in bringing Marathi poetry from the realm of fantasy to the realm of reality. As a result, Marathi poetry was reawakened, and entered a world where unknown facets of reality were exposed.

Dalit Poetry

Dalit poetry forms an important chapter in the history of Marathi literature. It is new and significant to the readers of poetry. Dalit poetry is produced in abundance. Dalit poets seem to have prioritised ideological motivations above literary rules. After 1960, Dalit poetry became incredibly powerful and motivating. It was poetry about human experiences, sufferings, joys, and pains.

The new awareness entered the Dalits' hearts and enhanced their views. During Ambedkar's lifetime, several poets composed socially conscious poems, and they were the ones who communicated

Ambedkar's ideas to the masses. Through Dalit poetry, awareness of injustice, oppression in history, and revolt against the pathetic life of ancestors started to emerge. Dalit poets, were motivated by the profound philosophy of the Dr Ambedkar. This was undoubtedly owing to the plight of people whose lives were being wrecked and who were fighting for their rights.

Poets like Namdeo Dhasal, Keshav Meshram, Waman Nimbalkar, Tryambak Sapkale, Daya Pawar, Yashwant Manohar, Umakant Ranveer, Arun Kamble, Ramakant Jadhav, Prakash Jadhav, Pralhad Chendvankar, Arjun Dangle, Ravichandra Hudsankar, Dharmaraj Nimsarkar, Baban Chahande, Damodar More, B. Rangrao, Meena Gajbhiye, Hira Bansode, Jyoti Lanjewar, Mallika Amar Sheikh, Bhimsen Dethe, Pragya Pawar, etc. contributed to the realm of Dalit poetry. They developed a paradigm focusing on humanity. These writers expanded the significance of Marathi poetry by broadening its boundaries. The works of Dalit poets are infused with Ambedkarite ideas. As a result, Dalit poetry now makes the reader introspective and compels them to ponder. Even now, the condition of Dalits has not improved. Consequently, these poets may be seen striving day and night for creating social awareness.

First Generation of Dalit Poets

During a period when prejudice was rife, Dr Ambedkar encouraged and inspired Dalits. During this period, the first generation of Dalit poets penned poetry that expressed tyranny and injustice against Dalits. The rebellious nature of their poetry was apparent.

Earlier poets also attacked inhuman customs and tradition in Hindu religion. It was, however, after Dr Ambedkar's *mahaparinirvan* that Dalit poetry flourished and spread far and wide. It assumed the form of movement. Newly educated Dalit youths began to express their sentiments through poetry. This poetry is remarkable for its assertiveness, anger and protest. They also wrote about misery and wretchedness that surrounded their lives. These poets disregarded the canonical norms of poetry and demanded different norms to be adopted to appreciate their works. These poets, generally regarded as first generation of Dalit poets after Independence, include Namdeo Dhasal, Keshav Meshram, Daya Pawar, Tryambak Sapkale, Yashwant Manohar, Waman Nimbalkar, Arjun Dangle and others.

Namdeo Dhasal the most notable among the first generation of Dalit poet's after Independence, was a taxi driver in Mumbai. He spent considerable time of his life in a locality called ***Golpeetha,*** the red

- light area in South Bombay /Mumbai and brought out a book of poems called **'Golpeetha'** itself. The poems in this collection gave an altogether different turn to the history of Marathi poetry. The poems are remarkable for their innovative style and bold new subject-matter. Total rejection of history and tradition by the Dalit literary movement is indicated by the following lines by Namdeo Dhasal -

Plato Einstein Archimedes,

Socrates Marx Ashok Hitler-Bitler Camus

Sartre Kafka Baudelaire Rimbaud Ezra Pound

Hopkins Goethe Dostoevesky Mayakovsky Maxim

Gorky Edison-Medison Kalidas Tukaram Shakespeare

Dnyaneshwar. Who are they?

I throw them away into the gutter-man-hole.[29]

— (Golpeetha)

Subsequently, Dhasal published seven collections of poems, but his reputation as a rebel - poet rests mainly on ***Golpeetha***.

Daya Pawar's ***Kondwada***, the collection of his poems, depicts the sufferings, agonies, protest and anger inherent in the movement of Dalit poetry. Pawar's autobiography ***'Balut'*** is a graphic account of the wretched life of the Dalits in India. Keshav Meshram was a poet, novelist and literary critic. His first collection of poems, ***Utkhanan***, is remarkable for protest and anger. Waman Nimbalkar's ***Gaokusabaheril Kavita*** is yet another landmark in the history of Marathi Dalit poetry. Yashwant Manohar is a poet and critic whose collection of poems ***Utthangumpha*** is an important contribution to the gamut of Dalit poetry. Other poets of the time include Tryambak Sapkale, Arjun Dangle, J. V. Pawar, Prahlad Chendvarkar, Prakash Jadhav and others.

Women poet's contribution to Dalit Poetry in Marathi is equally remarkable. Notable among them are Hira Bansode, Jyoti Lanjewar, Surekha Bhagat, Pradnya Pawar, Sandhya Rangari and others. Dual suffering of Dalit women - being women and untouchable - is well brought out in the works of these poets. Hira Bansode writes about her plight through the following lines -

What kind of life is this? A woman I am -

and Untouchable too.

My hopes and expectations lay shattered.[30]

— (Phoenix)

Second generation of Dalit poets in Marathi move a little ahead from those in first generation after Independence. These men as women are better placed in life as they had jobs in hand due to reservation and had a regular source of income. However, they are surrounded by their kinsfolk who are the worst victims of casteism. These educated young men and women are tortured within because they are constantly reminded of history and the inhuman treatment meted out to their parents. Consequently, their anger and protest sharpened and they speak out in a language which is moving and piercing at the same time. These lines by Ram Dotonde for example -

The vows that you and me repeat

have no potentials-

Reaching out to horizon

Doesn't bring the sky in range

We better do one thing -

Let's tear apart the caste itself.[31]

— (Galli Badalalela Morcha)

Other remarkable poets of this group include Baban Chahande, E. M. Narnaware, Bhimsen Dethe, Damodhar More, B. Rangrao, Yuvraj Sontakke, W. Kapoor, and others.

The uncertainties of poetic diction and style which the earlier poets faced disappeared now as these poets found themselves in much comfortable social position. Their poetic art reveals confidence and total control over the medium they handle. Most of them had received higher education and became acquainted with the movement of Black literature in America, Marxist literary theory, New literature in English etc. Therefore, their poetry offers deeper and larger human understanding and, at the same time, remains deeply rooted in Dalit poetic sensibility. They write about such international figures like Nelson Mandela, refer to the Harlem Renaissance and seek inspiration from Marxist ideology. This makes their poetry profound and their ideology more relevant.

There was a time when Dalit literary movement appeared stagnant. But it never lost its relevance. It spread out in other parts of the nation and in other Indian languages. Hindi, Gujarati, Tamil, Malayalam, Kannada, Telugu, Punjabi languages revealed potentials for Dalits literary sensibility and produced remarkable Dalit writers like Meena Kandaswami, Bama, Siddhalingayy, Lal Singh and others besides those in Marathi, Gujarati and Hindi languages.

Dalit scenario since the last twenty years has changed considerably. The socio - economic changes have brought about transformation in the life of the erstwhile untouchables; Untouchability has been abolished constitutionally, although it exists in the minds of the caste - Hindus. Wide spread of education and democratic values have created larger awareness among the Dalits. These factors have brought about changes in Dalit literary trends. There are certain regions in India where the Dalit community is on the forefront in every walk of life. In Maharashtra, the home state of Dr Ambedkar, they are combative, assertive and educationally, on a par with the so-called high caste people. In other states like West Bengal and Kerala the communists ideology has made them largely aware of the unjust social reality. Other southern states where Ramswami Periar, and others enlightened souls have steered the Dalit community out of the middle-age mentality, social situation is much better than what it used to be fifty years ago. In Northern states, however, no remarkable changes are noticed. In these states, the Dalits are still compelled to lead the life of misery and wretchedness. Many young men and women have to leave their homes in search of jobs in other states like Maharashtra and Gujarat. The percentage of literacy is miserably low; therefore, most of them have to adopt menial jobs leaving no scope for mental improvement.

However, there have been efforts by the government and other agencies to improve and ameliorate the social condition of the erstwhile untouchables. Consequently, they are gradually coming up on a par with their other fellow - countrymen.

This socio-cultural transformation has inevitably affected the Dalit literary creativity. Marathi Dalit writer no longer writes about the pangs of untouchability; rather he prefers to write about social hypocrisy and political professionalism which affect the common man's faith in the establishment. The Dalits in Maharashtra, particularly those who follow Dr Ambedkar's ideology, refuse to call themselves 'Dalit' because the term has derogatory connotations. They prefer to call themselves "the Ambedkarite" and their literature 'Ambedkarite literature'. Notable among those who pursue Ambedkarite ideology are the poets Uttam Ambhore, Mangesh Bansode, Sandhya Rangari, Prabhakar Gambhar, Nanda Taiwade, Sudam Sonule, Digambar Zade, Sunil Abhiman Avachar and others. These poets are staunch followers of Dr Babasaheb Ambedkar and show remarkable awareness about contemporary socio-political situations. Their poetic effort, certainly, will create a new chapter in the history of Dalit poetry in Maharashtra and elsewhere.

Short Story as a literary genre

Story, perhaps, is as old as humanity itself. Human communities entertained themselves by narrating experiences by individuals. The story came down from generation to generation in various forms. It transformed itself from prose narrative to poetry. Ballads are the narration of stories of individual heroes in poetic form. Grandmas narrated stories to put their grandchildren to sleep. This custom continues in all social groups from ages together. Stories have a special place in the Indian ethos. Folk tales are regarded as the source-house of country wisdom. Stories narrated by the ghost-king Vetala are popular and famous for their worldly-wisdom. The stories collected in the Sanskrit text called ***Kathasaritsagara*** are popular even today. The famous ***Arabian Nights*** have retained their popularity and relevance throughout the ages. In Europe and in America short-stories are written and read. Such writers as Maupassant, Gustave, Flaubert, and Balzac in French, Somerset Maugham, E. A. Bates, James Joyce in England, O'Henry in America have contributed remarkably to the growth and development of short stories as a literary form. In Indian languages such writers like Premchand in Hindi, G. A. Kulkarni in Marathi, Manik Bandopadhaya in Bengali, Kalki Krishnamurthy in Tamil and several others have made the short story as a literary genre most relevant. In India, it is an important literary form being practiced in all the major languages.

Features of short-story as a genre

Short story is a brief account of fictitious details. It falls into the category of fiction. Novel as a literary form is also fiction, but there is a remarkable difference between the two. Novel has a large proportion and spans into several hundred pages. It narrates the story of more than one generation, and like an epic, can include more than one location. Short stories, on the other hand, are brief and evoke the spirit of the subject-matter within a short span of time. Short story writers must have skill of imparting the desired effect with few countable words and pages. He has no freedom of relying upon extraneous elements and enlarge scope effective conclusion. That freedom is a privilege of the novelist, while a short-story writer has restrictions in this regard. Otherwise, his writing efforts will be ineffective.

Several short stories have abrupt ends and leave the readers awe-struck or, as in the stories of O'Henry, they have a twisting turn towards the end that brings out unexpected results. ***Gift of the Magi***, ***The Last Leaf, Mammon*** and ***The Archer,*** are some of the short stories of O'Henry which demonstrate his art and skill. Several other short story writers use this genre for social realism as in the case of Russian writers like Maxim Gorki, while Marcel Proust and James Joyce use short stories for inner working of the mind. Their short stories manifest *psychological realism.*

Thus, short story is an effective genre for evoking desired effect within a short span of time. It is a good source of entertainment also. Many readers go to short stories for amusement. That phase, however, is gone. Now, it has become a serious genre capable of amusement and enlightenment together.

Dalit short story is capable of evoking both these effects. They throw light on the pitiable condition of the Dalits in India, and, at the same time, entertain the readers through amusing events and occurrings.

Dalit short - story

The stories about Dalits examine topics such as poverty, famine, untouchability, and other types of prejudice that Dalits are subjected to. In the Dalit story, the traditional paradigm, which was the theology of the upper class, has been discarded. It acts as a source from which the group's voice can be heard. The fundamental feelings that are portrayed in Dalit narratives are grief, fury, wrath, rejection, and resistance. Through its incorporation of the Phule- Ambedkarite philosophical tradition, Dalit writing has added a fresh facet to Indian literary traditions. Therefore, the cultural awareness that Dr Ambedkar imparted was actualised in the narrative of the Dalits. Dalit stories provide a picture of the political and social movement that Dr Ambedkar initiated and established. The suffering and struggles that Dr Ambedkar and Jyotirao Phule endured throughout history have been recounted in the Dalit story. As a result, the ideology of Ambedkar is one of the aspects that makes up the Dalit story.

In the midst of the nineteenth century, the Dalit narrative started. In ***Shetkaryacha Asud,*** Jyotirao wrote about the misery of the poor for the first time. He highlights the tension between the exploiter and the exploited in this realistic and ideological work.

Many authors were inspired by Dr Ambedkar's ideals and began writing in periodicals like *Janta* and *Prabuddha Bharat*. Nirguna Kamble's short pieces in these journals conveyed the conflict between the Sanatani community's mentality and the newly awakened pariah. In 1953, Bandhumadhav published two collections of short tales, ***Aamhi hi Mansa Ahot*** and ***Petlela Aakash.*** Through his works and words, Bandhumadhav ignited the revolution. The narrative of Bandhumadhava effectively communicated Ambedkar's views from house to house. His ***Watani Katha*** is the powerful voice of an awakened society. It calls on Dalits to educate children and to fight injustice. He based his story ***Javetyanchya Vansa*** based on the American novel ***Black Like Me.*** Bandhumadhava shows a white man who turns black and experiences what a black person goes through.

The story is regarded as one of the most creative forms in Dalit writing. A significant number of Dalit story writers have established themselves in a prominent position within the annals of Marathi literary history. After the year 1960, a considerable number of unique Dalit stories began to emerge. Writers like Baburao Bagul, Yogiraj Waghmare, P. E. Sonkamble, Waman Howal, Tarachandra Khandekar, Arun Kamble, Pundalik Dhongade, Amitabh (Waman Nagarale), Bhimrao Shirwade, Sukhram Hiwarale, V. V. Bodhe, Anant Bhoyar, Ashok Lokhande, Avinash Dolas, Sudhakar Gaikwad, Dr Yogendra Meshram, Daya Pawar, Dr Prakash Kharat, Jalandhar Sonune, Arjun Dangle, Keshav Meshram, T. L. Kamble, Chandrakant Wankhede, Urmila Pawar, Dayanand Maske, Jaywant Hiray, Gorakh Bhalerao, Ramesh Patil, Bhimsen Dethe, Manohar Jilhe, Jaiprakash Gawale, Gautamiputra Kamble etc. were inspired by Dr Ambedkar's teachings and started to express themselves in their own distinctive ways.

Shankarrao Kharat is another famous Dalit short story writer. His stories, such as ***Bara Balutedar, Tadipaar, Sangava, and Titvicha Fera,*** amongst many others, depict the life of the lower caste people of the village, as well as various tribes, their superstitions, and the sorrows caused by traditional rituals.

Baburao Bagul, is the finest craftsman in Dalit fiction writing. He can be compared to Chekhov. Baburao's narrative represents a watershed moment in Marathi storytelling. Baburao elevated the life narrative of Dalit victims on the verge of social and economic abuse to a new level. Serious reflection on the lives of the lower caste contributes to the uniqueness of his narrative. His stories have appeared in two collections: ***When I Hid My Caste*** and ***Death is Getting Cheaper.*** Baburao Bagul's stories provide fresh meaning and expression. The story ***Death is Getting Cheaper*** shows the lower classes' social, political, and economic pathos.

Sukhram Hiwarale's short story collection ***"Vishwagangechya Kathi"*** was released in 1979, however he has been writing tales since 1956. The material of Hiwarale's narrative is derived from rural living. As a result, his narrative has taken on a more rustic tone. The plot highlights the conflict between dhamma and anti-dhamma traditional beliefs. The Ambedkarite thinking may be noticed in Waman Hoval's ***"Yelkot"*** and ***"Benwad,"*** two story collections that likewise deal mostly with the rural setting. Hoval depicts many superstitions, attitudes, hypocrisy, and prejudice of the upper caste in rural life, and mocks at the treasured superstitions.

Waghmare is regarded as one of the most influential story writers in Dalit literature. Waghmare's stories ***'Udrek'*** and ***'Begad'*** centre on atrocities committed against Dalit victims, the path of the Dalit community towards prosperity, and the agony of society and the suffering generated by the system in the position of Dalits.

Arjun Dangle's story collection. ***Bandhawarchi Manse*** depicts the disregarded society's myriad problems. He argues that the caste system, which oppresses the poor and prevents women from affording modesty, should be reformed.

The collection of tales ***Pad*** by Amitabh Padmapani (Waman Nagarale) puts attention on the challenges, hardships, and discrepancies encountered by the Dalit community at different levels.

Mahasagar, a collection of tales by Avinash Dolas, shows the hopes of today's Dalit youth and the reality that shatters these ambitions. ***Raktalaleli Lactare,*** a collection of tales by Yogendra Meshram, illustrates the struggle of the disadvantaged.

Prakash Kharat is a Dalit story writer who writes in a unique way about Buddhist culture. His story collection ***Andharacha Ast*** illustrates the oppressed classes assault of poverty. In his works, there is a roar of resistance and a scream of sorrow from the downtrodden class. Stories such as ***Dandakaranya, Raktapalavi, Nagananda*** attempt to resurrect old history and trace the gory pages of Indian culture in which lower caste people were tormented and treated worse than animals.

Vital, is a collection of short tales by Daya Pawar. The stories in ***Vital*** are all unique, yet they are linked by a common thread. All of the stories depict centuries of societal injustice, untouchability, and ugliness directed towards the depressed caste. This ugliness devastated several generations of Dalit people who lived in enslavement and ignorance. The collection of tales ***Vital*** was written with the intention of showing it to the world, making some steps to eliminate it, and publicly expressing the Dalit community's tremendous pain. B. Rangrao's *Desperate men and women: Ten Dalit Short Stories from Indian* written in Indian English becomes a valuable asset to the gamut of dalit Short Story.

Dalit short story as a literary genre is well developed in all the major Indian languages. Dalit issues were also taken up by non-Dalit writers like Premchand in Hindi, S.M. Mate in Marathi etc. Famous Indian English novelist Mulk Raj Anand wrote a full length novel called ***Untouchable*** dealing with the same issue. However, their approach to Dalit individual and society is that of a saint wishing well for the entire humanity, doing nothing concrete for its betterment. A Dalit writer, on the other hand, reaches straight to the core and suggests solutions. These solutions suggested by the Dalit writers turn out to be bitter and indigestive to the caste-Hindus; they are effective, nonetheless; Dalit literature has crossed the regional boundaries and has become a national phenomenon. Its spread is due to several factors. First of all, spread of education and democratic values made the depressed classes aware of their rights. Indian Constitution ensures freedom to every individual. Therefore, the educated Dalits all over India found it easy to express themselves through literature. In fact, most of the folk arts is dominated by the Dalits since ancient times. But that was side-lined and neglected by the canonical norms. The situation changed totally after Independence. Several progressive movements gained ground in the various states. Dr Ambedkar and his teachings continued to attract the masses. Consequently, new awareness spread out far and wide, and the entire nation awakened to new social reality. The movement of Dalit literature, which began in Maharashtra, became a power to reckon with. It challenged the old cultural norms and asserted its identity. This met resistance from every quarter, but the hands of clock could not be reverted, and the movement of Dalit literature grew up gradually. Today, it has become a major cultural trend in India today.

There have been efforts to establish counter culture in the West as opposed to the established one by those who envisaged a new world. The Dalits in India are doing precisely the same as the established culture refused to accommodate them as equals. Dr Ambedkar's efforts to procure equal status to the untouchables among the Hindus did not come off. Consequently, he relinquished Hinduism and adopted Buddha's Dhamma which is more a way of life than a conventional religion. This event can be compared with the Western event of counter culture, though in a different context. Buddha offered a systematic and thoroughly perceived enlightenment, a confident way towards personal salvation to every individual. Not that all Dalits in India embraced Buddhism as the Maharashtrians did, yet resentment against ill-treatment they receive at the hands of the caste-Hindus can be felt and observed at large. This resentment often turns out to be anger, protest and resistance to the establishment and manifests itself through literature in all the major Indian languages.

Notes

1. Kumar, Tila. "Hinduism, Hegemonism and the Dalit Question." Electronic Research Journal of Social Sciences and Humanities, Vol. 3, 2021, www.eresearchjournal.com/wp- content/uploads/2021/12/3.-Hinduism-Hegemonism-and-the-Dalit-Question.pdf. (p.16)
2. Kumar, Tila. "Hinduism, Hegemonism and the Dalit Question." Electronic Research Journal of Social Sciences and Humanities, Vol. 3, 2021, www.eresearchjournal.com/wp- content/uploads/2021/12/3.-Hinduism-Hegemonism-and-the-Dalit-Question.pdf. (p.16)
3. Kumar, Tila. "Hinduism, Hegemonism and the Dalit Question." Electronic Research Journal of Social Sciences and Humanities, Vol. 3, 2021, www.eresearchjournal.com/wp- content/uploads/2021/12/3.-Hinduism-Hegemonism-and-the-Dalit-Question.pdf. (p. 23)
   https:/www.macmillandictionary.com
   https://www.orfordlearnersdictionaries.com

4. Zelliot, Eleanor. From Untouchable to Dalit. South Asia Books, 1996.(267)
5. https://www.thefreedictionary.com
6. https://www.dictionary.com
7. https://www.collinsdictionary.com
8. https://en.wikipedia.org
9. "Dalit Literature and Aesthetics" | Kervan. International Journal of African and Asian Studies." www.ojs.unito.it, www.ojs.unito.it/index.php/kervan/article/view/1676. (p.173)
10. "Dalit Literature and Aesthetics" | Kervan. International Journal of African and Asian Studies." www.ojs.unito.it, www.ojs.unito.it/index.php/kervan/article/view/1676. (p.174)
11. "Dalit Literature and Aesthetics" | Kervan. International Journal of African and Asian Studies." www.ojs.unito.it, www.ojs.unito.it/index.php/kervan/article/view/1676. (p.174)
12. Raj Kumar. Dalit Literature and Criticism. Hyderabad, Telangana, India, Orient Blackswan, 2019. (p.139)
13. Kumar, Tila. "Hinduism, Hegemonism and the Dalit Question." Electronic Research Journal of Social Sciences and Humanities, Vol. 3, 2021, www.eresearchjournal.com/wp- content/uploads/2021/12/3. -Hinduism-Hegemonism-and-the-Dalit-Question.pdf. (p. 20)
14. Chandrakant Mhatre. One Hundred Poems of Chokha Mela.
15. CreateSpace, 2015. (preview p. 15)
16. Anand Teltumbde. Dalits. Routledge Chapman & Hall, 2019. (pp. 93, 94)
17. Rāmacandra Kshīrasāgara. Dalit Movement in India and Its Leaders, 1857-1956. M.D. Publications Pvt. Ltd., 1994. (p. 38)
18. Anand Teltumbde. Dalits. Routledge Chapman & Hall, 2019. (p. 96)
19. Raj Kumar. Dalit Literature and Criticism. Hyderabad, Telangana, India, Orient Blackswan, 2019. (p. 105)

20. Brueck, Laura. "Good Dalits and Bad Brahmins." South Asia Research, Vol. 30, no. 2, July 2010, pp. 125–144, 10.1177/026272801003000202. Accessed 16 Dec. 2020.
21. Bhongle, Rangrao. Saviour of the Nation: Dr B. R. Ambedkar and India. New Delhi, N. D. Publications, 2019.
22. "Namdeo Dhasal - Two Poems." The Daily Write, 5 Apr. 2021, thedailywrite.net/namdeo-dhasal-poetry/.
23. Dalit Sahitya Part 1 Sankalpana ani Swaroop (MA Part II).(p. 68)
24. Dalit Sahitya Part 1 Sankalpana ani Swaroop (MA Part II).(p. 71)
25. Dalit Sahitya Part 1 Sankalpana ani Swaroop (MA Part II).(p. 73)
26. Dalit Sahitya Part 1 Sankalpana ani Swaroop (MA Part II).(p.75)
27. Dalit Sahitya Part 1 Sankalpana ani Swaroop (MA Part II).(p.75)
28. Namdeo Dhasal. (n.d.). Golpeetha (2017).
29. Hira Bansode, Phoenix. (2001).
30. Ram Dotonde, Galli Badalalela Morcha.

Chapter - II

Authors: Life and Works

2.1 B. Rangrao (b. 1950)

B. Rangrao is the pen-name of Dr Rangrao J. Bhongle, Professor and former Head, Department of English, University of Mumbai, Maharashtra State, India. He is retired and lives in Mumbai with his family.

Rangrao was born in a poor Mahar community in Maharashtra, which once was counted among the untouchable castes. His native place is in Amravati district in Vidarbha region– a village on the bank of river Purna which recurs in his creative writing like a metaphor. His parents were field labourers - illiterate and helpless, yet determined to educate their children like their mentor and messiah Dr B. R. Ambedkar, whom they followed throughout life. Rangrao was brought up amid poverty who went to school often ill- attired and without means. However, he had developed love for reading and writing and always stood first among the school children. He was assisted by scholarship by the Central Government of those days awarded to students belonging to Scheduled Castes and Tribes. He walked ten kilometres daily to attend high school classes in a nearby village and returned home in the evening. He went to Amravati, a district place in Maharashtra, for further studies and completed post-graduation in English literature from a Government institution. He stood second in order of merit from Nagpur University in 1974 and won the Pt. Sitaram Silver Medal, something highly creditable for a boy in the Mahar community without educational background and financial support.

Rangrao was called to join as lecturer in English in Vidarbha Mahavidyalaya, Amravati, a Government institution of high educational repute of those days. While imparting instructions on literature to students, he also participated in Dalit movement of the time. Those were the days when the movement of Dalit Panther was in full swing in Maharashtra. Rangrao was a part of the movement. He courted police arrest for retaliation of atrocities on a Dalit woman and fought for her rights. He was disappointed after the split in the movement and decided to concentrate on writing. His first book of poems called ***Oedipus*** was published in 1979. It contains poems of protest and anger and of Dalit sensibility revealing inner working of the mind of an angry Dalit young man. The poems in the book uphold human values and concentrate on 'man' as an individual. Rangrao quotes Albert Camus, the French philosopher in defence of his stand as a poet —

> **I have chosen Justice......so as to keep faith with the earth.**
> **I continue to believe that this world**
> **has no supernatural meaning.**
> **But I know that something in the world**
> **has meaning — man — because he is the**
> **only being who demands meaning for himself.**
> **This world contains at least the truth of man,**
> **and our task is to justify him in the face of**
> **destiny itself.**
>
> — (Oedipus, 1979, Introduction)[1]

Oedipus was well received by readers and students of Dalit understanding. His second book of poems entitled— ***Andharachya Kavita*** came in 1982. The poems in this book, however, are of personal sensibility. Most of these poems are of frustrated love which often turns philosophical. Elements of existentialism can also be traced in these poems. The book, however, remained neglected because Rangrao himself had turned against personal sensibility in literature and was a powerful spokesperson of social responsibility of writers. His participation in Dalit literary movement began to grow. He became noted writer in Dalit literary circle. He regularly published poems and articles in journals like *Asmitadarsha, Samaj Prabodhan Patrika* etc. However, he refused to be associated with any group, as Marathi Dalit literary movement was divided into two groups – one headed by Gangadhar Pantawane claiming to be pure Ambedkarite — another carried on by Baburao Bagul, Namdeo Dhasal and others who openly talked of Marxist ideology as an asset to Dalit literary movement. Rangrao was friendly with Pantwane, Bagul, Dhasal, Yashwant Manohar and others and yet remained isolated, pursuing studies and writing.

Meanwhile, Rangrao was transferred to Mumbai where he found a larger scope for literary creativity. His first novel ***Soma*** was published in 1987. ***Navyawata Navi Walane,*** the book of Marathi literary criticism, came out in 1989. It received the prestigious Maharashtra Sahitya Parishad Literary Award in the following year. University Grant Commission (UGC) granted him three years' Research Fellowship. He worked on C. P. Snow's novel sequence ***Strangers and Brothers*** for Ph.D. degree. He submitted his thesis to the University of Mumbai and was awarded Ph.D. in the year 1991.

Rangrao left the State Government collegiate services and joined Mumbai University, initially as Reader in English in 1991. He was appointed to the post of Professor in English in 1995. His third book of poems ***Vedana Samvedana*** was published in 1992 by Pras Prakashan, one of the prestigious publishing centres in Maharashtra. This book fetched him the Asmita Darsh award for poetry in 1993. As Professor of English in Mumbai University, Rangrao participated in the various literary conferences, made presentations, delivered speeches etc. He was invited by Otto Von Guericke University, Magdeburg, Germany, as DAAD Professor in 2003, where he held lessons on Indian English Poetry for the German students.

Rangrao's second novel in Marathi ***Timirangan*** was published in 2007. This novel depicts the situation after the Ambedkarite movement, particularly the political scenario, became ineffective after the split. The protagonist in the first novel ***Soma*** appears as a strong Ambedkarite with total commitment to the society in this novel. Independence brought nothing new in the lives of the Dalits and downtrodden. They continue to suffer as before. Their plight worsens after the Ambedkarite political strategy failed and the so-called Dalit leaders are sold out for personal gain. The followers of Dr Ambedkar, like the protagonist in ***Timirangan,*** are helpless before the establishment and their confidence seems to be dwindling away. The novel is remarkable for the stream of consciousness technique adopted to reveal miseries and helplessness of the protagonist. It also presents collective consciousness of the Dalit community which looks forward to social transformation.

Rangrao's stature as an academician and social thinker grew up gradually. His literary creativity also became explicit through books he published from time to time. ***The Moon at the Window*** is a collection of poems in English which reveal the poet's Dalit sensibility and, at the same time, his command over the art of poetry. He had been teaching literature and practising it at the same time. This added grace to his profession. He was a poet and critic simultaneously. T. S. Eliot says in one of his essays that practising literary artists are in a better position as a critic. Rangrao is a poet and critic; therefore, can offer better literary criticism on the books written by others. While in the University he edited critical books on Contemporary American Literature and on Contemporary Indian English fiction. Both the books are assets to the teaching profession in colleges as well as in universities. His book entitled ***Revelations: Essays on English Poetry*** (1995) is an ambitious study dealing profoundly with various trends in English poetry since eighteenth century. There are essays on Romanticism, Victorian poetry, T. S. Eliot's modernism and the postmodernist trends in Contemporary British Poetry. Essays on ***"In Memoriam"***, Edward Fitzgerald's translation of ***'Omar Khayyam's Rubaiyat'*** are captivating indeed!

Rangrao retired from the teaching profession after having taught English language and literature for 36 years. His third novel in Marathi — ***Eka Amrutachi Gost*** was published after retirement. The book is a milestone in the history of Marathi novel. It is a postmodernist novel dealing with history and its impact on contemporaneity brought forward through a protagonist, who claims to be 'amurt' i.e. 'abstract', not made of human traits. The novel is remarkable for several things. Perhaps, it is the first novel in Marathi written in postmodernist technique. It goes beyond tradition and modernity, and traces the elements of postmodern culture. Several men and women in history come alive — Shivaji Maharaj, Sambhaji, Bajirao Peshwa, Mastani, Jyotiba Phule, Dr B. R. Ambedkar and speak for their contemporary relevance. Narrative techniques include extracts from Sanskrit texts, Panchatantra, Arabian Nights, popular songs from Hindi movies etc. There is a combination of seriousness and light-hearted elements often evoking laughter. All these result in an authentic literary text in the genre of fiction contributing magnificently to the gamut of Marathi novel.

B. Rangrao had already proved his literary calibre before yet another important book on Postmodernism appeared in 2016. This book is an anthology of essays by the author on postmodern literary trends in Indian languages. The author argues that classicism and modernism cannot be separated as both the ideologies uphold the elite values in life and literature. Spread of education and of democratic values after the fall of the Empire brought about fundamental changes in the world outlook. The traditional concept of culture underwent thorough change, all that was canonical came to be looked down upon, the social classes neglected by history — Dalits, slaves, blacks, aboriginals, women — started asserting themselves, they began to speak for themselves, asserting their identity. This gave rise to new concepts of arts and literature demanding new literary standards, new measures of artistic values. This was obviously an anti-thesis to the modernist concept of creative arts. This was postmodernism arriving at the cultural scenario around the 1950s. B. Rangrao further argues that this created inevitable opposition to the old canons in arts and literature. New voices were made fun of and derided. They were said to be below average and below standard. On the other hand, new artists and writers have denied the old standard and declared their judgement useless, because it is biased and founded on wrong notions about man and the universe. This difference or "differance" as Derrida calls it, was inevitable. The new phase of history called postmodernism allows binary differences between man and woman, black and white, low and high, culture and nature, rich and poor etc. This is one of the determining factors of postmodernism as the current phase of history.

Literature of the Dalits in India, women's literature, African-American literature, literature of the aboriginals, queer literature, memoirs of prisoners, confessions of lunatics — are all welcome because they reveal human experiences, and humanity – or man — is what matters above all today. Baburao Bagul has a poem called 'Man' in which he eulogizes man as the firstborn on the earth. **"You were born before the Vedas, you were born before any religion was conceived, you were first to welcome the sun, the moon, the rain, the wind, and the stars. You were first to fill space with your ceaseless energy and ever expanding consciousness."** Classicism and modernism failed to realise this amazing form of man and concentrated only on groups they created for themselves. They came to believe in "the Best and the Rest". This discrimination drops down in the postmodern situation and encompasses within its range the entire humanity with its various facets and forms. This underlines the relevance of Dalit literature in Indian languages.

B. Rangrao's book on postmodernism, though written in Marathi, is a landmark for the entire contemporary Indian literature. Presently, the book is prescribed for literary studies in several Universities in Maharashtra.

B. Rangrao has edited ***Marathi Dalit Kavita*** (2004), a representative collection of Dalit poetry in Marathi, for Sahitya Akademi. He has written prolonged ***Introduction*** to the anthology elaborating various features of Dalit poetry. The comments he offers on the subject and the references he draws to prove and justify his points are irrefutable. Therefore, the anthology he edited for Sahitya Akademi can be found on the table of all serious students and readers of Marathi Dalit poetry. While comparing the experiences of Dalit woman with those of black woman in America, he quotes Toni Morrison, the Nobel Prize winner African-American woman novelist, pointing out that these experiences have gone into the making of their literary creativity, poetic creativity in particular. One cannot avoid the temptation of quoting the passage here, again—

> **Edging into the life from the backdoor.**
> **Becoming. Everybody in the world was**
> **in the position to give them order —**
> **white women said — 'Do this'.**
> **White man said — "Come here".**
> **Black man said — "Lie down".**
> **The only people they need**
> **not take order from were**
> **black children and each other.**
> **But they took all that and**
> **recreated it in their own image**
> **They ran the house and they knew it.**
> **When white men beat their men they**
> **cleaned up blood and went home to**
> **receive abuse from the victim.**
> **They beat their children with the one hand**
> **and stole for them with the other.**
> **The hands that fell trees also cut**
> **umbilical cords, the hands that wrung**
> **the neck of chicken and butchered hogs**
> **also nudged African violets into bloom,**
> **the arms that loaded sheaves, bales and**
> **sacks rocked babies into sleep. They patted**
> **biscuits into flaky ovens of innocence**

and shrouded the dead. They ploughed all day and came home to nestle like plume under the limbs of their men. The legs that straddled a mule's back were the same ones that straddled their men's hips. And difference was all the differences there was......

— (Introduction, xiii)[2]

These books are considered as authentic sources of Dr Ambedkar's life and mission, his ideology. They offer exhaustive comments on Indian history, politics and sociology, economics, religion, and Dr Ambedkar's active involvement in them. The books depict Dr Ambedkar's image as social revolutionary, a profound scholar, practical strategist, and a great patriot who opposed the canonical concept of nationalism and strove for welfare of every individual within the national context. Nationalism, according to Dr Ambedkar, is not a vague concept expressing love for land, mountains, rivers, forest and the sky, but a concrete plan and its implementation towards the people's well-being, readiness to share their sorrows and happiness and authentic efforts to ameliorate their plight. Nationalism cannot be a political means to exploit weaknesses of the masses.

B. Rangrao has created a place for himself as a Dalit Indian English writer. He had already published ***The Moon at the Window*** — a collection of poems in English in 1999. ***Desperate Men and Women: Ten Dalit Short Stories from India*** enhanced his position as an Indian English writer writing about Dalit issues and sensibility. The book is being read and discussed at various literary circles and prescribed for study in Indian Universities. A detailed account of the stories included in the books follows in the forthcoming chapters.

2.2 Baburao Bagul (1931 - 2008)

Baburao Ramchandra Bagul is the full name of Baburao Bagul. He was born in 1931 in Vihitgaon, a hamlet two kilometres from Nashik Road station and close to Deolali Military Camp in Maharashtra. Bagul's exact date of birth is unknown. His parents were illiterate and ignorant therefore his original birth date was not registered. 1931 is thought to be Bagul's birth year. When the bomb blasts at the Bombay ports in April 1944-1945, took place, Bagul was around 14 or 15 years old and in the fourth grade of study. Maybe, Bagul must have used this as an information to figure out his birthdate.

His father's financial condition was bad. He owned a small land where he used to farm through which he would earn a livelihood. To make money, his father would travel to nearby villages and gather and transport goods using a bullock cart. Bones were formerly bought by his father and sold to the traders. His mother used to take care of the housework. His parents would sometimes sell bananas or vegetables at the station or on the street. This was the kind of life his parents used to lead. Bagul grew up in this environment.

As a kid, Baburao had poor health. He was fearful and fragile. However, the intellect was sensitive. During his studies, he was subjected to the discrimination that Dalit children faced. Because of his narrow neck and huge head, children mocked him as 'Dokmasa.' Because of inferiority complex, he was unable to study at the time. Because of his mother's excessive indulgence and the master's usage of a cane, he never completed his schooling. He could only finish his education till fourth grade. Later, in 1948, he enrolled at Mumbai's Dadar Vidyamandir for English instruction. He was disappointed that he could not get the education he desired. His schooling ended with matriculation.

Baburao has enjoyed reading since childhood. Since the age of four, he has enjoyed penning poetry and songs. These songs projected Dr Ambedkar's optimism, humanism, battle for rights, equality, and revolution. Bagul was born at a time when there were many social awareness conflicts. At that time, the social enlightenment and truth-seeking ideologies of Chhatrapati Shahu Maharaj and Jyotirao Phule were becoming more and more prevalent. Dr Babasaheb Ambedkar conducted Satyagraha at Mahad's Chavdar Lake in 1927. The satyagraha for the entrance to the Kalaram temple was also underway in Nashik. Baburao Bagul was impacted by the winds of change at a young age since he was born into the brilliant backdrop of such a transformation. Like other people of the Mahar community, Bagul struggled with the issue of untouchability. They found inspiration in Shahu, Phule's social revolution and struggles, and Dr Babasaheb Ambedkar's theories of human emancipation. His ideas have become rebellious as a result of the Kalaram Mandir entrance and other Satyagrahas. His works, especially the short stories he penned, continue to exhibit this rebellious spirit.

Dalits developed a feeling of self-awareness as a result of Dr Babasaheb Ambedkar's Mahad Satyagraha in 1927. The Kala Ram Mandir entrance Satyagraha in Nashik in 1930 gave the Dalit psyche a sharp edge of identity. It was obvious that the young Bagul was impacted by such a setting. Mass awakening movements led by social reformers like Mahatma Phule, Chhatrapati Shahu Maharaj had acquired traction in Maharashtra prior to Babasaheb Ambedkar. The Dalit community was particularly agitated in 1925 by the Patitpawanbuwa social movement in Nashik and the surrounding area. The reason for this is the aforesaid social reformers' ideological drive. Dadasaheb Gaikwad, Dr Babasaheb Ambedkar's right-hand man, spearheaded the Satyagraha campaign and performed an excellent job of raising Dalit consciousness. Gaikwad had taken the initiative to open wells and water features that belonged to the government. Bagul was impacted by the thoughts of all the revolutionary movements of this era. It is clear that Bagul's development as a writer was benefited much from the work of these movements.

In later years, Bagul moved to Mumbai in order to further his education. He had acquired a vast amount of knowledge by that time. He was also aware of the surroundings. Reading was one of his passions, and as a result, he was able to assimilate the perspectives of some of the greatest thinkers in history. He took a close look at working class life after moving into the Matunga labour camp in Mumbai. He became familiar with the realities of their existence since this settlement was essentially labour- intensive. Mahar caste people predominated in this camp, and they were all followers of Babasaheb Ambedkar. Because these folks were labourers, they were often influenced by the Communist Party, Lal Bawata, and others. The winds of World War II began to blow throughout the world during this time (1944-1945). Hitler's declaration was also issued at the time, and the Indian independence fight was taking a revolutionary turn.

As Matunga was a workers' community, Stalin's name was unavoidable. There was also a Communist Party organisation in this settlement. Bagul was familiar with Shahir Annabhau Sathe and other communist activists. Meetings of the Communist Party and Dr Babasaheb Ambedkar were held in the neighbourhood. Bagul has been attending such sessions since he was a youngster. While he was in high school, he became interested in the revolutionary movement. He was captivated by the revolutionary movement from the age of 16 to 18. During this time, he studied Maxim Gorky, Lenin, Ambedkar, and Marx, and his thoughts took a new turn. He got immersed in poetry, revolutionary philosophy, and literature. He used to go to meetings of the Scheduled Caste Federation, Communist Party, and Socialist Party. During this time, he started a youth group called Yuvak Sangar Pathak and thought about starting an armed revolution. He also studied politics and philosophy. Dalit women suffered as a result of persecution in the villages, and he believed that the communities where such oppression took place should be set on fire.

Bagul, who had been "active" from childhood, engaged himself in Scheduled Caste Federation events. He used to astound folks by engaging in debate with elderly individuals. A book of Gorky's translation slipped into his hands, at which point Marxism became his philosophy, and he was attracted to the Communist Movement. Regularly attending the gatherings, he met Mulkraj Anand, Sardar Jafri, Krishnachandra, Balraj Sahni, Annabhau Sathe, Amar Sheikh, Gavankar, Jambhekar, and others. He states, **"I was in a mental state. I was in a somewhat strange mood of melancholy and belligerence"**. During this time, he desired to compose poems and lead an armed revolution. His poetry reflects the revolutionary thoughts. Describing the state of his mind, Bagul says —

"My head was full of poetry and thought, like the continuous flow of water from the Gangotri. It was full of thoughts and poems. I wanted to write plays, poems, novels, to make speeches, to make revolutions. But I didn't have much opportunity to say this in the labour camp. My friends were not at the intellectual or mental level as I was."[3] (self.trans) (qt. Memoir of Baburao Bagul)

He wished to write about this inner ideological struggle. His mental struggle to express itself was evident from his mood at the moment. He needed readers and mentors, neither of which he was able to get; nonetheless, he persisted in writing as and when he could.

The story ***Daulat*** was published in the magazine *Aahar* in 1952. The response was positive. Later, a story called ***Turung*** was published in *Yugantar*. The story ***Bohada*** got well-known in Acharya Atre's *Navyug*. Following that, his first collection of stories, ***Jevha Mi Jaat Chorli Hoti*** (When I Hid My Caste), was released in 1963. It drew attention of the critics.

Although Bagul was influenced by the communist movement, Dr Babasaheb Ambedkar's ideology became more important to him as he progressed in life. The communist philosophy eventually faded away. He established his unique style of fiction writing. This set him apart from Annabhau Sathe and Shankarrao Kharat. Bagul's 'Katha' established an autonomous manner of expression soon after. Bagul has worked at several occupations since he was a youngster. He was a compounder, he wrote receipts and distributed food grains at the ration store, wrote bills in the laundry, rolled gasoline or oil cans, job at the trade union office, as a porter on the trains, recruiting in the blacksmith department and transfer to the same department, moved to the paint shop and resigned from there. For the rest of his life, he effectively used his experiences in his creative writing, notably in stories, which made them honest and realistic. As a writer, he has carved himself a distinct niche in Marathi literature.

Position of Baburao Bagul in Dalit Literature

Baburao Bagul is known as the architect of the Dalit short-story. He has a flexible, complex style of writing. Early on, he attempted to communicate his feelings via poetry, but he was not satisfied. He believed that poetry was an inadequate form of expression. As a result, he quit it up. His heart was on fire with anger over the atrocities on Dalits. He was moved by the working class's horrific suffering. He has gone through the challenges of this life. In an effort to portray his revolutionary ideas, he also attempted to compose plays. However, he felt that the dramatic form was restricted, and one day he came upon a story that, in his opinion, was the ideal vehicle for expressing his literary vision. Short tales, thus, became his preferred literary form. His first story, ***Daulat,*** which was published in *Aahar,* was liked because it was different from other stories. In this narrative, the anguish of the oppressed victims—the Dalits, the poor, the downtrodden—was shown for the first time. Authors of tales at the time included Sharkarao Kharat, Annabhau Sathe, and Bandhu Madhav. Bagul's work differed from theirs in terms of texture. It had more incendiary ideas and a more specific allegation. A short story from *Yugantar* with the name***Turung*** was published around this period. The story ***Bohada*** from Acharya Atre's *Navyug* became famous, and Baburao Bagul rose to prominence as a story writer. His first book of short stories, ***Jevha Mi Jaat Chorli Hoti,*** (When I Hid My Caste) was published in 1963. The name Baburao Bagul became well-known in the literary world. Today, Bagul is regarded as one of the major architects of the Dalit narrative. Two collections, ***Death is Getter Cheaper*** (Maran Swast Hot Aahe) in 1969 and the short novel Revenge (Sud) in 1970, were published one after the other. These tales demonstrated how masterful a job Baburao Bagul had done in defining the Dalit identity.

Baburao Bagul is exceedingly sensitive and introspective, and it is because of this reflectiveness that he became a Dalit thinker. Bagul felt unhappy and restless because of the social, economic, political, and cultural disparities around him, as well as the large number of Dalit victims living in this system. Bagul considered all of this introspectively and wanted to take action against them. His opinions on these problems are clearly articulated in his lectures and publications. He has also spoken as the chairperson of various Dalit literary forums and conferences. Through these speeches, he was able to articulate his ideas in a very tangible way.

Baburao Bagul is a revolutionary commentator of Dalit life

Bagul is the author of 'Ambedkar Bharat,' a biography of Babasaheb Ambedkar. This demonstrates his intense interest in and careful study of Dr Ambedkar's life events. This biography also discusses Dr Ambedkar's life and work and their relevance today. The first part of ***Ambedkar Bharat*** was launched in 1981. ***Part 2***, came out in 1995. Previously, biographers such as Dhananjay Keer and Changdev Khairmode had written on Dr Ambedkar's life and mission. These are extensive biographies that are drawn in great depth. They are, nevertheless, descriptive and narrative. Baburao Bagul's **Ambedkar *Bharat*** is distinct from them.

Why should Baburao Bagul's book have been called ***Ambedkar Bharat?*** As in ***Mahabharata,*** sub-stories come after the main story. This book is almost the same as it is put together. Stories follow each other in **Ambedkar *Bharat.*** Baburao Bagul penned seventeen tales, all of which included allusions to mythology and continued to have significance in our times. Karna in Vyasa's ***Mahabharata***, Eklavya, Shambuka in ***Ramayana*** are the inspiration behind ***Ambedkar Bharat.*** What Karna, Shambuk, and Eklavya went through under the *Varna* System, Dr Babasaheb Ambedkar also went through it in twentieth century. With Babasaheb Ambedkar's rise, this country got a new ***Mahabharat***, and Dr Ambedkar became Adinayak and Mahanayak. So, Baburao Bagul was moved to write a glorious biography of the man. This is the clear intention behind the phrase ***Ambedkar India***. Bagul says, **Adolescents and young Dalit boys and girls should be well-educated, their minds and tendencies, which are tired and worn out, should be enlightened and bright.** This was his intention behind writing **Ambedkar *Bharat***. This inspired him further to write about the oppressed and the downtrodden.

Baburao Bagul used the Jatak story form for delivering the tales in ***Ambedkar Bharat.*** The Jataka stories are those of Buddha's former lives. In India, storytelling has been practised since ancient times. In truth, the human mind's attraction with storytelling is global and everlasting. This practice gave rise to Jataka tales. Every Jataka story starts with

Bodhisattva's birth in Amkya's womb. This is the first scene in the narrative. Bagul has used this style of storytelling in ***Ambedkar Bharat***.

In the first volume of ***Ambedkar Bharat*** contains Dr Babasaheb Ambedkar's life from childhood to graduation, his appointment at the state of Baroda, his disappointment therein and coming back home on hearing the news of his father's ill health. The second volume contains his further education (D. Lit), confrontation with the congress and Gandhi, the positions he held in the British Government etc. The third volume narrates his further life till *Mahaparinirvana* in 1956. The biography provides a perfect depiction of Dr Ambedkar's life and its relevance to modern India.

Bagul as a Literary Critic

Besides being a creative writer, Bagul is also known as an eminent Dalit literary critic. He has explained his own position as a writer from various platforms and at the same time, expressed views of Dalit literary movement. He has defined the term 'Dalit' on the platform of Dalit literary conferences held at Nagpur in 1978. According to him — 'Dalit' is the one who opposes all kinds of injustice, social, economic or political. Dalit is not caste, but a notion which explains all the efforts to eliminate discrimination based on caste, creed, gender or race. According to Bagul, Dalit writers and artists should concentrate all their creative energy on 'Man' alone — man without caste or creed, without race or gender — 'man' as a human being. Man alone came down to earth before any religion had arrived. Therefore, he reigns supreme in the universe. Man was there, before the Vedas were composed, man was there before Islam or Christianity arrived on the earth. All the literary efforts, therefore, deserve to be concentrated upon man and his dignity. No effort can be tolerated against human dignity because that is not only unjust but also against the divine scheme.

Dalit literature has chosen 'man' as its centre; therefore, it is revolutionary and also scientific at the same time. Dalit literature has capacity to lead the world literature, hence every Indian should follow the norms laid down by the Dalit aesthetics.

Bagul further says — The majority of the people of India — the Dalit, working people, those who fought for freedom, who provide food, clothes to the country, who give India 'new places of pilgrimage' and shape the future of India, do not get to see, read or hear their life depicted. Dalit literature had given all this to this society now. Therefore,

Bagul welcomes Dalit literature wholeheartedly — as *Krantividnyam* (Revolutionary science) of today.

Bagul actively participated in the "Dalit Panther" movement as well. Even there, he worked for change. He has done more than most people to help the Dalit literary movement. Bagul deserves a lot of credit for keeping the Dalit literary movement going. He also played a big role in making *Pragat Sahitya Sabha* and *Dalit Sahitya Parishad*. Bagul stayed in charge of these fronts, but he did it by being a hard worker. As a leader, he didn't stand out or be in the spotlight. He stayed out of the spotlight and kept writing and expressing himself through writing. So, Baburao Bagul is more important to Dalit literature as a writer and thinker than as an activist.

Inspiration and characteristics behind Bagul's writings

Baburao Bagul's works are inspired by the revolutionary ideas of Buddha, Marx, Phule, and Dr B. R. Ambedkar. Buddha saw common people's misery and servitude. Buddha's mind was overcome with compassion, and he then revealed the path out of their misery. Marx observed exploitation and proposed the road of comprehensive revolution to eliminate it. Phule saw the extreme social inequalities, as well as the untouchables' ignorance. For this, Phule campaigned for societal change. Dr Ambedkar was moved by the plight of the Dalits. He also saw the Dalit people' inequality, helplessness, and vulnerability. As a result, he abandoned Hinduism and converted the masses to Buddhism, giving them new identity. The man in Bagul arose, and he, too, was concerned by Dalits' suffering, poverty, illiteracy and inequality.

Bagul's position as a writer further enhances in view of the fact that his writings — short stories, novels, plays, criticism — manifest larger influences. On the one hand, we come across Indian mythological characters like Karna, Eklavya, Shambuka, on the other hand, there are references to world classics and their writers who believed in social commitment and worked out accordingly. He led the life of a poor artist despite the recognition he received from the state and reading masses. He also received various awards for his creativity but failed to exploit fame towards material gain. Nevertheless, he was loved and respected for his vast human understanding and literary creativity. All his books — the two collection of short stories ***Maran Swasta Hot Aahe*** (Death is getter cheaper) and ***Jevha Mi Jaat Chorli Hoti*** (When I Hid My Caste) are considered as landmark in Dalit literature. His novel ***Sud*** (Revenge) stands apart in the entire history of Marathi novel. The collection of essays on Dalit literature ***Dalit Sahitya: Aajche Kratividnyan*** offers insightful progressive thoughts and understanding of contemporary literary issues. Bagul's literary image in Marathi is that of literary Godfather who cast influence and provided guidance to several upcoming Dalit writers and artists.

Baburao Bagul died a poor man at the age of 78 leaving literary legacy to young and upcoming writers.

2.3 Ratan Kumar Sambharia (b. 1956)

Ratan Kumar Sambharia was born on January 6, 1956, into a poor family in the village of Bhada was in the Rewari district of Haryana. He is one of the outstanding short story writers in India, a sharp critic, and a supporter of new social innovation and technology. His father was an impoverished agricultural labourer. His mother, Gujri Devi, was a devout and efficient housewife. As the youngest child of his parents, he was lavished with attention. His mother affectionately referred to him as 'Ratna.' During those days there was less importance to girls' education, therefore his parents did not pay attention to his two sisters' education. When his mother enrolled him in school, the teacher asked his mother Ratan Kumar's birth date. His mother started counting the tips of fingers to remember the years when he was born. The silence of his mother was accepted as ignorance by his master and he voluntarily wrote his date of birth as 1.6.1956. It stated that he turned six on the day of his admission.

Ratan Kumar Sambharia's financial condition was very poor, his father used to repair roofs of the house and was very skilled at it, but due to poverty he was unable to repair the roof of his own house. Whenever it rained the roof leaked and to collect water all the utensils of the house were insufficient. He has grown up in such a poor environment.

Despite the various problems faced by Sambharia, he did not leave studies. His sisters supported him as they thought that they were not able to get education but his brother Ratan Kumar should. In the early days of schooling Ratan Kumar was not interested in studies and did not pay attention in class. His master once slapped him and the fear of this made him concentrate on studies.

During his childhood, Ratan Kumar endured the ravages of poverty, but this did not deter him and he continued education. While studying in the village school, he took part in various competitions which encouraged him to move ahead in life. When Sambharia was in VI std, he was inspired by the story ***Idgah*** by Premchand from his Hindi textbook. This story is about child psychology, which depicted the grandmother's plight and the grandson's attachment to his grandmother. Sambharia was deeply touched by this story and this gave him impetus to write stories himself.

When Ratan Kumar was in the VIII std, he had participated in the play called ***Eklavya*** in which he himself played the role of Eklavya. In the play, Guru Dronacharya asked Eklavya for the thumb of his right hand in exchange for teaching archery, whereas, Guru Dronacharya had never taught him archery. Asking for the thumb in exchange of fees was something which was never witnessed by the world. Ratan Kumar was deeply moved by this and was disturbed by the discrimination against the poor and low caste boy done by a Guru. At that time, he felt as to why he participated in such a heinous play. While the story of ***Idgah*** planted seeds of superiority, idealism and devotion to duty in him, ***Eklavya*** planted seeds of hatred for the tradition superstitious belief and disbelief in him.

Good results give wings to the students. The same thing happened with Ratan Kumar. When the results of class 7th came, he felt as if he had got wings, but the flapping of the wings soon subsided when he remembered the poor financial condition of his family. His father was an agricultural labourer. He could hardly take care of the family. Ratan Kumar had neither good clothes to wear nor money to pay fees. Fees were arranged somehow and they did not let the economic deprivation become a hindrance into education. To continue education further he took admission in B. S. Ahir Higher Secondary School. But the untimely death of his father made life more difficult. He used to wear short pants, a half sleeved shirt and broken slippers and walk seven kilometres away from village to attend school. On Sunday, when school was closed, he used to work on labour fields to wage livelihood. He has also faced the bitter experience of caste in his academic life. Even the poison of caste is dissolved in our society. Although caste is constitutionally prohibited, it remains in the minds of people everywhere. It becomes more visible in villages where people know each other by caste alone. Ratan Kumar experienced it all as a school boy. As his village did not have school beyond VIII std, he had to go to Rewari for further studies, where, again, he faced several difficulties. This made him strong and capable of facing life bravely. He obtained B. A. degree from Ahir College and did B. Ed from Satish Public College of Education, Rewari.

When Ratan Kumar was studying in Ahir College Rewari, there used to be 'Prep' in the college, which was equivalent to XI standard. He had enrolled in 'Prep' in the college. One of the subjects he opted for was Hindi literature. The college used to publish a magazine *'Phoenix'* which he found useful for his creativity. The magazine offered scope for his creative efforts. Principal of the college, who was the editor of the magazine, encouraged him by printing several of his poems and short stories. He published his first short story ***Ghunghat*** in *'Phoenix'*. Then came ***'Chathi Ki Raat'*** which made him famous and labelled him as "progressive writer". The short story ***Chati Ki Raat*** deals with bad social customs and their ill impact on the society. Ratan Kumar found in Prof. Rampal Yadav — the principal of the college— true advisor, a friend and "guru". With the principal's help he could publish many of his compositions, and made himself known as a young writer. He became a member of the literary committee of the college and found himself in a position to advise others as well. He discussed with other members of the committee subjects like superstitions, social disorder, unequal laws etc., which were chosen for creativity of the young writers.

After passing graduation in 1976, he wanted to become a teacher. There was lack of trained educated teachers in those days in the tribal dominated districts of Rajasthan, Udaipur, Dungarpur, Banswara, Chittorgarh. The name of Sambharia was registered in the planning office of Udaipur and with the new academic session, he was appointed as a temporary teacher in Gadwas, the government primary school of Dhariyawad Panchayat Samiti, Udaipur. In that one teacher school which was closed for years, he faced many problems. Dronacharya's remarks about Eklavya always kept revolving in the mind of the writer. He was always afraid that he might share this tragedy. On the day Ratan Kumar opened the school, two or three half-naked children had come to school. Later, more than 45 children were in front of him in school dress. The area around the school belonged to the tribals. There were forests all around. The name of the school was that of tendu leaves. Cobras came out of the holes besides other frightening factors. Sambharia thought that he should run away from there, but his financial condition had tied his feet and was not able to leave the job.

Ratan Kumar continued to write stories and articles. He published an article on the condition of his school, suggesting measures for improvement. The authority was hurt by the details he offered. Consequently, he was sacked from the job. He took another job of an accountant which helped him earn livelihood. He came down to Jaipur and published short stories regularly in journals like *Rajasthan Patrika, Dainik Navjyoti, Rashtradoot*, etc. His first collection of short stories

Samaj Ki Naak came out soon, which was released at the hands of the then Chief Minister of Rajasthan — Shri Shivcharan Mathur. However, this did not improve his financial condition and had to face difficulties at home.

Sambharia was selected as translator for All India Radio in 1992. His literary creativity began to flourish here. He developed contacts with other talented people in various fields like sports, education, literature, music, etc,. He himself was comfortably settled down now, and began to publish from time to time. He earned diploma in journalism which helped him procure the post of public relation officer in All India Radio. He continued to work there till his retirement in 2016. After retirement he decided to dedicate himself to writing, and published several books on a variety of subjects.

Caste system in Rajasthan, like other regions in the Northern region, is life threatening. Ratan Kumar narrates various examples of caste-barriers of which he himself was a victim. He suffered a great deal at the hands of the upper caste people — the Marwari, Bania, Brahmans and others — He ate his food sitting on the ground while others had dinner on the dining table. He drank water from distance so that he would not contaminate others. He often found himself in suffocating conditions and wondered how he could survive in the face of these adversities. He recalls — he suffered from mental agony, faced discrimination, had economic crisis at home, — something which might have broken down others. He however, faced these circumstances stoically, steered himself out of these harrowing experiences and proved his 'metal', a pure gold – "Kundan" in the society.

Ratan Kumar Sambharia started writing from the college days. He published short stories, plays and wrote a few poems. His favourite genre is short story which offers enough scope for literary vision. Most of his stories depict rural life and the people therein; also his personal experiences as a man belonging to an oppressed community. These stories have found place in several national magazines and journals. Getting published in *Hans* was very prestigious during those days. Therefore, he sent his short story ***Swarg Ka Marg*** (Path to Heaven) to *Hans*. He received the letter of approval — a postcard — signed by Rajendra Yadav — the renowned literary critic and editor of *Hans*. His joy knew no bound. He showed this letter to all his friends. Ironically, this story is yet to be published in *Hans*, while other journals carried his stories regularly. The number of short stories he published till now is around 250 — and many of them in renowned magazines and journals. Ratan Kumar Sambharia became a household name to the readers of Hindi Dalit short stories.

Major Themes in Ratan Kumar Stories

Ratan Kumar writes mostly about Dalit life in Indian villages, particularly from the Northern regions of the nation. He has published ten collections of short stories in Hindi – he was born in Haryana, but settled down in Rajasthan. Therefore, the language of his creativity is a unique combination of Haryanvi and Rajasthani. This makes his stories popular in Haryanvi and Rajasthani; yet remains an influential literary output in Hindi language. There is profound influence of Premchand on Ratan Kumar's creativity. Ideologically, he is an Ambedkarite, who practices teaching of Dr B. R. Ambedkar in personal life and in social interaction. He has published an important book on Munshi Premchand entitled — ***Munshi Premchand and Dalit Samaj***, also attempted a biography of Dr B. R. Ambedkar entitled — ***Dr Ambedkar: Ek Prerak Jiwan***.

Ratan Kumar Sambharia has published around 250 short stories so far. Major collection of his short stories include — ***"Hukum Ki Duggi", "Kaal Tatha Anya Kahaniya, Khet Tatha Anya Kahaniya", "Dalit Samaj Ki Kahaniya".*** His creativity has been rewarded by various prestigious awards — some of them are —

1. Navjyoti Katha Samman.
2. Felicitation by Vice-President of India, 2005.
3. Kathadesh Akhil Bharatiya Puraskar.
4. Rajasthan Patrika Creativity Award.

Ratan Kumar Sambharia is one of the highly educated Dalit writers in India. Like B. Rangrao, who made his way to the top out of nothing, Ratan Kumar also had to struggle to reach out to prestigious position in the Rajasthan Government set-up. The details of the struggle he underwent is well preserved in his autobiography — ***Shabd Badalte Yug***, which is a graphic account of the writer's journey from zero to top achiever. Besides earning diploma in journalism after graduation, he went on to obtain other degrees like B. Ed, BSc, B.J.M.C etc. This shows his thirst for knowledge and faith in personal efforts to achieve success. His creativity, education and determination reveal the kind of man Ratan Kumar is — self-made, progressive and a creative genius. His literary output and personality make it clear that he follows Saint Kabir, Karl

Marx and Dr B. R. Ambedkar, who together have cast profound impact on his life as a thinker and creative writer.

Notes

1. B. Rangrao. **Oedipus**. Maharashtra Sahitya and Sanskrity publication, 1979.
2. **Marathi Dalit Kavita**. B. Rangrao (ed) Sahitya Academi Publication, 2009.
3. Ingale, Dr Malti. **Baburao Bagul: Vyakti ani Vangmay**. Devyani Prakashan, 2011.
4. Singhal, Deshraj. "RatnakumarSambhariya Ka Katha Sahitya_srijanKeVividhAayam." Handle.net, 2015, hdl.handle.net/10603/312506, http://hdl.handle.net/10603/312506.
5. Snehlata. "RatnakumarSambhariyaKe Sahitya Mein Samajik Chetna." Handle.net, 2019, hdl.handle.net/10603/303803, http://hdl.handle.net/10603/303803.

Chapter - III (A)

Thematic Analysis of the Text Desperate Men and Women: *Ten Dalit Short Stories from India*

–B. Rangrao

Desperate Men and Women: Ten Dalit Short- stories from India is a collection of short stories by B. Rangrao. The book was published in 2013 by Kalpaz publication, New Delhi and is an object of literary discussion since then. The stories in the book were discussed in a literary conference in England in 2015 and papers were presented on them. In India, the stories are discussed and studied on various platforms. The book is said to be the first of its kind, an expression of Dalit creative sensibility, a pioneering attempt by a Dalit writer to write short stories in English. There are others who wrote biographies, social documentaries etc. but B. Rangrao stands apart among others as a creative writer in Indian English.

Here is an attempt to analyse the short stories in the book:

1. Childbirth

Childbirth is depiction of a Dalit woman who delivers baby on her own, without any assistance from a doctor, or maid. The story is set against rural background in Maharashtra; where farming and harvest is always at the mercy of rain. Farm labourers, particularly women, help the farmers to weed and protect crops from unwanted grass, raise it and ultimately reap the harvest. So, there are naturalistic details of the clouds, wind, greenery, farming activities, etc. There are poor women from among the Dalit community who have to earn daily wages to run families. There are days when there is no work. Consequently, they have to starve, as there is no other source of income. These women must work, even if they are handicapped, sick or pregnant. Rakhma is one of these poor Dalit women. She is at the advanced stage of pregnancy, and, in fact, her days are over. But she must go to work, otherwise, her two sons, who wander aimlessly in the village street, and her good-for- nothing husband who smoke *bidis* continuously lying down idly— will starve. Rakhma joins other women and goes to work on the farm. These working Dalit women suffer more or less in the same manner. They have similar stories to narrate. One of them has a drunkard husband who quarrels and beats her daily. Another tells how the *Patwari* stared at her lecherously when she was adjusting her "pallu". Third one narrated the story of her mother-in-law who was raped by the Patil in the village. Her father-in-law takes revenge by murdering the Patil and is imprisoned for the life. Sufferings and torture are permanently associated with the lives of these poor Dalit women.

Rakhma starts working efficiently along with other women in the group. The pangs of childbirth, however, strike her in the middle of the work. She knows her days are over and she must return home to deliver the baby. She comes back home staggering only to find out that there is nobody at home to assist her. Her two sons and husband— all are absconding. All the neighbours have gone to work as it was a working day. She is alone at home and helpless. The pangs become unbearable. She lies down on the ground, unties the clothes and tries to push down the baby from the womb. She is successful. Her baby comes tumbling out. She cuts the umbilical cord herself and tries to soothe the crying baby. She is terribly hungry as her belly has been evacuated. Pangs of hunger begin to torture her. There is nothing in the house to eat. The pathetic condition is effectively brought out by the author —

Childbirth leaves both mother and the baby hungry. While the baby brings it down to the earth, mother's hunger is evoked by the space in the stomach left by the newborn. This hunger is so strong that animals are often said to eat up their own progenies. Mother scorpion is killed immediately, unable to withstand the pangs of hunger. God has created hunger, but the creator has failed to produce means to pacify it. Something similar happened in the case of Rakhma. (p.19)

The hungry Rakhma does not know what to do. Her newborn baby is crying out of hunger, and she is equally hungry herself. She is reminded of a grocery shop nearby, stands up with great difficulty, wraps herself with a tattered cloth and walks out bleeding profusely. She comes to the shop and picks up a handful of groundnuts as there is no one at the counter. The owner of the shop mistakes her for a thief and shouts at her — **"hey, keep the stuff, you thief. How dare you...."**. She is deeply disturbed, and the thought of her baby lying lonely in the house deepens her disturbance. She is weak, fragile and helpless. Yet she walks hastily towards the baby. As she crosses the threshold of the house, she collapses like a tree that falls in a storm. No movement of her body is noticed. No noise is heard except the piercing cry of the baby. Is she dead or alive? Is the mother in her awake to take care and feed the hungry baby? Or is the baby left to the care of the raging elements? These are the questions left to the readers to answer.

Whatever the answers to the questions raised above — helplessness of the weak and the poor is affirmed. This is the Dalit life and such situations frequently occur in it. Social system in India has always been an enemy to the Dalits — even nature is equally unsympathetic towards them. Rain in the story plays a negative role. Whenever the Dalit women want work untimely rain falls like curses on them and the work is ruled out. No work, no food. The entire family has to sleep without food. When it rains heavily the houses of mud leak profusely. The entire family keeps awake till the rain stops. The flooded rivers take away their cattle, even helpless men and women are drowned in floods.

In ***Childbirth*** rain is a symbol of sorrow and misery. It stands for destruction. When Rakhma is trying to push the child out of the womb, a pattering sound on the roof is heard. When Rakhma feels pangs of hunger, rain outside seems to be mocking at her. When she walks back home with handful of groundnuts, rain pours down heavily. When she finally reaches home, she collapses and it is raining heavily. The concluding passage in the story convincingly asserts this truth —

Rakhma had turned back by now and started running towards home. The thought of her baby lying alone and unprotected brought her back to herself. She held the groundnuts in her fist but forgot to put them in mouth. Hunger seemed to have disappeared. By the time she reached home she was exhausted totally. She crossed the threshold and before she could reach out to her baby, collapsed. She lay motionless in a pool of blood, unaware of the life of her own, of the baby she had begotten. *Rain had gathered momentum outside and began to fall fiercely.* (p. 20)

The story is remarkable for several other things. It portrays the Dalit life realistically. Arrival of rainy season, agriculture prevalent in the Indian villages, the role of farm labourers in farming, etc. are important traits of the Indian agriculture. The author has made them appear authentically. Position of Dalit women in the Indian social set-up also has always been a cause of concern. She has to suffer from dual victimisation— as a woman and Dalit at the same time. Her position is like that of the Black woman in America who is also a victim of gender and race simultaneously. Rakhma's position is badly placed in this trap of dual predicament. She is poor and Dalit, therefore is unable to support herself financially — a caste – Hindu women would have certainly been better off, — Rakhma is totally helpless. No one in the world comes forward to help her. She delivers the baby like a cow, she-buffalo, or like even a bitch — who eats up her own newborn puppies to satisfy hunger. Rakhma being human, cannot do that. Therefore, she must suffer. That is her fate and predicament.

Rakhma's predicament is also linked with gender. Her man— a good-for-nothing husband — thinks he has rights over the women. He does nothing to help the family and spends time idly smoking *bidis* continuously. Her two sons — the urchins — are not taught to help their mother. Being boys, they are set free to wander in the village streets and return home only to eat. It's a strange world for Rakhma to live in. She lives in it and, probably dies in it.

Other women in the story are in similar position. They narrate their experiences in the course of gossiping. These experiences are those of Dalit women who are also victims of casteism in India. The drunkard Dalit man behaving violently with other members of the family, the *Patwari* looking at a Dalit woman while she adjusts her sari, a Dalit woman raped by Patil — and her husband imprisoned for life for murdering the Patil — all are the traits and characteristics of Dalit life in India. The author has brought them out effectively and to the desired impact on the readers' sensibility.

2. Death of a Rich Man

This is the story of a Dalit boy called Satya who is enrolled in school register as Satyawan Tryambak Meshram. Satya does not like school and the lessons therein and mostly stays away from it. He spends most of his time on the bank of the river with his friends who are from other Dalit communities. These boys either swim in the river water or wander along the river bank teasing each other, giggling and indulging in things that really do not suit their age. They are aware of the fact that whenever someone in the village dies, the dead body is either buried or cremated on the river bank. This offers them a chance to collect a few coins hurled across the corpse in the funeral procession, also a few more left on the place of the cremation. This is the time for them to 'earn' and help their parents who are always annoyed and angry at their waywardness. Satya's case in particular, is noteworthy. His parents had enrolled him in school in response to their leaders' appeal who were inspired by Dr Ambedkar's insistence on education and his call to **"educate, unite and agitate".** They knew their son's dislike for school, therefore they wished that he should at least work and help them to run the family. Satya, however, was good for nothing.

The village wherein Satya lived had all the castes and communities living peacefully together. There were rich Marwaris with huge *haveli* and hundreds of acres of fertile land spread across the village. The poor villagers, men and women from backward communities, worked on these lands and earned their livelihood. Therefore, they respected the rich Marwaris and maintained respectful distance from them at the same time. Seth Jhabarmal — a rich Marwari in the village in his late eighties, was sick for quite sometimes. He suffered from various ailments. The entire village knew about his condition and prayed for the old man to live longer, or at least die in peace. Satya and friends knew this as well, and waited eagerly for the Marwari's death so that they could 'earn' a few coins. So it happened. Seth Jhabarmal died at the ripe age. The news spread in the village like wildfire. A large number of villagers gathered outside the *haveli* in desperate hope of last *darshan* of the Seth. Satya and his friends were also present at the gate of the *haveli* and were overjoyed to see the dead body being taken out on a ladder. A huge funeral procession moved slowly towards the river bank where Seth's dead body was to be cremated. The chant of "Ram Nam Satya Hai" was heard in the chorus. Coins of one rupee or of bigger value were hurled across the corpse. The boys wanted to collect the coins before they fall down on the ground and earn their share. A kind of race began to leap up in the air and catch hold of the coins. Men in the procession were accustomed to this and did not really mind the disturbance. They, however, were insensitive towards the boys falling on the ground and trampled upon their bodies.

Satya, who was weak compared to other boys, could collect none as the stronger and swifter boys succeeded in their efforts. Satya was desperate and wanted to earn at least a few, so that he could please his father who, otherwise, would not allow him to enter the house. He, therefore, made the last effort — the last and the best. He leapt up in the air, aiming at a coin above the head of the men in procession. But he missed the coins even this time and fell down on the ground like a pumpkin dropped down. The men cursed the boy, called him filthy names and walked ahead treading upon his weary limbs. The procession moved ahead towards the river banks; Satya's body, however, lied motionless on the ground. They were still chanting "Ram Nam Satya Hai", but it could not reach Satya's lifeless ears. Was he dead? Or was he alive? The last passage of the story portrays this —

Most of the boys had their catches. Satya had none. 'Shall I have to go without any?' He asked himself, 'How shall I show face to my father? If I fail and go home without the catch father will surely beat me up.' He shuddered at the thought of beating. But all is not lost, he told himself again, 'Coins are still being hurled. I shall make another effort, the last and the best'...... Sound of the coins brought him back to himself. He caught sight of the coins flung in the air, and, like the baby Hanuman leaping towards the rising sun, leapt towards the coins. He missed them and fell on the ground like a huge pumpkin dropped down. This disarrayed the procession for a while. The men cursed the boy, abused and called him names. They, however, soon resumed their positions and moved ahead to cremate their dead trampling upon the limbs of the boy. The funeral procession of Seth Jhabarmal reached the graveyard while Satya's motionless body lay unattended in the street. The chanting sound in chorus was heard once again—Ram nam satya hai.... Ram nam satya hai.... (p. 25)

The story is remarkable for several other things. It portrays the Dalit life realistically. It shows that respect and importance is given to the dead of the higher caste but not to the injury of the lower caste. The story in this manner, presents that aspect of life in India, which existed along with pleasant ones, but was never recorded in literature. The irony becomes explicit towards the end of the story when the readers want to know the condition of Satya, and temporarily forget the death of the rich man. The title of the story, thus, is ironical and evokes the memory of Arthur Miller's play ***Death of Salesman*** wherein death is treated in somewhat similar manner.

3. Farewell

'Farewell' is a story depicting atrocities in the name of caste. The story is once again set in rural background where farming decides livelihood and is a main source of income and crops like wheat, sorghum, corn, rice etc. are harvested and reaped. B. Rangrao, who has spent his childhood in a village, is a master of portraying life in Indian villages—

It was a small village in the remote Indian countryside surrounded by thick forest on one side and by hillocks on the other. At the daybreak when the sun rose slowly behind the hillocks the entire horizon appeared brightly lit as if in a painting by Ravi Varma. The birds left their nests in search of food and cattle were let free to drink at the river and to graze. The entire village came alive after the peaceful night. Young girls were seen rushing towards the river with pitchers on the heads while elderly men and women engaged themselves in preparations for the day's work. As the day progressed and the sun became sober in the afternoon the familiar calm prevailed till the evening when the villages would interact and bustle in the narrow dusty lanes. (p. 27)

This is the story of Lakhan and his wife Jamuna who are from Dalit community and field labourers. They lived with two children and Lakhan's old parents. Lakhan loved his parents and took every care to make them happy. Jamuna shared her husband's sentiments and was happy to look after her in-laws.

Superstitions have always been a part of Indian social life. Poverty and ignorance prevailed everywhere. Independence did little to ameliorate the plight of the poors. So, when an epidemic broke out in Lakhan's village everybody thought it was the curse of the Goddess whose temple lay in dilapidated condition for several years. It was necessary, therefore, to re-construct it immediately. The construction work began. Everybody contributed to it. Some paid cash for the material, others offered labour for the construction work. The epidemic continued to take lives of the people — the poor and the Dalits, in particular because they lived unhygienically and ate under-nutritious food. There was no medical assistance, only continuous *puja* in the temple and prayers asking for blessings from the Goddess. Eventually, it happened. Several old men and women succumbed to the deadly disease. Lakhan's father was one of them. He died for want of medicine. The entire family was deeply aggrieved. There was nothing Lakhan could do, except blaming fate. However, he gathered courage and started preparing for the old man's funeral. Relatives were called upon along with a few neighbouring caste-men. Dead body of his father was taken out in procession. Four men shouldering the ladder walked ahead while the rest followed. The funeral procession was not allowed to go further by the village chief, who asked Lakhan to divert because the temple of the Goddess is ahead on the street. The Goddess who is already displeased will be infuriated if an untouchable's corpse is carried along side of the temple. It is for the benefit of the entire village, the village chief explained. Lakhan, however, was not convinced. How can the Goddess get angry because of a man's dead body who had served the Goddess while living? He himself has contributed to construction by working hard for two weeks in a row. This is unjust, thought Lakhan, and asked his men to move ahead, let whatever may happen.

Lakhan has to pay heavy price for his audacity. The entire village boycotted him for his defiance and disobedience. Nobody gives him work, even Jamuna is sent back from work by her workmates. He is not allowed to buy things from the shop, not allowed even to draw water from the well. Lakhan goes to the village chief and pleads his case, but is beaten up severely. He receives a message through one of his acquaintances — the chief is willing to lift the boycott if Lakhan sends his wife Jamuna to the Chief's *wada* just for one night. This was adding insult to the injury. Lakhan's wreaths with pain and helplessness. The family would not survive without people's support beyond a couple of days. What shall they do? They finally decide to leave the village and settle down somewhere else — maybe in one of the neighbouring villages. It was difficult to make the mind, but there was no alternative left. They, therefore, leave the village with heavy hearts and disappointment.

B. Rangrao has explored human psychology while narrating Lakhan's plight. He has also delineated the nature of relationship among the members of Dalit family — Lakhan loves his father to the extent of earning enmity with the village chief. He enquires about his parents' welfare first when he returns home from work. The children come next. He loves his wife and feels insulted when the village chief talks ill about her. The entire family is bound with love and affection about each other and is deeply disturbed when they are compelled to leave the village. Lakhan does not feel regret about the defiant stand he adopted to protect his father's honour. The author makes it quite clear—

They left the house with heavy heart and came near the shrine. Lakhan's old mother folded her hands in the direction of the Goddess and muttered something to her. Lakhan remembered the day when he refused to obey the chief's command and took his father's dead body to the graveyard through the same lane. He was also reminded of the punishment meted out to him. 'Is he *contrite* about the act? No, not at all', he told to himself. On the contrary, he was proud of what he did. He performed the filial duty to satisfaction. He loved his father and was ready to suffer for the sake of love. (p. 36)

'Farewell' is about the atrocities inflicted upon the Dalit communities in the Indian villages. The elements of casteism are always strong. The Hindu Gods and Goddesses also seem to be unfriendly with the untouchables. The village chief declares that the Goddess will be displeased if the corpse of an untouchable is taken by its shrine. The whole community believes in what he says. This becomes main cause of Lakhan's displacement. The story also reveals how the caste hierarchy operates in the village structure. The village chief is invariably from the higher caste who practically rules over the entire population. His decrees are to be obeyed and followed. Those who resist them must suffer. So does Lakhan because he had defied the chief's decree. Casteism vanishes when it comes to the basic instinct. The chief has an eye over Lakhan's beautiful young wife Jamuna. He believes that the Dalit are poor, therefore vulnerable. He wants Jamuna for a night, then he would lift the decree of boycott on Lakhan's family. But he is wrong. Lakhan burns with anger when he hears about it, even though he is helpless. Lakhan wreaths inside when he realises his helplessness and decides to leave the village. They have spent sunny days and celebrated several occasions in this village. Lakhan's father was a respected man in the village, who was approached for advice by many people in critical times. Everyone honoured the old man as he would share everyone's sentiment. Lakhan wonders why it all has come to the end all of a sudden? Why all those whom he trusted as friends and acquaintances turn hostile for no fault of his? Why has the whole village become his enemy? He bids farewell to the village with heavy heart, as he is unable to forget the old days and the memories associated with them. The author comments —

They came out of the village and halted at a place to have a last look. Lakhan turned back and saw the cluster of small houses. He could locate his house which stood apart from the huts that surrounded it. He was not certain if he could ever come back and occupy the house again. He must bid farewell to it, temporarily though. He looked ahead on the way and started walking. Jamuna followed him with her children and the old mother-in-law. They soon disappeared in the thick forest. (p. 36)

"Farewell" should be a milestone in the history of Dalit writings.

4. When the Sun God Refused to Set

Each of the short stories in the collection is an example itself. 'When the Sun God Refused to Set' is a combination of myth and reality. It offers a very good example of psychological working of a Dalit man, who has suffered throughout life, yet fights the surrounding stoically till he ultimately succumbs to death.

Raghoba, a Dalit man, has lost his wife when he was young. He refused to remarry despite insurmountable pressure from the relatives. He, instead, decides to raise his two children — girl and boy — and take proper care of them. However, he can never forget sweet memories of the days he spent with his wife. He loved her very much, and he loves his children equally. He lives in a small hut with his children and is happily settled. Raghoba enrols his children in school, and when his daughter– Kala– comes of age, he marries her off to a suitable young man. His son – Babu – goes to school and reaches upto tenth standard without difficulties. Raghoba wants his son to continue education and makes preparations to send him to taluka place for higher studies. Raghoba's day starts with praying to the Sun with folded hands. Other things follow only after the prayer. That has become his daily habit. Time passes on. Age has started telling on Raghoba's nerves and he always falls ill. He gets delusions in which he behaves improperly. He, however, is unaware of that and is under the impression that there is nothing wrong with him. Babu comes to know about his father's illness and decides to stay home to take care of the old man. He gets a small job in village *Grampanchayat* and earns enough to make the two ends meet. Raghoba asks his son to get married and bring "Laxmi" in the house, so that peace prevails and they live happily together. Babu agrees, unwillingly though.

Trouble starts on the first night of Babu's marriage. Raghoba is extremely happy and is often found talking to his dead wife who would have been equally happy seeing her new *'bahu'* at home. He gets delusions once again. When his son and daughter-in-law are together during their wedding night, he enters the room. The girl is deeply disturbed. Babu tries to explain the situation and his father's illness to his bride. She is convinced. Raghoba's delusion returns the next night and he again walks into the place when the young couple are engaged in love-making. Babu is extremely annoyed and shouts at his father, sending him away. Raghoba comes back to himself and realises the blunder he has committed. He loved his son so much that he would not forgive himself for causing disturbances in his joyous moment.

Next morning the sky was overloaded with clouds. The sun did not appear. Babu did not see his father moving about as usual. As it was late he went to wake his father. Raghoba was no more. He passed away during the night itself.

The story offers a beautiful blending of myth and reality and opens up the psychological workings of the mind of a man who is deeply drowned in love for wife and children.

5. And Quiet Flowed the Purnamai

'And Quiet Flowed the Purnamai' is an interesting love story set against the caste discrimination in the Indian social structure. It also offers a bitter comment upon missatched marriages when a young woman is married off to an old man. Once again, the river plays an important role in the narrative structure. Purnamai — Purna, the mother, is what the river named. The episode in the story occurs in a village situated on the bank of the river Purna. The story opens with sweet reference to the Purnamai —

Not very long years ago, the river Purna had enriched the villages situated on its bank. Those were the days when the villagers took pride in their association with river whose sweet water quenched their thirst. A dive in the river would free them from the weariness of the daily routine; the sins they committed inordinately would be washed away in the flow of the river. Purna for them was as holy as the Ganga itself and they all affectionately called the river Purnamai – Purna, the mother. (p. 47)

The story further takes the reader into an old mansion of the Patels who had once ruled the neighbouring vicinity, but now are frustrated lots because the government after independence has taken away all their glory — the unaccountable land, the rights, the authority and the unquestionable terror once they exercised over the less privileged. Gone are those days now. The land is distributed among the tillers, the rights are given to the government administration and the authority no longer entertains them. Yet, the Patel's have maintained pride and would not marry less than three times even if they have nothing to feed their wives and children. They would strictly adhere to *Dharmashastras* and the restrictions laid therein.

Viren Patel is the last inheritor of the great Patel clan. He has already married twice before, and brings third bride to the enormous mansion, which needs repairs and renovations from every side. The mansion was the symbol of power and glory the Patel's had enjoyed once. ***"Now it appeared like scrotum of an old man suffering from hydrocele; trying to uphold itself from one side and in total disruption from another."*** Viren is popularly known as Viru Patel. He is in late sixties. His third wife Lila is young and beautiful, who finds her husband's unproductive approaches uninteresting. She even hates the old man who sleeps besides her snoring loudly. She wants to go out of the mansion and breathe freely, as the atmosphere inside is almost suffocating. Her husband arranges her trips outside with his old servant's daughter Bijli as a companion. Lila visits Bijli's house one day and meets her brother Baiju who is on vacation from college during Diwali or so. Lila's visits to Baiju became quite frequent and the two fall in love with each other. Lila finds in Baiju a man of her dreams, young and virulent. Baiju, who is scared initially, responds to her approaches, and the two often are engaged in love making.

Baiju belongs to an untouchable community. Though educated, he is ignorant about the ways of the world. Youthful Lila is equally so. They never imagined the consequences of their union. Their love story soon spreads out in the village. Viru Patel's first wife, Sushila, is infuriated at the realisation that Lila has spoilt the prestige of the Patel clan. Viru himself is ashamed of himself for allowing Lila to wander in Dalit locality. The entire Patel community takes it as a matter of honour. An untouchable boy having spoilt honour of a Patel woman goes against their lofty sense of invincible tradition. They decide to kill Baiju and restrict Lila's movements within the mansion. A mob of about twenty five armed men march towards Baiju's hut. Before they could reach the Dalit locality, Lila approaches Baiju and takes him away towards the river where they could hide and protect themselves from the violent mob. The men trace the two lovers and follow them in rage and apathy. As it seems difficult to escape, the lovers jump down into the river where the water is deep and current powerful. Baiju knows swimming, but, in an attempt to protect his beloved, is totally exhausted. As the water current takes them away further, both are drowned.

The love story reads like one of Romeo and Juliet, Laila-Majnu or Heer-Ranjha. But this one is different because the tragic element here is caste. It manifests the social difference between the high profile Patels with a profound sense of caste superiority and the low graded, downtrodden into the changing times after independence. Independence brought little cheers to the people; it seems. The rich have lost age-old glory, and the poor have become an object of their apathy. What really is missing — is enlightenment. Political theories or systems of governance have little impact unless the people are enlightened. Precisely the same situation prevails in India today. Untouchability is prohibited constitutionally in free India, but in reality, it remains intact in the minds of the people. More so, in rural vicinities. Even rivers are divided according to the caste. The author has brought it out clearly—

Purnamai offered her water equally to all the villagers who were divided into castes and communities. There were the Brahmins, the Patels, who counted themselves among the Kshatriyas, the traders who ran small shops and grinding mills and the lower castes treated as untouchables. The Muslims also formed a sizable portion of the village population. The untouchables, however, were a caste apart. They toiled the whole day and received a tiny share in return which was never enough to feed their kinsfolk who lived huddled together in hut-like apartments. These castes served others in the village-cleaned their courtyards, reared their cattle, procured wood for cooking meals, lit the pole lamps to lighten the streets, ran with messages from village to village and, in absence of doctors and medical facilities, the untouchable women supervised their childbirths. The traditionally assigned jobs were performed with immaculate perfection, and if, by chance, anything was missed out, or gone wrong, they received abuses and humiliation. They were being oppressed by the social order for centuries together and no one, not even God whom they worshipped day in and out, would liberate them from the dehumanising social apathy.

There were three separate *ghats* along the river flow used by three different communities. The first one, from where the water ran downwards, was used by the higher castes, the Muslims used the next, and the last one was given to the untouchables. There was the fourth ghat allocated for cattle to drink. These spots were compartmentalised institutions and no one would trespass from one to another; not even animals would dare to drink from a spot preserved for the human beings. (pp. 47, 48)

The story offers elaborate comments on caste as artificial which dissolves when it comes to human hearts melting together. Lila belongs to high caste Patel community and finds nothing wrong in giving into Baiju's masculinity, or pulling Baiju towards her female needs. The love scene between the two is controlled yet convincingly effective. The author has portrayed it in almost Lawrencian style —

Baiju realised that the young woman needs love and was gradually drawn towards her. Lila was already in deep love with him. She would forget everything in presence of Baiju including her marital status and the caste barrier that separated the two. The urge that had remained unfulfilled till now would push her into Baiju's arms whose kisses and caresses would send her wild with passion.

She would tear his shirt open and reach down to his groins. Then the nature would follow its own course.... (p. 55)

The story moves onto the various levels and puts forward issues like decline of the old glory of the erstwhile rich communities like the Patels, mismatched marriages like the one between Viru Bhai and Lila, and their consequences, intensity of human passion when deprived etc. Yet, it revolves around the vital factor - caste. Therefore, it is an important literary creation by a Dalit writer.

6. A Tale Told by a Scavenger

A Tale Told by a Scavenger is yet another interesting story wherein the protagonist is the narrator himself. Form of the story is oral— as if the narrator relates his experiences to listeners. He talks to the listeners in the middle of the narration— **"Will you be so kind as to lend your ears to this tale of a poor scavenger...** This gives an impression of live narration of the story.

This is the story of a scavenger — a *"bhangi"* as he is referred to in Indian languages. It is a strange story assuming the form of a mystery. The narrator protagonist is called Sukha– Sukha Billu Bhangi — as his name appears in the register book maintained by municipality. He is a scavenger — cleaner of toilets, sweeper of streets, and, when required, lifting what every filth is dropped in public places. Sukha has inherited this job from his father, and considers himself lucky because he has got this job without efforts while several educated young men and women are unemployed and looking for jobs. He is aware that times have changed, that manual cleaning of toilets are replaced by flush, defecating in the open is prohibited, yet social condition of the scavengers remains the same. This scavenger, Sukha, however, has a mysterious tale to narrate....

As he was returning home from work in the evening, he came across a scene wherein a woman was beaten up by several men with lathis and iron rods. She was screaming with pain, and, at the same time, abusing and cursing her husband and in-laws. The men abandoned her as she fell unconscious and lay motionless. They went away, but one of them called Sukha by name asking him to clean the spot. Sukha came to know that the woman had urinated and defecated profusely and was smeared with the filth. He washes the woman with a bucketful of water, cleans the spot and is about to go when the woman moans with pain. Sukha feels pity for her and helps her rise. She further requests him to take her home as she has nowhere to go.

This woman is called Mukta, as the reader comes to know in the course of narration. She is a mad woman from a Brahmin family. The reason for her madness is not revealed, but everybody thinks she is mad and is abandoned by her husband and other family members. She spends the night with Sukha's family against his father's will, who resists her presence in the house. They have to leave the house, spend night in the village temple, relieving and freshening themselves at the public lavatory. They go to Sukha's distant relative - an old woman who lived alone at the other end of the town. She is happy to receive them. They spend night together on a bed giving in each other physically. That was Sukha's first experience which made him extremely happy and developed love for Mukta who appeared quite sane, sober and good looking. Mukta, however, turns out to be mysterious woman. She disappears in the town and is never traced despite several efforts by Sukha. On the other hand, Sukha is badly beaten up in a locality where Mukta is said to be living.

The caste factor, once again, is predominating in the story. However, it operates on a different level. Mukta is Brahmin by caste. She is insane, abandoned by her kinsfolk. Sukha not only takes pity for her miserable condition but also invites rage and enmity of her parents. He takes her away to his distant relative as no one in the neighbourhood is ready to accept them. He spends nights with her first in a neighbouring temple, second, in the old woman's cosy bedroom. They both seem to have enjoyed a great deal. It is a reincarnation for Mukta who appears sane, sober and beautiful. She abandons Sukha, who has abandoned everything for her. This kind of infidelity and ungratefulness is unheard of. Why does she desert him? Is it to make him follow her and receive inflictions and abuses by her Brahmin caste men? The story concludes this way —

I had come far ahead in the town and presently found myself at the place where I had come across Mukta, two days ago, as the mad woman. I did not have precise notion of her residence but could guess the locality, now that I knew she was a Brahmin woman. I moved towards my guesswork, the posh territory of the town and began to call out her name loudly. Several windows opened up at the mention of Mukta. The name seemed familiar to many as I could locate curiosity oozing out of every face that peeped through the window. I looked around to see if Mukta responds, but my looks came back to me unresponded and the intimidating silence did not speak to me. I stood still in the midst of the road as I heard the noise from my back. "Here is the swine that defiled the sanctity of Brahmanism, the scavenger who polluted the woman of our caste."

A group of about seven able-bodied men with heavy sticks in their hands came running towards me. They grabbed me by throat and began to shower punches on my body. "Get him down", someone shouted and shouted and felled me like a tree on the ground. Now they began to beat me with sticks. I screamed for help which did not come from anywhere around. So they could have their own way and continued thrashing me till they fatigued, or perhaps till I lost my consciousness. (p. 69, 70)

Thus, the story portrays a clash between two castes; scavengers and the Brahmins, in which the former is badly beaten and defeated physically and spiritually as well.

7. Cobbler, Cobbler Mend My Shoes

Desperate Men and Women contains stories that give expression to different aspects of Dalit life. Here is a story that deals with life of the cobbler community, its sorrows and sufferings and the journey towards social stability. It is the story of Sadashiv Kalel, *chamar* or cobbler by caste, who has suffered a great deal in the past. Presently, better days have come. His son and daughter-in-law both are working in Government institutions. Their only son, who has started going to pre-primary school is left to the care of grandfather– i.e., Sadashiv. The child is learning his lesson loudly by heart. "Cobbler, cobbler mend my shoe......." and Sadashiv the cobbler, is sent back to his past when his father mended shoes of the village people, and ran the family labelled as untouchable......

Sadashiv retired as a primary school teacher. He wanted to learn more, obtain degrees and be Professor, Doctor or Engineer as a few of his classmates have gone up to those positions. But his father was a poor shoe-maker, a *chamar* who had no other source of income except mending shoes and *chappals* of the village folk with which he could hardly manage to survive. Sadashiv's mother would help her husband; even that was inadequate to earn enough to feed the family. Besides, the stigma of *chamar* caste would follow them like a shadow wherever they go. Sadashiv recalls....

They were always hungry, Sadashiv and his two sisters, for there was little food left after the day's meal. His mother would take care of the two girls at home, while Sada, as he was endearingly called by his parents, was supposed to go to school. He, however, was always found sitting by his father learning the art of stitching shoes, handling mallet and leather-scraper. That was the God-given profession of the *Chamars*, his father would tell him, No *Chamar* would go hungry if he

knows his profession well, while others — the *Mahars* and the *Matangs* will starve, or beg for food for lack of specific profession in the face of drought or famine. Therefore, each one of them should learn it. Sada would listen to him carefully, not to learn the profession and emulate his father, but to offer him assistance to dispose of the heap of shoes and *chappals* each one of which was labelled as urgent... (p. 72)

Untouchability and poverty go hand in hand. The untouchables were never allowed to pursue respectable jobs; they did not possess means to procure wealth. They always had to rely on pity of the high caste people. Even if they earned for themselves, as the cobbler community in India did, they never received credit for that. On the contrary, they were ill-treated and looked down upon. In the present story, protagonist's father earns for himself and for his family, yet he is always abused and scolded for little delay in completing the work at hand. The author has portrayed incident in which Sada's father was unable to complete work within the given time. He is beaten for that by a caste Hindu. There is another incident in which the little Sada and his family had to wait for hours to get left-over in a marriage feast. When his sister cries for food is driven away from the site and the family had to starve for want of food at home. Ironically, it was Sada's father who rushes to help the bride whose footwear needed mending. The untouchables served the society and affluent individual with equal sincere zeal and efforts, but they never received their due. On the contrary, were abused, humiliated even beaten up to death. The story has a scene where Sada's father is shown as a humble docile servant of the rich —

Everything went off well as planned by the Deshmukh family, everything except one. Next morning when the bride was about to leave her parent's house and go ahead with the groom she found her chappal's belt come off. She won't wear any other pair as this one represented the marriage sanctity and matched the garments she had put on. Men were sent for Sada's father who was the only shoe-maker available at that time. The man did his job well, stitched the belt properly, and held the girl's foot in hand placing it inside the footwear to check it properly. Cobbler, Cobbler mend my shoe.... (p. 76)

As Sada goes to school his knowledge and awareness broadens. He becomes aware of the fact that the shoe-making is a prospering business. It is an industry in itself. The Bata shoes company is famous throughout the country. The Batas have amassed wealth out of shoe-making. Why not his father do something similar. Or, at least seeks job in a shoe-making company. After all, his father is expert in shoe-making and mending shoes. He is disappointed at the realisation of his father's helplessness. He himself is unable to do anything in this direction. He feels dejected at the thought of his personal inability. He even shows awareness of the movement of the untouchables and Dr Ambedkar's dedication to it. He also knows what Congress and Gandhi are doing for the untouchables. However, he decides to keep aloof from these movements and follows the cobbler's profession; because —

He thought of cobbler's profession as noble, for it was like serving humanity in general, helping men as women in their critical moments. Therefore, he would ask his people not to forego the profession, rather pursue it with traditional zeal and comingle it with a sense of dignity. The gentry, however, would never treat the cobblers as a civilised class and looked down upon their profession as filthy. Like the rest of untouchables in the village, they were also counted among the unholy castes. (p. 77)

Sada's father dies during the cold of winter season. The author offers realistic comments on the Indian winter. While for some cold days of winter are pleasant, offering relief from heat and humidity, for the poor the winter is the most upsetting season. The bitter cold pierces the skinny limbs of the poor. There is no food to keep their bodies warm, and no clothes to ward them off from wintry waves. The sick and the old cannot stand to the biting waves that often bring cough and cold. Most of them breathe their last during winter. Sada's father, who is old enough to cause concern, dies unexpectedly during winter. There is no one who could support the family, hence Sada's mother takes over the little shop where his father used to attend to the customers. Sada tried to dissuade his mother from doing so, instead, had offered his services to look after the family. His mother, however, refuses his advice and sends her son to school and works herself to bring up the children. She was well acquainted with the cobbler's tools and could handle anvil, the scraper and the stitching material effectively. In spite of abuses and humiliating experiences from customers, she continued her work and brought up her children. Sada had obtained teacher's training and was soon appointed as a primary teacher.

Sada's past, thus, was extremely painful, filled with sorrows and sufferings. He, however, could overcome those days and set himself towards bright future. He has a son who is an administrative officer in the state government and a daughter who is married off in a respectable family. He is reminded of those painful days his own miserable past, but soon decides to forget those days and look forward to better days ahead—

Cobbler, Cobbler Mend My Shoe. Get it done by half past two……… Sadashiv Badaji Kalel, the grandfather of the child reciting his poem, was overwhelmed with the memories of past. The warm touch of tears running down his tears brought him back to the present. He looked around and noticed his grandchild smiling at him. He smiled back at the child and wondered if the little one shared his sentiments. "No, why should he", the old man told to himself, those days were marked for me alone. My progeny shall live happily ever after. The creator of the Universe has rectified his mistake. No one shall command his fellow being now, no one shall compose such filthy verse and no one shall recite… Cobbler, Cobbler Mend My Shoe…. (p.78)

Thus, the story brings out miserable past of the Dalits effectively.

8. Loneliness of An Ex-Soldier

This is the story of a young soldier called Wasu who has retired from the army after serving it for fifteen long years. Wasu was a brave soldier and well-known for his courageous acts. He had carried his wounded lieutenants on shoulders fearlessly amid the shower of bullets from the army camp and saved their lives. The whole battalion grew sentimental when he retired and returned home in his village after fifteen years.

Wasu was Mahar by caste and a staunch follower of Dr Ambedkar. He decided to teach the Ambedkarite principles to young boys of his community and held regular meetings in which he appealed his community men and women to renounce discriminatory customs and not to celebrate festivals that are expensive and based on untrue stories. He also taught them not to bow down to Brahmins and other caste-Hindus who think themselves superior.

This disturbed the village atmosphere which, till the arrival of Wasu, was running smoothly. The followers of Dr Ambedkar who agreed with Wasu, were ex-communicated. Young boys in the village from Wasu's community were framed into false allegations. Caste-Hindu women drawing water from well refused give water to thirsty Wasu when he returns home from work. And then — Wasu's young sister Suman — Sumi — as she was called — disappeared. She was found dead the next day with her young body mutilated and her clothes tattered. She was obviously raped and killed mercilessly.

Wasu was dumbfounded and awe-struck. Those men and women from his community, who were his followers till yesterday refused to side with him. His lonely struggle began. He went to the police authorities and reported the matter. The police, however, did nothing to give him justice. The police van came after two days, discussed the matter with the head of the village panchayat and went away. The matter did not progress beyond the initial stage. Wasu, the brave soldier in the Indian army was left alone and helpless, drowned in loneliness and desperation.

The story, thus, is about the injustice meted out to the Dalits even after Independence. The soldier who fought for the nation's security, was insecure in his own homeland. This is the general truth that prevails everywhere in India after Independence. It is pathetic but true.

9. Kultha Rangan

Kultha Rangan is set in the Southern state of Tamil Nādu when the entire region was stirred by the Periyar movement. It is the story of a woman called Kultha who is caught in a series of disasters and who is ultimately left alone to suffer. Dalit movement encompasses within its range welfare of every individual, and is particularly considerate towards the plight of Indian women who are counted among the *Shudras* in the social structure.

Kulatha's parents had come down to Madras in search of job and settled down as fishermen. They would go to the sea on fishing boats and return with considerable amount of fish which would offer them rich source of livelihood. Kulatha was their only child and was brought up with love and endearment. As a child she would wander in the market place freely and enjoy with the boys and girls of her age. She had watched the rising waves of the sea and basked beneath them. She would observe the sun setting into the ocean and the distant water bidding farewell to him. Men and women were genial, supporting and loving. She loved the village and was happy with her parents in it.

Kulatha's happiness, however, proved short-lived. Her parents, who went away on the boat on the sea, did not return. Their boat was caught in a cyclone and drowned. Kulatha was left alone. As she grew up Kulatha looked beautiful, though dark complexioned, she had remarkable face and figure. Several men approached her with proposals, several flirted with her, but she refused their approaches and decided to live on her own. Fate, however, had something else to offer. In view of her loneliness, four men raped her in her own house, leaving her exhausted and motionless. The news of her devastation spread out in the village. Everyone blamed her for what had happened, because they believed it was Kulatha's excessive frankness that had invited the disaster. Kulatha had no face to show as people in the village would mock at her, scold her at times, and she would return home crying, cursing her own self. One of the four men who had raped her approached her one day and agreed to give her shelter and protection from the village folk provided she accepts his proposal to be his "mistress", a keep who shall live as his personal property and will have no relationship with others. Kulatha rejects the proposal and sends the man out, shouting at him, calling him names.

Kulatha leaves the village and moves out towards the city of Madras, the metropolis where people are too busy to enquire about anybody's past, and where life seems to be comfortable. She finds a job at a construction site where several men and women, young and old, were employed. She joins them as labourers and soon cumingles with them sharing their joys and sorrows. Everyone respects Kulatha as a sincere worker and the one who is always ready to help others out of difficulties. Those were the days when the city of Madras was a witness to the state-wide social movement. Everyone in the region was overwhelmed with the principles forwarded to the masses by the leaders and spoke-persons of the movement. There were gatherings and meetings where the leaders would explain the cause of the stir and appeal the listeners to join it. They talked about tamil 'asmita', the ancient glorified past of the South, and about bright future for every individual including women, rich or poor. Kulatha would attend these meetings on non-working days, listen intently to the speakers and would be deeply impressed by the entire scenario. She would linger on after the meeting got over, and help those who cleaned the place and wind up the proceedings. There was dedication and sincerity in her work, and a total sense of commitment which was noticed by one of activists of the movement. He was called Rangan and held respectable place among his friends and colleagues. His devotion to the cause of the movement was beyond a trace of doubt. He had pledged to live for the cause and die for it.

Rangan was attracted towards Kulatha not only for her good looks, but also for dedication she revealed towards the movement. He falls in love with her and asks for her hand in marriage. Kulatha is startled by the proposal. She considers herself as nobody compared with Rangan, Besides, her miserable past would never leave her alone. Rangan, however, is drenched in love from top to bottom and would often express his love for the woman. Kulatha had to give in. They get married in a simple ceremony. Rangan's colleagues and friends were happy because they all loved Rangan and had great regards for his personality. Rangan's wife Kulatha was also an object of respect and regards for all of them.

Kulatha's life once again, bloomed like flowers in the spring. She profusely thanked God for the wonderful man – that Rangan was. She was now officially called *Kulatha Rangan.* That was recorded in all the official documents and the woman came to be called Kulatha Rangan. Life seemed to be on the right track till the day Kulatha's husband brought a friend for tea at home. Kulatha was taken aghast, because the guest was the same man from her village on the sea shore who had raped her and had come with the proposal of concubine. The man looked at Kulatha and a strange spark of acquaintance appeared in his eyes. He went quietly with Rangan but left Kulatha in deep state of turmoil. She was deeply disturbed and expected another calamity on the way. Rangan came back home late at night. But he was not in his usual self. He was drunk and could hardly control the balance. He went straight ahead to the bed and collapsed upon it. Kulatha was frightened to see her husband's unseen avatar. After having babbled to himself, he went to sleep immediately. He did not go out the next day, instead, lay on the bed till noon. Kulatha tried to wake him up. He did not rise in the morning. He remained still in the bed till the noon turned westward. Kulatha sat beside his bed trying to talk to him. He refused to respond. She went out to kitchen to prepare the evening meal. It was almost nine o'clock at night when Rangan got up from bed. All of a sudden, he started sobbing, holding head in hands. Kulatha rushed to him asking – "What happened, what happened, tell me what happened?" He turned hostile at the touch of her hand, "Keep away, keep away!" he shouted at her. At her next move, he pushed her away — calling her slut and debauch. Kulatha tried to plead her innocence, tried to explain the situation. He was in no mood to understand her. He asked her to get out of his life, presently get out of his house. He pushed her out physically and shut the door against her. The author describes Kulatha's plight —

It was dark outside and cold. The stars gleamed away into the sky as if to mock at Kulatha's plight. The noise of insects and the occasional barking of dogs were heard, and an owl's hooting away somewhere added horror to the scene. Kulatha turned back and looked at the house. She had spent happy hours and enjoyed the bliss of marriage inside it. Suddenly, it had turned hostile. Where shall she go now, alone –no, she was no longer alone — but carrying Rangan's child in her womb for more than three months. She thought of reminding Rangan of that, but she decided not to, for Rangan would

not think of it as a suitable reason to let her in. She moved away in the dark like a sleepwalker knowing not its destination. (p.99)

The story is remarkable for several things. First, it deals with the plight of a woman exploited by patriarchy. Kulatha was insecure from the day she lost her parents to the ocean. Her innocence is mistaken as frailty and men around her thought that she is easily "available". She is raped by those whom she knew as friendly men. The society blames not those men, but the girl for the "misdeed". Rangan's hypocrisy is well exposed. He is a respected leader of a movement meant to uplift the poor and the helpless. Ironically, it is the poor and the helpless who is deserted by him. His love and affection evaporates after he comes to know about Kulatha's past. He is broken inside as if he is made of hollow sticks of wood. Kulatha, on the other hand, gathers courage and decides not to return to her husband who has pushed her out of the house. She accepts fate stoically and walks out into the dark leading to unknown destination.

The author delineates a realistic picture of coastal life in Madras presidency of those days. Here is an imaginary village called Silampatti situated on the coastal line –

Silampatti was a fishing centre which supplied fishes to markets and to other towns in the province. It offered regular employment to a number of families including those who were not fishermen by profession. Kulatha's parents had migrated here in search of job when she was thirteen. They made best of the opportunities and settled down here as a fishing caste. Kulatha was their only child who was brought up with loving care in conditions available to the poor. They went to the sea early in the morning and returned home at the sunset. Cyclones and hurricane often strike the coastal regions and rendered life inoperative. They take way the working folk into the deep sea and drown them. Human lives are perished by nature's atrocious moods. Kulatha's parents went to work on a certain day and never returned. She was left alone and destitute. Thus, began her ordeal...... (p. 91)

Like the rest of the short stories in the book ***Kulatha Rangan*** should also be a milestone in the realm of Indian short stories.

10. Confessions of a Graveyard Keeper

This is a humorous story replete with amusing sarcasm. The protagonist is a narrator himself who narrates the events in his life in an amusing manner. His parents were *chandals* attending the dead in the graveyard. They worked on the bank of the river Ganga at Benaras — that holy place where the dead were hurled out into the river water which Gangamai carried away quietly. The narrator grew up watching his parents attending the dead on the bank river. He noticed the boats crossing the river, and watched the women bathing in Ganga water. He had his first successful masturbation here on the bank of river Ganga.

The protagonist lost his father unexpectedly. The boy and his mother were sent away as the widow was not allowed to touch the dead and watch the funeral rites. They came to a place called Rampur and worked at a graveyard under the supervision of an old man called Anda Bhurji. This Anda Bhurji was drawn toward the young widow and allowed her to stay in the graveyard with her son. The old Anda Bhurji often visited their house and sent the boy away on some pretext or other. The women did not mind Anda Bhurji's approaches, because she was in need of support, and was sure about the old man's ineffective dangling crotch. Anda Bhurji died in course of time, and the entire charge of graveyard came to the narrator and his mother. The narrator is married to Anda Bhurji's youngest daughter who is very talkative and as dark as tar. The protagonist narrates numerous events which are amusing and funny. His mother dies and is not allowed by customs, to be buried in the graveyard which was exclusively reserved for the upper castes. He, however, dares the convention and buries his mother's dead body in the graveyard itself.

The time passes on and he continues to be the sole keeper of the graveyard. His wife loses his front two teeth. That makes her keep her mouth shut and remain silent.

The story is extremely amusing and readable. A Dalit boy, as the protagonist has no inhibition in narrating what he does or sees. Therefore, there are references to women bathing in the Ganga River, leaving the breasts uncovered, the mating couple in the temple courtyard, elopement of Muslim girl with a Hindu boy etc.

This story is also remarkable for the Dalit ethos, the discriminatory Hindu customs and the suffering they cause to the untouchables. Humour and pathos stay together in the short story named ***Confession of Graveyard Keeper.***

Anguish and Desperation on part of the characters in the stories is visible throughout the texts. Rakhma's anguish and desperateness while delivering the child all alone without assistance is explicit. So is Lakhan's when he is compelled to leave his native place. All the characters, in the stories, in fact suffer from these traits because they are tortured by the caste

– Hindus and utterly helpless. Ex-soldier's loneliness, Kultha Rangan's wretchedness, miseries of Sadashiv, the shoe-maker — everyone suffers from incurable anguish and desperation. The unnamed scavenger, Butya, the gravedigger is also caught into insurmountable misery and have to face the situation that is beyond control.

Major Themes in *Desperate Men and Women*

While caste and its ill-effects on individuals and the society are the major themes of the stories in ***Desperate Men and Women***, there are several other social issues that come up and attract the attention of the readers. The first and foremost among them is the plight of Dalit women in India. They suffer from dual victimisation — being women and Dalit simultaneously. ***Childbirth*** the very first short story in the collection, offers the best illustration. Rakhma, the protagonist in the story, suffers tremendously. Other women characters have their own stories to narrate and each one of them is equally moving. They are all ill-treated in their own house by their men folk. They all discuss their plight while working together on the agricultural farms. One of them tells her husband is always drunk and beats children. The other one exposes the lecherous intention of a *patwari* while she was adjusting her sari. The third woman has a more tragic tale to narrate. Her young mother-in-law was raped by a Patil when all other members had gone away to attend a religious function. Enraged, her father-in-law murders the Patil and is imprisoned for the life. The family suffers as its head is in jail and there is no working man in the house. In fact, Dalit women's sexual exploitation by high caste men in India is not uncommon. Their helplessness, hunger and poverty compel them to lie down to satisfy carnal desire of the high-caste, rich men.

Rakhma in the story is prototype of the Indian Dalit woman. She is poor, helpless and committed to her family. Her husband is good for nothing – does not work and spends time idly smoking *bidis*. He is indifferent towards his wife's plight who is pregnant with nine months gone and needs assistance. On the other hand, he thinks it is his right to live on his wife's meagre earnings and spends time smoking *bidis* doing nothing. Rakhma knows it all and decides to go for work to feed her husband and two children. Her courage and sense of commitment is remarkable. Her ability to move and work even in that condition is also noteworthy. Her decision to beget the baby on her own is the top of a woman's credibility. She comes back home and realises that there is no one at home to assist her in childbirth. Therefore, she lies down on the ground, parts her thighs away from each other, pushes the baby, who comes tumbling out in the world. She cuts the umbilical cord herself, with a sickle and finds out something to eat, as the evacuated belly needs to be filled in. There is nothing to eat. She leaves the crying baby alone and comes out in search of food. She is bleeding profusely and half-clad. It's raining that makes her body shiver with cold. She picks up a handful of groundnuts from a shop and returns home quickly. However, she is totally exhausted and collapses before she enters the house. The baby is crying inside and the rain outside falls heavily.

This kind of situation in a woman's life is rare indeed, and indicative of her courage and stoicism. Dalit women in India often undergo such ordeals and face the situation bravely. Most of them survive and a few die as well. What happens in Rakhma's case is open to speculation. Rain is a symbol of destruction in the lives of the Dalits as it blocks all the ways to move and work. No work, no meal. Several Dalit families go to sleep without food as it rains continuously rendering everything wet and slippery. Rakhma presently is in this conditions, she is a woman and Dalit. The author has brought out the pathos in the story remarkably well.

Women characters in other short stories in the collection confirm Dalit women's dual victimisation. Jamuna, Lakhan's wife in ***Farewell,*** faces the similar situation. She is young and good-looking. The village chief has an eye on her adorable appearance. He demands her to stay with him for a night to lift up the ban that has been imposed on her family by the entire village. This was adding salt to the wound for Jamuna and her husband, who instead decide to bid farewell to the village itself. The high-caste Hindu men are often lured away by Dalit women's flexible physique, well-built and attractive. They find worth-touching while their men are untouchable. This is well depicted in the story —

The chief avoided Lakhan and looked at Jamuna who was listening to the arguments as a mute witness. "Your women are the only human beings amongst you untouchables. Look at her, she is so beautiful and worthy of a man's desire. She can set you free if you so desire", said the chief while staring at Jamuna lustily.

"What do you mean?" Asked Lakhan who had suspected the man's lecherous intention, "what do you mean by that?"

The chief smiled and, looking at the men stood surrounding him, said — "tell him the meaning."

"Lakhan", said one of them, "It's simple. Send your wife to *haveli* **tonight and tomorrow you will be free". (p. 33)**

This is socio-economic conditions of the Dalit women in India wherein they live and die eventually. In ***When the Sun God Refused to Set*** there are women characters like Kala and Baby who suffer from their men folk and get nothing in return. ***Quiet Flowed the Purnamai*** has a woman character, who is not Dalit by birth, but suffer tremendously for flouting the social norm. Lila is married to Viru Patel who is thrice old in age than the young Lila. She, in fact, is his third wife and hates his ineffective sexual advances. She, therefore, is naturally drawn towards young Baiju with whom she develops physical relations. Baiju is a Dalit by caste, therefore a scornful object to the Patel clan. They decide to kill him for his misdemeanour and avenge the humiliation. Lila, however, is aware of his innocence and protects him from her husband's wrath. However, both of them are drowned in the river in an attempt to escape from the violent mob.

The author has effectively depicted the young Lila's physical yearnings and her powerful desire to set herself free from the suffocating atmosphere in the Patel mansion. The story also exposes the high caste Hindu men's love for tradition even though they are ruined by it. Their hatred towards the untouchable community has also been laid bare. There is a high-caste woman characters in stories like ***"A Tale Told by A Scavenger".*** Mukta, as she is called, is an interesting woman character who is declared mad by her in-laws, but gets cured after sexual intercourse with the scavenger. Suman, in ***Loneliness of an Ex-Soldier***, is another Dalit girl who is raped and killed brutally by the high-caste Hindu men.

Kulatha Rangan depicts one more powerful woman character form the Dalit community, who suffers and faces the situation bravely. Kulatha was brought up with love by her parents, who were, unfortunately, gulfed down by the ocean while they were working on a ship. She is left alone and helpless. Her innocence and frankness is misunderstood by her work-mates who rape her and leave the young girl astounded. Kulatha is blamed for what has happened to her and the rapists are let at large. Life becomes difficult for her; therefore, she leaves the native place and comes down to the city of Madras in Tamil Nādu, which, during those days, was stirred with the Periyar movement. She finds work and shelter in Madras and is involuntarily involved in the movement. She impresses everyone by hard work, sincerity and commitment to the cause. Rangan who is one of the leaders of the movement falls in love with her. He is able to persuade her to marry. They live happily together till one day, Kulatha's old acquaintance in the village appears unexpectedly. He recognises her immediately. He reveals Kulatha's past poisoning Rangan's heart and mind against her; Rangan, who once loved her immensely, turns against her. He drives her out of the house. She is left alone to suffer once again.

Kulatha's story is typical of a Dalit woman who is abandoned for no fault of her. She was abandoned by her workmates earlier, now she is abandoned by her husband who thinks of her as characterless. She is a victim of caste-system and of patriarchy at the same time. Indian Dalit woman's condition is a precarious and pathetic as that of a black woman in America. Tony Morrison, the 1992 Nobel Laureate for literature, depicts the image of a black woman, which has striking resemblance with that of a Dalit woman in India — Morrison writes —

Edging into the life from the backdoor. I becoming. Everybody in the world was in a position to give them order – White woman said — "Do this", White men said "Come here", black men said "lie down". The only people not take order form were black children and each other.

But they took all that and recreated in it their own image. They ran the house of while people and knew it. When white men beat their men they cleaned up blood and went home to receive abuse from the victim. They beat their children with one hand and stole for them with the other. The hands that fell trees also cut umbilical cords; the hands that wrung the neck of chickens and butchered hogs also nudged African violets into bloom, the arms that loaded sheaves, bales and sacks rocked babies into sleep. They patted biscuits into flaky ovens of innocence and shrouded the dead. They ploughed all day and came home to nestle like plume under the limbs of their men. The legs that straddled a mule's back were the same ones that straddled their men's hips. And difference was all the difference there was. (Morrison, p. 23)

This is precisely the image of a Dalit woman in India who is a victim of caste system and patriarchy at the same time.

B. Rangrao's stories also deal with other social issues like mismatched marriage as in ***Quiet Flowed the Purnamai***, military personnel's helplessness after retirement as in **Loneliness of an Ex-soldier**, etc. However, the author makes it clear in the ***Preface*** itself that his stories are not "social documents", neither do they have "political connotations". They are "projection of social reality perceived by a creative mind which has itself undergone and experienced much that it portrays in the stories". He writes further —

Caste is the major underlying factor of Dalit experience. Other factors like class, gender, race or creed deviate the focus from the main issue and lead it towards another form of essentialism, which, in turn, leaves the Indian social reality half perceived. Creativity, of course, results out of personal experience and its understanding, and cannot be a matter of comparison. Therefore, no claim can be laid towards superiority of these stories in English, but they are *Dalit* in essence, that is confirmed. (Preface)

Thus, B. Rangrao's short stories are basically about "caste", though they also deal with other social issues when and where required.

Notes

1. B. Rangrao, **Desperate Men and Women : Ten Dalit Short Stories from India**. Delhi, Kalpaz Publications ; New Delhi, 2013. (p. 19)
2. *Ibid.* (p. 20)
3. *Ibid.* (p. 25)
4. *Ibid.*(p. 27)
5. *Ibid.* (p. 36)
6. *Ibid.* (p. 36)
7. *Ibid.* (p. 47)
8. *Ibid.* (p. 47, 48)
9. *Ibid.* (p. 55)
10. *Ibid.* (p. 69, 70)
11. *Ibid.* (p. 72)
12. *Ibid.* (p. 76)
13. *Ibid.* (p. 77)
14. *Ibid.* (p. 78)
15. *Ibid.* (p. 99)
16. *Ibid.* (p. 91)
17. *Ibid.* (p. 33)
18. Upanisha, S, and Dr Grace Priyadarsini. "Turkish Online Journal of Qualitative Inquiry (TOJQI)." Turkish Online Journal of Qualitative Inquiry (TOJQI), Vol. 12, no. 6, 2007, pp. 8488–8494.
19. B. Rangrao, *Desperate Men and Women: Ten Dalit Short Stories from India.* Delhi, Kalpaz Publications; New Delhi, 2013. (Preface)

Chapter - III (B)

Thematic Analysis of the Text *When I Hid My Caste*

— Baburao Bagul

Baburao Bagul's ***When I Hid My Caste*** was published in 1963 by Abhinav Prakashan, Mumbai. Since then, the book has sixteen reprints, latest being the one republished in 2018. These stories were translated from the original Marathi into English by the famous translator Jerry Pinto, under the title ***When I Hid My Caste.*** Bagul's short stories are supposed to be the landmark of short stories in Indian languages. They are the revelations of the Dalit sensibility and offer astounding facets of Indian social reality.

Here is an attempt to analyse the stories in the book.

1. Prisoner of Darkness

"Prisoners of Darkness" is about men and women who are surrounded by darkness, ignorance, poverty, miseries and wretchedness. "Darkness" in the title of the story stands for the wretchedness which had darkened their past, present and future at the same time. They are men and women who have been deprived of amenities of life — they are desperate men and women who have struggled throughout life and are defeated. Therefore, they are angry, hostile towards each other and disappointed about life in general.

The story depicts the life of Devram Deshmukh — Deshmukh, generally, is a high caste village chief. The Deshmukhs, traditionally, practice polygamy and marry more than once and bring different women at home. Devram's father has a young woman called Banoo. She is young and beautiful and has complete sway over his father. The old man was totally under her influence and did not bother about the family welfare. Devram hated this young Banoo, but was unable to do anything because his father, though old, was all powerful. The old man died and Devram's anger and hatred towards Banoo bursts out like a volcano —

The evening, a young woman adorned by the departing sun's warm love, proceeded to the west and darkness fell. It was at this melancholic moment that Ramrao Deshmukh's body was ablaze on his funeral pyre. His son Devram, bare-chested, his massive body as hard as rock, spun around form the pyre; the heat pressing down upon the corpse's chin had caused the skull to explode; the sharp crack eliciting a wall of grief from all those who had been close to the dead man. Devram punched the air with a fist as powerful as a hammer. He gnashed his teeth and between sobs, he shouted — "Banoo, You......" (1)

Devram's anger and hatred towards Banoo is so intense and all pervasive as if it covers the entire surrounding. He hates Banoo, not only because she was his father's "keep", but also because she belonged to untouchable community, and a "Murli" — a girl "given up" to God to serve Him and the society. Banoo loves Deshmukh whole-heartedly, and, in fact, is happy as "keep" of the village chief who provides her everything necessary to lead a peaceful life. She has even neglected her son Daulat — born out of wedlock, and has reconciled with fate. Devram, late Ramrao's son, however, an eye on her beautiful body and, at the same time, wanted to kill her for polluting and entering the Deshmukh mansion. When he enters her room with a gun his intention becomes clear. Banoo mistakes him as aggrieved deeply by his father's death and tries to pacify his grief and anger. She even agrees to leave the mansion to stay elsewhere with her son. He, however, orders her not to leave and stay with him as his keep. Banoo tries to explain that she is his father's wife; hence his mother even though has not begotten him. He refuses to accept Banoo's argument and is bent on killing her. She somehow escapes from the mansion and runs out for fear of life. She knows that Devram has turned out into a beast and can kill her mercilessly. She runs out through the village lanes with her clothes unwrapped and shattered. The villagers pass filthy comments as they notice her running in that position. She was a *murli* after all, meant for everyone's sexual gratification. Therefore, they think it's their right to have her at least for a night. The villagers are as beastly and ruthless as Devram himself. No one comes to her rescue. On the contrary, they laugh at her helplessness and enjoy the women's misery. One of them even tries to molest her. He tries to hold her from behind but his efforts are terminated by sudden attack by someone. The man who saves Banoo was none other than her own son Daulat. Devram, in the meantime, reaches the place where Banoo was surrounded by the violent mob. He tries to rape the woman in that situation. Banoo appeals her son to save her from the beastly Devram who has already pushed the boy with a powerful stroke of fist. Daulat somehow raises himself up, controls his balance and pierces the knife into Devram's body. Devram reels as if in whirlwind and falls down on the ground the next moment dead. The mob dismantles and scatters away with fear and intimidation.

The story ends with a profound sense of panic and amazement. The violence and aggression have deep impact on the reader. How do these people live? How do they die? They are not human beings but prisoners of darkness. This darkness around them has dehumanised them. They struggle with themselves and with the world outside which is equally hostile. The author brings this out effectively towards the close of the story —

As she bore the ignominy and shame — as she would to the end of her life — Banoo slipped her arm out from under Devram's body and struggled to prise the knife out of Daulat's fist. Her blouse was in tatters; her sari, clenched between her teeth, was torn. A curtain of black hair flowed past her shoulders. And hand struggles to free the knife from Daulat's grasp. There was blood everywhere.

The gully was silent, the village still. The image of Maruti, which faced the village, hands folded in the flickering light of the lamp placed before it, sometimes appeared angry and sometimes sad. (18)

"Prisoners of Darkness" is remarkable for many things. It exposes the *'Vaghya-Murali'* tradition in Maharashtra wherein girls of certain untouchable castes are 'married' to God, meaning thereby that they must make themselves available to whosoever demands them. Invariably, it's the worshipper in the temple (pujari), or the village chief who lays claim on the young girl's body. Needless to state that the young unfortunate girls are left to nowhere after their prime youth is over. Afterwards in old age, they live in miseries and die in the similar conditions. Banoo in this short story lives with the old Deshmukh who seems to be kind enough to take care of her. However, his young son Devram is drawn towards her lecherously and wants to 'keep' her after his father's demise. The woman for him and for the entire village is no other than a 'murali' whose womanhood is never looked upon with dignity. This tradition in

Maharashtra existed for several years and flourished during the Peshwa rule when all kinds of discriminatory social customs were encouraged. Today it seems to be on the decline and the traditions like Murali, Devdasi etc. have lost their significance.

The story also depicts the relationship between the mother and son. Banoo's illegitimate son Daulat lives away from her as a bastard. He knows his position and that of his mother in society. Therefore, they hardly meet or communicate. Nevertheless, he comes to her rescue when her life is in danger. He kills a villager called Kashinath and Devram Deshmukh who was bent on raping before he could kill her. Daulat kills the man and saves his mother's life and dignity.

Thus, the story is a moving account of the life of the oppressed and untouchables in Indian society.

2. Bohada

Bohada is a mask of God, Semi-God or mythological hero to be worn in order to enact that character. This is done in festivals and fairs in some parts of Maharashtra, in Nashik district in particular. This is honour given to high caste men while the Dalits or the oppressed are supposed to watch. There are several customs prevalent among the Hindu wherein only high caste men have privileges to perform certain rituals. Putting fire for Holi dump or taking bullocks under the bunch of flowers on the day of "pola" — the festival when farmers worship bullocks as a token of gratefulness towards the animals. Similarly, Bohada is a privilege of the High caste men. They enact certain God while others watch the show.

Bagul's short story **Bohada** depicts a character — a young man from Mahar community called Damu who revolts against the customary ritual of Bohada and declares that he will enact the God Narsimha by wearing his mask. This is unexpected and unheard of to the men assembled in "chawadi" — the office of the village chief. The men in the assembly include a brahmin, a Deshmukh, a Muslim, and a few others from the so-called higher castes. This announcement by Damu – a Mahar by caste, sends them into dizziness, and each one of them begins to question Damu. Their response to Damu's revolt is noteworthy —

Anger began to rule as Ravana had ruled in Lanka. Bhagwan Deshmukh's pendulous round cheeks began to vibrate. Jagannath cracked his hunter and began to curse. Raghu Arighala began to abuse even as he tried to twist his Brahmanical pigtail, his *shendi* into

a knot. Karim Chacha began to pluck white hair from his beard and ask questions.

Through it all, there in the village gateway, at the edge of the square, stood six-feet Damu, a warrior, adamantine in colour and in body. He kept looking at the people in the square. On his face was the peace and the restraint of a powerful man. (20)

While Damu's revolutionary demeanour has starling effects on everyone, the assembled men grew conscious about the status in the village set-up. "Jagannath always felt that he should be acknowledged as Shamrao Deshmukh's son: that Bhagwan should accept him as his half-brother; that he should have right to residence in their wada. As none of this happened, people called him a member of the cow- herding colony, which is why this fatherless boy was always angry."

The Muslims in the village have certain rights which are denied to Mahars, Matangs and Chamars even though they are members of the Hindu community. The caste-ridden Hindus feel insulted if they are referred to by caste below theirs. A *Kunabi* is humiliated if he is called a Mahar; even a Mahar feels humiliated if called a Matang. Caste-pyramid in Hindu social structure is so compartmentalised that even a Mahar would not give his daughter in marriage to a Brahmin or a Kshatriya. That would bring social stigma upon his social honour. The men assembled in the village office reveal this through their responses to the challenges thrown by Damu, the Mahar. Interestingly, as this important issue is discussed in the village office, not a single woman is noticed at the council. Women among the Hindus were not allowed to participate in such important discussion. Their place was within the four walls of the house. The story does not contain women characters at all. Dalit life and the Dalit experiences was no better than the canonical structure wherein women were treated as secondary. This is evident from all the self-narratives of Dalit women writers. Mallika Amar Sheikh's ***"I want to Destroy Myself"*** is the best example.

Bohada has several things to declare. It is a story of a revolt of a young Dalit against the tradition. Damu is a part of the Hindu social set-up. Therefore, he wants to live on equal social level with others. Bohada cannot be a prerogative and monopoly of the high castes. It should come down to the Mahars, Matangs and the Chamars who were deprived of human rights and dignity. Damu declares openly that he is going to play bohada this year. The Patil opposes his stand and that ignites the spark of social conflict. Others ask him to pay in view of the fact he is too poor to pay the amount of 200 rupees. Damu agrees to pay the amount. The council raises the amount to 600 rupees. Damu decides to face financial crisis at home and pay the said amount. He does pay the amount because that alone will break the old canons, that alone will offer opportunities to the oppressed to prove their worth, that alone will pave a way to social equality.

Damu plays bohada enacting the avatara Narishma heroically. The entire village is impressed. The Mahars are convincingly pleased, whereas the Patil and his friends are jealous. They cannot digest Damu's impressive performance and his superiority in the act. This comes out through their conversation —

We haven't had Narsimha like that in twenty years' — Karim chacha said to an old man. (31)

And the Patil was saying — 'Now we should have no more bohadas'

And the Mahars were saying — "Next year, we will dance to the five Pandavas. And let them bring down death or destruction, it will be all the same to us." (32)

The story also brings out local customs in rural Maharashtra and their impact on the village life.

3. Streetwalker

Baburao Bagul's definition of 'Dalit' goes much beyond 'caste' and covers, within its range, everyone who is exploited socially, economically, or in the name of religion. First story in this collection ***Prisoners of Darkness*** depicts the plight of a 'murali', who is by decree of religion, married to God and is sexually exploited by everyone. ***Streetwalker*** depicts the miseries of a prostitute, who, in the face of profound grief, has to maintain false pleasantries and beautiful appearance in order to attract customers. The socio-economic conditions oppress the individual to the extent of ethical violation, and one becomes a mere beast forgetting the social norms. Bagul was strongly influenced by the Marxist ideology wherein economic exploitation is social norms. Bagul was strongly influenced by the Marxist ideology wherein economic exploitation is said to be the main cause of human misery. Bagul carried these impressions throughout his life and worked them out in creative writings. His stories prove, time and again, that Ambedkarism should be accompanied by the Marxist ideology.

Streetwalker is the story of a prostitute called Girija, who, like the rest of her community, believes in superstitions. She has visited Haji Malang, the popular local deity, whose blessings enhances wealth and improves business. This popular belief attracts a number of visitors to Haji Malang, Hindus and the Muslims together, and a fair or 'Mela' is formed on certain days in a year. Girija has brought "prasad", that is, God's offering to distribute among the kinsfolk and eat it herself. That would enhance and improve her "business" and fetch money which she badly needs. She has just returned from Haji Malang and is in high spirit, as she thinks it a good time to start.

She comes to the restaurant which is her favourite place to sit and watch around targeting customers. The owner of the restaurant is well acquainted with her, and, is in fact, her landlord whose address she uses for postal communication. The man takes pity on the woman, knowing her well enough, and does not mind her presence as she attracts customers who would enjoy a cup of tea and biscuits boosting her own business further. Girija gives him 'prasad' and orders tea. She has not paid the earlier debt, yet the owner asks the waiter to give her tea. A few moments later, the owner breaks the news to Girija that there is telegram for her. She is taken aback at the mention of telegram and requests the owner to read out the content. Her son who is away at village is seriously ill and the treatment requires money. Girija is deeply aggrieved. She loves her son and decides to earn enough to treat his ailment.

She comes out in the street in search of customers. She is young and quite good looking. The news has darkened her face, but she tries to keep it brightened as much as possible. Prostitutes generally are poor and ill-fed. They suffer from all sorts of diseases. Girija, however, did not have any major ailment and her looks attracted customers quite often. Today, however, she had no desire to offer herself to an unknown man while her son is suffering away at a village. Yet, she needs money to treat her beloved son. Therefore, she must find a customer. She stands at the corner of a street, making signs to the passers-by. Men look at her making lewd faces or uttering abuses. No one seems to be interested. **"Why, have they lost their virility today? Have they all turned out to be impotent?"** She asks herself. A man approaches her. How much? He asks. Five, she tells him. So much, will Two do? He enquires. No, she tells him. The man goes away. Her ordeal starts again. There are other women standing at distances. She notices men dealing with them. A few of them go with the customers. Girija curses her fate. She prays to Haji Malang whose 'prasad' must send customers. She tries to improve her looks, leaves her breasts half covered, removes sari from her flat belly. God, send some customers, she prays again. After a long wait, a man approaches her. He looks quite young and handsome but looks don't matter, she tells herself. Come, whosoever must, and eat me away, take each part of my body to the butcher's device if that quenches your thirst and pacifies your hunger. Men are hungry from time immemorial. They have eaten away women and belched out with satisfaction. We are food, they are stomach, they eat us, eat out flesh and bones, eat our souls away and depart.

Finally, a man arrives. He agrees to pay five rupees and the two go to a nearby room. Girija pretends to be a nice woman who is drawn to prostitution only recently out of need. She tells him that she was a dancer in *Tamasha* and lost her job out of misunderstanding with the *shair*. She played every trick to attract him and draw as much money from him as she could. Even though he appeared to be a nice man, rich and all. But he wants 'it' in his own way. Standing. Girija suggests lying down on back. He refuses. The two make a way out. The man falls upon her like a hungry beast. Girija wants to forget everything — her son, his illness, need of money, but cannot. She does not respond to the man's violent strokes, is as still as a dead body. The man is exhausted, but infuriated. He dresses up angrily, calls the woman few dirty names and leaves her naked body with the banging of the door. She tries to raise herself, but the man holds her by the neck, pushes her back and goes away quickly. A few moments later, Girija comes to herself. She looks around and realises that the man is gone. He has not paid. She gets up abruptly at the realisation, wraps he naked body with the end of the sari, comes to the door and yells out — "hey, you....". The man is gone away and is nowhere to be seen. She lies back quietly motionless. The story ends. It brings out irony of the situation, and irony of fate in the context of the poor woman. Reader is taken aghast and does not know whom to blame. The man who wants full satisfaction for his money and does not receive? Or the woman who fails to respond to the man's needs. The story open-ended.

Baburao Bagul reveals larger human understanding through his short stories. His characters include beggars, labourers, untouchables, field workers, prostitutes, pimps, sex-agents — and all types of destitute and desperate men and women. When he began writing stories, the Marathi literary world was dominated by the Brahmanical tradition — G. A. Kulkarni, Gangadhar Gadgil were his contemporaries. These writers were highly esteemed. Bagul's stories came as sharp contrast to their writing. Therefore, he did not receive the expected response from the existing literary critics. His Dalit sensibility reached to prominence as the movement of Dalit literature became powerful rejecting the existing literary canons. His stories were always compared in literary seminars, workshops etc. with those of G. A. Kulkarni, and Gangadhar Gadgil who wrote out of Romantic and Modernist literary concepts. Bagul, on the other hand, exposed social reality and laid bare its nauseating facets: The characters he wrote about were neglected altogether or treated to create personalities. Bagul, like Namdeo Dhasal, raised them up to human level and pleaded for their honour and dignity. These characters are victims of social surroundings and the society, they need not to be blamed for the precarious condition they often found themselves in. This was new to the literary world based on the canonical assumption of human existence. This was also a challenge to literary authority. Therefore, if faced resistance from the establishment and had to struggle a great deal in order to receive acceptance from the readers.

Bagul is not only a social thinker, but also a fine artist who draws various nuances out of his literary creation. His language is always convincing, rough though at times. And he has capacity to enter into the heart of the situation. Girija's portrait in "Streetwalker" is beautifully drawn. In a subtle style of storytelling, he makes Girija's plight visible —

Her docile body, racked by terrible pain, pushed to the extremes of endurance, came back to life, such was the effect of the rage she felt. Her upper lip peeled back to her nose and became a straight line. In her muscles, strength began to gather. Her eyes filled with rage of the serpent. Her face grew red with anger. She dragged her blanket into a makeshift covering and burst out — 'You pimp, where do you think you're off to? Drop that money!'

At the very door, he paused for a moment, startled by her altered avatar. He grew alert, watching her, knowing that she was about to pounce. When she did, he got her by the neck and flung her aside carelessly as one might fling a cat.

And she fell, a mother maddened by love, burned by her own sorrow, she fell and she lay where she had fallen. (42,43)

Earlier, Girija's plight as a mother who is giving up her body to unknown men is well brought out. Mother and prostitute are at loggerhead with each other —

Working up some foam with the soap, she scrubbed her face. Then she dried it on her dirty blouse. She set the mirror in front of her, and the sight of her face undid the control she had exercised over

her tears. The sobs burst from her; the mirror dropped from her hand. She cried and cried and did not stop until her mind grew quiet; then she applied herself again to the task of beautifying herself. She oiled her hair and parted it. She pulled it back into a loose bun...... (34)

The story, thus, is a realistic portrait of a mother who has turned to prostitution in order to feed her family. Bagul has convincingly brought out the truth that no woman turns to prostitution willingly, rather, the social condition and surrounding factors compel her to do so.

Prostitutes and their wretchedness has been a favourite topic to write about to Dalit writers. Namdeo Dhasal, for example, had named a collection of his poem as ***Golpeetha,*** an area in South Mumbai inhabited by the prostitutes. Prakash Jadhav, another Dalit poet in Marathi writes about the issues in many of his poems. Baburao Bagul's sympathy as a writer goes towards these unfortunate women. ***"Streetwalker"*** is an example.

4. Gangster

Baburao Bagul's art of storytelling is unique and effective at the same time. No other writer in Marathi or in any other Indian language tells the story of a single person placing him amid hostile social surroundings. His psychological approach combined with sociological hostility make his art superb. ***Gangster*** is about an unknown criminal hardened by the circumstances and who is insensitive about human sentiment. The story narrates his transformation from insensitive gangster to a sensitive human being who helps out a young woman in need. He is presented in a manner that gives out an authentic picture of a criminal like him —

He pounded the ribcage of the staircase, his footsteps thumping as he walked. He struck the door with a powerful fist. The door took the blow and opened. Peace evaporated from the room behind it; it began to darken with fear. Seeing the angry demon standing there, the Bohri treasurer sitting inside began to stammer and stutter....

His iron-coloured face swelled up with anger. His bone-white teeth flashed in a menacing grimace. His small red eyes gave him the look of a cruel bear from Africa...

He gave the old man a buffet and grabbed the money. He rushed out, and ran down the steps, his feet keeping pace with his racing heart. The slap of his slippers ate up the distance as this magnificent, iron- chested man, black as night, his hair curly, his face

thrust forward, stormed down the road, as if he were a wild animal about to pounce on its prey. (44, 45)

After having fetched the money from the old Bohri he walks out towards his destination. He comes to a paan-shop where all sorts of meaningless activities go on. "One was using the juice of tambul to redden his lips. The second was cleaning his face with an air of deep appreciation for his own efforts. The third was pulling the ears of his collar up. The fourth was trying to fluff his hair out to make it look a little more luxuriant.... The *paanwala* was terribly frightened. He handed the *paan* out to the gangster without raising head. He gave him money drawing it out of the inflated wallet. He leaves the place without causing further trouble. The people who watched his every movement heaved a sigh of relief as things went back to normal.

The gangster is moved within by a sweet girl who has asked him a favour. No one has ever asked him for anything before. No one has trusted him, in fact. His very appearance frightened the people away. He is so moved within that he started thinking of love. "Does she love me?" he asks to himself, "Does she?" This thought of love shaken his entire person — rough and beastly. He shouts again — "Does she love me?" —

This terrible cry exploded from his burning heart like a bullet out of a gun. His feelings surged and stormed, a flock of startled bats in his head. His unease increased; it was as if electric jolts were shattering his peace of mind. He felt like a wounded wild animal, frothing at the mouth. (46)

He keeps on repeating — "Does she love me?" But he was not to receive the answer. He was a gangster who had fought with his own boss, who has committed all sorts of crimes — murder, theft, treachery, robbery, — even rape. He had been a member of Hong Kong gang, then they shifted to Singapore. He was an active criminal wanted by legal authorities — the police. He could successfully evade the police, and presently was in Bombay — the present day Mumbai. Even in Bombay his movements were restricted; he was not allowed to move out during day-time. He recalls certain events in the past. While in Singapore, he had confronted a white woman from Germany — a prostitute, in fact. But she had declined his offer, sending him away. He wanted to give her all the money he had, she wanted nothing from him. Now he is overjoyed because a beautiful Gujarati girl has asked him a favour. Jayantiben, as the girl is called wanted money for her mother's funeral rites. She had approached everyone; no one came forward to help her. Finally, she requested this man explaining the situation. He could not believe in what he saw and heard. A beautiful Gujarati girl asking for help. The greatest moment in his life. He brings money from the old Bohri. That was dacoity. He gives that money to the one who is needy. That was generosity.

Bagul has depicted the situation skilfully. It exposes the inner working of a gangster. He is a die-hard criminal who has committed every possible crime, yet is deeply thirsty for love and affection. The Gujarati girl's request for help is the greatest thing that has happened in life. The girl, of course, does not love him. Knowing that fully well, he decides to help her further. He joins as one of the pyre bearers of her mother's dead body. As the funeral procession moves on, he cries within. His heart weeps.

In his heart, a pain began to grind, as if deep inside him something was being born. He might have discovered what this was if he had wept. But he had never wept in life. (50)

Gangster is one of the finest stories in Indian literature. It reveals the author's mastery over the art of fiction writing. It places Bagul among the great writers of social realism.

5. Dassehra Sacrifice

Dassehra Sacrifice is yet another short story dealing with religious customs and rituals prevalent among the Hindus wherein a big fat powerful he-buffalo and a Mahar are at stake. Buffalo is killed inevitably, but the Mahar, if failed to control the animal, is killed by the neighbouring village chief. This is a custom and a ritual since long and was followed meticulously in Maharashtra till recently. The Constitution banned such practices, but the memories still linger on. Bagul, who was born during pre-Independence time, must have watched the event that is why he portrays it so vividly in the story:

The entire courtyard was glowing beautiful, filled with people. On the steps in front of the temple, the village folk sat, and the Untouchables were in the open maidan, where they endured the warm love of the last rays of the setting sun. Some people were sitting under a tree awaiting the *seema pujan;*and some others were sitting on the branches of the tree. But all eyes were fixed, eagle-like, on the *Maharwada.* Every heart was filled with an intense eagerness. And that eagerness was translating itself into a symbol. The symbol was the God of the Mahars and it was already growing, enlarging, becoming so big that it would soon touch the horizon. Others were

thinking of the ways of the buffalo and their chests were already thundering in fear. (51)

Patil, or the village chief is, of course, presiding person of the event. Then follows the description how the Patil enters the place where the sacrifice is to be performed. Sitting on a decorated live horse, the Patil wears high-bounded *pagari,* holds a sword by the waist and appears, as if, he has just returned victorious from battle. Patil is greeted with due politeness by all the village folks. The Mahars bent down and offered *johar* to the Patil. Others folded their hands, still others shouted Patil's name revealing their loyalty towards the village chief. Patil felt flattered and was deeply pleased. The crowd now waited intently for the he-buffalo and Deva — the Mahar, who would sport with the animal and kill it eventually, or get killed in the process if failed in his job. The sacrifice is applicable to both — the animal or the man — a Mahar, who, otherwise also, is treated no better than an animal.

The two appeared on the scene — the he-buffalo and the Mahar. The animal, raised and brought up especially for sacrifice, was huge, powerful and ferocious. A bottle of home-made liquor was poured down its throat. This had driven him mad. On its huge forehead *shendur* was smeared and a garland of flowers hung around its neck. Its eyes turned red and it looked so horrible that someone's death by the animal appeared ascertained. The Mahar who was walking along with the animal was called Deva — In his late Thirties. Deva — the Mahar looked as strong and powerful as the he-buffalo itself. He was dark-complexioned, tall and well-built. His face, adorned with an upturned moustache, and brilliant eyes, appeared confident. The crowd cheered at the sight of Deva, who waved his hand to the crowd in return. There were other three — all of them Mahars– to assist Deva in case the animal retaliates during the process of cutting parts of its body. Even they looked strong and confident. The he-buffalo, in the meantime, had turned wild with the noise the crowd and at the sight of the people wearing colourful dresses. This was a festival — Dasshera— celebrated for the victory of the Good over the Evil. It was the day when Pandvas had returned after fourteen years of exile and had procured their weapons kept concealed on the *apta* tree. Everyone was in high spirit and wanted to enjoy the occasion. They shouted, cried and called encouraging names loudly to Deva and his assistants. This had maddened the animal further and it looked even more intimidating.

The process of sacrifice began. The honour of initialling the same goes to the Patil. That was his privilege. The Patil comes forward, and the animal looks at him ferociously. The Patil steps back, but takes heart and goes ahead a little. Deva assures him his safety. Patil cuts the animal's ear with the sword. The animal turns violent and it pulls Deva and his colleagues who had held it by strong ropes. All the four try to stop the animal which seem to be more powerful than all of them put together. Patil now emboldened a little, and with a swift movement he cuts another ear of the animal, then the tail. The animal now turns completely wild, and uncontrollable. It pulls all the four Mahars with indomitable strength, they being dragged by it. Patil gets suspicious because practically, failure in sacrifice would mean his humiliation. He has no active role in the process expect from distance. Yet the whole affair stands for his honour, being chief of the village.

Deva knew his business well. The other three were equally determined. They, however, seemed to be exhausted. It was Deva alone who must control the animal and kill with a powerful stroke of the sword he carried along the waist. But the animal had turned ferocious, wild and uncontrollable. He pulled all the four with its enormous strength, even tried to attack the men with its sharpened horns. Last year, the animal had overpowered the men and had trespassed the boundary entering into the neighbouring village. The animal was killed by that village people by arrows and all. The man, in charge of the animal was butchered mercilessly. That was a big insult to the village and to the village chief. He experienced the pangs of insult throughout the year and wanted to avoid this year by whatever cost he must pay. He had confidence in Deva's skill and strength, which now seemed to be dwindling away. The animal was bleeding, the drops of blood had made the ground red. The animal pulled the men till the boundaries. They were exhausted – they, expect one — Deva, the Mahar. Considering the crisis in the move, he acted swiftly. He gave a powerful stroke of fist to the right side of the jaw. The animal turned left and took the other way round. It ran towards the centre. It was the time to act, Deva realised and lifted the sword with both hands and brought it down swifty upon the neck of the animal. The head of the animal fell apart within no time. The job was done. Deva was victorious. The sacrifice accomplished.

Bagul describes the event with meticulous details. He offers impressionistic descriptions that are important ingredients of great art. All his stories are remarkable for the artistic values.

It was a great festival for the Mahars. The sacrifice of the he-buffalo's head was a great feast. They buried the he- buffalo's head and brought the rest of the carcass into the Maharwada. They would feast upon the meat and celebrate the festival. It was a day of celebration to Deva's wife as well —

Deva's wife laughed and wiped away her tears as she emerged from the terror of what had seemed like imminent widowhood, and she turned in all four directions and made salutations to the elements in praise of his victory. (61)

6. Monkey

William Wordsworth, the famous nineteenth century English poet, has defined poetry — **"a spontaneous overflow of powerful feelings".** This definition marks intensity of the experience which can be of a few moments — appearing spontaneously and lost. Baburao Bagul's short stories fall into this category. He chooses human experience as a subject-matter which may not last long, but is full of intense feeling and emotions. His stories are really short — covering not more than 4-5 pages, but depict those human experiences which leave the reader aghast. And, these human experiences are varied — a prostitute's last effort to earn and treat her sick child, a single event of controlling intoxicated powerful he-buffalo, or, as in the present short story — a wrestler's inability to decide for himself.

Monkey is the story of a wrestler called Bapu has to win the wrestling bout scheduled in the village fair. Bapu had lost the bout last year to a wrestler belonging to his in-laws village that too, to a man belonging to the caste below his. He considered this as a great insult and instantly decided to avenge it in the following match. He has worked on the plan throughout the year. He did not touch his young beautiful wife Sakhu in order to practise *brahmacharya.* He has left home from the village and has come down to live in a hut in his farm, so that there is no confrontation between the spouses. He ate *Khurak*— a mixture of dry fruits, dates and jaggery in order to build strength, regularly. He exercised until the sweat of his body drenched the ground. He practised the art of wrestling for hours together because he must win the forthcoming match and take revenge against the last year's defeat.

He, however, was often attracted towards his beautiful wife — Sakhu was not only beautiful, but also caring and duty-bound. Her husband was away from home since the last six months; she had not seen him because her mother-in-law, Bapu's mother, had warned her strictly not to meet him. Bapu must observe celibacy till he wins the wrestling match. Poor Sakhu had no alternative but to follow the orders. Today, however, she must go to the farm in order to carry her husband's meal, as her mother-in-law has gone away somewhere. There was no sign of her returning home. It was time for her husband's lunch. He must eat on time, otherwise, he will lose strength and lose the match as well. Bapu has already come to know that his mother has gone away to a *mantrik* to procure some *tawij* or threads for him.

This will help him win the match. The thought of Sakhu coming to the farm unsettles Bapu mentally. He is filled with passion but tries to keep it aside. A battle between the desire for Sakhu and the decision for celibacy tortures him. Bagul describes his position with that of a buffalo tormented by a horsefly —

Over the last two days, his naïve, blind, immature mind had been filled with lust for Sakhu; that he should feel this made him angry and this would initiate a battle between the desire to deceive and the desire to keep his promises. He was a buffalo tormented by a horsefly……(62)

But now that the competition was close, his mind was playing tricks on him. After the last defeat, he and his mother had decided that his wife was the enemy — but memories of Sakhu now tormented him. So that these should not return, and in so returning, ruin his vow of celibacy, he prayed to both Bajrangbali and Vetaal……(63)

Sakhu, however, has already arrived at the farm, and is close to the hut he lives in. Bapu is enraged at her. **"How dare she break my celibacy and come to the farm"**, he thought, **"Does she not know that her presence would attract me towards her".** He is terribly angry, and, yet calms down a little at the thought of her beautiful smiling face and the desirable body. But this terrifies him again and he thinks of the wrestling match that lies ahead. Sakhu had already come inside the hut. She was carrying a basket of food on her head and looked so caring. But Bapu was not pleased. On the contrary, he yelled at her — wanted to drag her out of the hut. He held his wife by the neck and pushed her away. Sakhu's sari disarranged a little, making her young breasts visible. Bapu looks at her and is fascinated. He lifts her up and holds her against his chest, pressing tightly. Sakhu asks him to leave and eat first as the food would turn stale. He leaves her and pushes her against the wall. She is physically hurt and, in fact, her nose starts bleeding. "Get out," he shouts at her again, get lost from here". Sakhu gets up with difficulty and starts walking out slowly. The movement of her body make Bapu's heart throb loudly. He wants to pull her towards him once again — wants to …… But he notices his mother walking towards the hut with quick steps. The old woman has realised the situation and is terribly angry with Sakhu for spoiling her son's chances of winning the wrestling match. She walks straight inside the hut and starts cursing Sakhu. She orders her to walk away from Bapu, abusing her, calling her nasty names. The poor girl walks away quietly.

Bapu's mother is bent on her son's victory in the match by whatever the means are available. She has already approached the *mantrik* who had assured her son's victory. She asks her son to forget Sakhu till the match is over and concentrate upon his efforts to win the match. She convinces him that celibacy alone will save him from being lost. He must practise it till the end. He obeys his mother's instructions and follows the rule. The wrestling match takes place in the fair. It is arranged with great pomp and show. Bapu is defeated once again. All his hopes are lost. His mother is deeply upset and holds his daughter-in-law responsible for her son's defeat. Bapu himself is profoundly hurt as he could not take revenge against his opponents. He feels ashamed of himself and holds his wife responsible for the loss. His mother is equally convinced about Sakhu's interruption in Bapu's celibacy and for her lack of co-operation in his adventure. They decide to kill her. The story ends with Bapu sharpening his axe.

The story moves on different levels. First of all, it brings out the inner conflicts in the mind of Bapu, the wrestler. He is deeply hurt by his defeat in the wrestling match, more so because it happened at his in-law's village. He wants to prove to his wife that he is not inferior to the people of her *maher,* her parents' place. Therefore, he wants to practise celibacy as it is an essential ingredient for improving physical strength. Yet, at the same time, he is deeply drawn towards his beautiful young wife. This conflict is at the centre of the story. Bapu's inability to makeup mind is, perhaps, also the cause of his second defeat.

The title of the story ***Monkey*** is apt because Bapu, the wrestler, apes his mother's instruction in the same way a monkey does. He is strong physically, but mentally he is as fickle-minded as a monkey. At a time, it comes that he cannot think at all. All his daily routines are determined by his mother and he follows them meticulously. And he thinks that his wife is responsible for his defeat and humiliation. Both — the mother and son — plan to do away with the young girl.

Sakhu's position is precarious. She is young and beautiful and knows her duties towards the family. Like any other young woman, she is eager to meet her husband and her mother someday. Therefore, she doesn't mind her husband's cruelty and violence when the two meet inside the hut. She is a perfect "Bhartiya Nari" tolerating her husband's misdeeds and misbehaviour and willing to give in to his animal desire —

But how could she answer the question? The blind worship a Hindu woman offers her husband, the tug of a new attraction had brought her there. She had been curious about how he would now look after all the pains he had endured, and it was this dangerous curiosity that had lured her there. How could she talk of these hopes and fears as she lay unconscious? And even had she been conscious, how could she, a respectable girl, speak as she took such a beating...... (68)

Thus, the story is yet another example of a nice artistic creation of Baburao Bagul.

7. Competition

Bagul's characters are men and women in the streets. They are low by caste, poor and often without a sense of dignity, but human beings, nonetheless. They often quarrel, abuse, call nasty names to each other, even fight like rivals, but are always filled with human sentiments and ready to share each other's grief and sorrow. The story ***Competition*** has such people — two women, in fact, who are involved in petty rivalry of small business, of selling bananas on the street, in front of a mill where workers come out in large numbers and buy bananas. Presently, an old women called Yamuna is quarrelling with a Brahmin customer Pande, who had not paid credit long due to him. Pande did not listen to Yamuna's argument on the other hand, he looked on and off at the fair back of Chandra, a young woman selling bananas beside her. But Chandra was not interested in Pande or his arguments, for he was a habitual customer who did not pay. The quarrel goes on for quite some time and the Brahmin frees himself from the old woman's ferocious grip.

Yamuna has a son away at the village who repeatedly asks for money. He sends her letters demanding the same. The old woman tries her best by earning as much as she can and sends him money by money order. Recently, the situation has changed. The workers who come out the mill's gate do not come to her, instead they go to Chandra and buy bananas. Chandra was shy initially, and she had picked up the tactics of a selling woman, young and beautiful, and attracted the customers. Yamuna's business goes array. Chandra would often let the end of her sari drop down the shoulders, revealing half of her youthful breasts. She had also learnt the manner of talking to customers and attract his attention. **"Oh sir, please come and take what you like, this is all yours"** — The customers would look at her drooping sari first and then buy bananas. The number of customers increased she started earning a good deal, and seemed to be happy. That has spoilt Yamuna's business. The old woman who sold bananas to everyone with loving kindness and earn money enough to maintain the expenses, is now out of business. Customers do not come to her any longer; they go to Chandra and buy all her bananas. This has created a spark of enmity between the two women. Yamuna holds Chandra for her misfortune. It was she who had brought Chandra, and offered space beside her and buy bananas. She was her distant relative and often helped her improve the small business. Chandra has now turned against her. The old Yamuna cannot see men doing all sorts of merry-making with Chandra, and the young woman responding to them positively. A man called Kisan, is especially interested in her and even offered Chandra a proposal of a keep. He will spend money on her lavishly, buy everything for her and keep her happy. Chandra does not exactly reject the proposal, though does not agree with it. This has encouraged Kisan who keeps on visiting Chandra without any solid reason. Chandra's behaviour angers the old Yamuna, who tries to dissuade her from doing so. Chandra, on the other hand, is annoyed at Yamuna's unwanted advice. The two women start quarrelling, coming to blows and wrestle with each other as if on the battle ground. Men gather to watch scene. Kisan rushes forward to see if Chandra is hurt, and, in doing so, he touches Chandra, inappropriately. Chandra realised his intention and shoos him away as if he is a dog. Chandra's transformation from a coy, inexperienced young woman to a ferocious fighting woman is amazing. The author has brought it out —

It was she who had set Chandra up to work there. She told every single person she knew that Chandra was her nephew's wife, a daughter-in-law to her. And so the immortal and the lustful were forewarned and spoke to Chandra as they ought rather than as they wanted. Not too many brought from her as they feared the old lady's suspicion. But then unhappy Chandra did not so much as look at her customers. It was as if speaking to them was an effort that cost her much. When she accepted money or gave the change, her melancholic face would brighten up for a bit. If someone's gaze fell upon her beautiful body, she reacted as a sparrow caught in a fire might. She would rush to cover herself up. In fear and shame, she would pull her pallu from her forehead, right down to her nose. Seeing such

discomfiture, the voyeur would be embarrassed; and because of this some well-behaved workers would never buy from her.

But in just one month, the mild, melancholic Chandra had changed completely. Her head was up, her gaze became bold, the pallu of her sari only got to her head to slip back to her blouse and if it fell off her breasts, she didn't bother too much. Her hair took a new look and her soft full lips took on the rich red of the *paan* she now chewed …. (75)

This change in her appearance deeply affected her behaviour and attitude towards her work. She became a staunch rival of the aged Yamuna who looked upon her as relative. Chandra's husband was T. B. patient and needed regular treatment. Therefore, she must earn enough. Yamuna knew this and always co-operated with her. Chandra, on the other hand grows malicious towards the old woman and is somehow bent on ruining her. Chandra is disillusioned soon. Kisan has started treating her almost like a prostitute. He even intends to earn money using young Chandra. Her realisation brings reconciliation between the two women. Yamuna even tries to overpower Chandra by bringing a young prostitute to beat Chandra. But the final reconciliation bridges the gap between the two women. The competition comes to the end.

And tears began to glister in the old lady's eyes. Without wiping them away, she wept and putting a hand on her head; she said. "Child, I made a mistake. His wife is pregnant. I was greedy for a grandchild and in that greed, I made a mistake. I attacked a married woman. Forgive me. I could not see your young life, its suffocation, because of my anger. I could not see how you were burning through the day and the night…. Sati Savitri brought her husband back from the door of death. You should do the same. May God bless you….

The old lady pressed her trembling lips together as she wept and quickly placed her hand on Chandra's head in blessing. And Chandra fell at the old lady's feet and kissed them repeatedly. With no control, her body was writhing and she was sobbing and saying, "Aatya, please forgive this sinner. Please take me to your breasts." (88, 89)

Thus, the competition comes to the end. The story denotes change in human behaviour, misunderstanding and the final reconciliation. It shows human understanding on the part of the author.

8. Revolt

Revolt is a story of dehumanised social condition in which Dalits are compelled to live. It narrats the plight of a scavenger boy — *'Bhangi'* as the community is known in India — who revolts against the social condition and wants to throw away the stigma of untouchability cast upon him by the establishment. The boy is called Jai and has received education till matriculation. Independence and the Indian constitution has created scope for the oppressed to reach out of their miserable plight, yet the existing social norms which cannot easily be removed, fall heavily upon their psyche. Jai's parents have been cleaning public lavatories since generations together, living with the human waste, their mentality has almost become like it — static, unchangeable and stinking terribly. Jai's father – Parabhu – is sick, therefore, the contractor has given his job to Jai and is asked to join with immediate effect. He is married but has not seen his wife's face who is ignorant and tradition bound. In fact, he hates the surroundings and wants to get out of it as early as possible. Therefore, he does not speak even with his mother who is a symbol of social humility and slavery. He wants all his kinsfolk to quit the dirty job and do something else. He himself has decided to apply for a clerk's job in government office, which, he is sure to obtain. His parents, his sick father in particular, are impatient about Jai's decision. They want him to accept the Bhangi's job which has come to him without efforts. He, however, refuses the assignment and has different intention. His young wife is equally against his move, because she has been experiencing her old in-laws' sufferings and dearth of peace at home since she has entered the house as a child bride. The young girl's predicament is well brought out by the author —

For here was a man who could snarl at his father like an animal when the latter lay on his deathbed; a man who could ignore poverty and deprivation in his own home; a man, who though he was physically male, would not so much as look at his own wife. And, for her part, his wife began to see him as stupid, unfeeling and intensely selfish. She began to look at him from behind the veil of her *ghoonghat;* and his physical beauty excited her. That she should be thinking of such thoughts — and in the presence of her father-in-law – made her feel ashamed of herself. She bowed her head again and applied herself to pressing his feet. (91)

This is a typical situation in the families of unlettered oppressed communities in India. Marriages take place early in childhood when the brides and bridegrooms do not even know the nature of their relationship till they grow up and consummate the marriage which, now, is old by several months or even by years. In Jai's case, consummation has not happened yet, as he hates his young wife for being unlettered and tradition bound like his mother. Parabhu, his old and sick father, tries to persuade him to accept the offer of the job for which there are several others willing. He explains the condition in the house, "I cannot work any more," the old man tells his son, "Your mother is weak and frail, and this girl, your wife, needs support as well." Jai, however, is adamant and refuses to take his father's advice. On the other hand, he asks his father -

Just for this I should become a Bhangi? Give up my education to clear up the dirt of the village? Carry filth on my head? If you wanted me to do that kind of work, why did you have me educated? Why did you let them light these lamps of independence, knowledge and humanity inside my mind? (92)

Parabhu, the old man understands nothing of the things his educated son mentions — independence, knowledge, humanity etc. The only thing he understands is servility, slavery and cleaning public lavatories. He wonders why his son has grown so disobedient? Why does he not care for his family – the old sick parents and the young helpless wife? Jai, however, lives in a different world – Education has brought down upon him enlightenment, a sense of human dignity and a fair, respectable way of leading life-something which is badly missing in his own house and in the houses of innumerable untouchable brethren. He represents a new sense of Dalithood, — angry, irreconcilable, and revolutionary. He, however, is sensitive enough to his parents' sufferings. He cannot tolerate to see his mother's helplessness. The old woman implores him to keep the family out of the present condition. He agrees to take up the job against his will, out of a sense of filial duty and obligation towards the family. He goes with his mother where jobs are assigned to the men and women assembled to carry on their duties. He is given a cart wherein he would put the dirt assembled from the lavatories of a particular Bombay suburban. His mother accompanies him. The sight of public lavatories sends him in wilderness. He saw accumulated human waste with maggots and flies, blood-stained clothes, balls of used cotton wool, bandages and gauges strips.... All this filled him with revulsion — the author describes his condition in the following words —

The stench emanating from the thirty-two toilets filled his throat. His breath was plucked from him. Darkness swam before his eyes. He closed them. Then he began to understand why his eyes had grown heavy, where his pain had come from. His brain was thrashing about

like a fish thrown on the burning sand, his veins seemed ready to burst upon and were beating against his forehead and the back of his head, and it seemed as if someone had shoved a churn into his stomach and was rolling it about again and again and the nerves of his stomach seemed ready to rip their way out of his mouth. He closed his lips firmly. The strength went out of his legs, which had begun to tremble, so he stood still, He began to look around with his eyes peeled…. (100)

Jai undertakes the work despite the nauseating feeling. He is drenched in filth as the basket of filth slips aside, his co-worker is to annoyed by Jai's lack of skill in handling the devices. He scolds him, calling names. Jai, who is already filled with revolt against the job, retaliates. The two start abusing each other, and are engaged in physical skirmish. Jai is out of sense with anger and protest and beats the man with a powerful fist. The onlookers assemble and watch the fight, but none interfere as they are afraid of being polluted by the Bhangis who are fighting against each other. Jai overcomes the opponent who lay flat and motionless like a corpse.

Jai's fight against his own caste man is a symbol of protest – a sort of revolt against the filthy tradition of carrying human waste on head and cleaning public toilets by his community. His mind and heart are filled with anger and hatred towards the tradition. He is an educated man, though not highly, and has learnt lessons about human dignity. He is an angry young man who wants to put the entire system upside down. The author indicates the Indian social structure formulated by Manu wherein every individual is trapped in the prison of his own caste, wherein the untouchables are oppressed down to the level of beasts.

Bagul's story and its protagonist can be compared with Mulk Raj Anand's Bakha in ***Untouchable,*** the famous novel written during pre-colonial time. The difference between the approaches of Mulk Raj Anand and Baburao Bagul towards the problem of untouchability is explicit. Mulk Raj Anand, who carried the impact of Marx and Gandhi at the same time, leaves his protagonist in the existing condition, waiting for the Mahatma, whose speech is heard some where in the distance, or waiting for Industrial Revolution in India which was in the waiting. Bagul's protagonist, on the contrary, is angry, restless and bent on changing the social structure without waiting any further. This was the difference between Gandhian ideology and Ambedkarism. Bagul, being an Ambedkarite, upholds revolt and social change —

When the carter fell at last, lifeless, a corpse, the rage began to recede from Jai's body. He hugged his mother to his chest and shouted — "Maa, break my fingers... cut off my hands... slash open my body, throw away my corpse."

A man who has soaked himself with petrol begins to scream, a cry that tears through the heart, so Jai screamed.

And Bhani could only wonder if her son had gone mad; this shock made her teeth chatter...

The people stood and watched. But no one could make sense of the flame of revolt that was burning inside Jai. There was no way for them to understand it. For their minds had been murdered long ago by Manu. (103)

9. Pesuk

Pesuk in folk-tales is an evil spirit in the form of a woman. The tale narrates the discomfiture of a Hindu woman who is tortured by her rich husband and his relatives, because she has given birth to a child by a man other than her husband. Jaidev is a rich landlord, a Kshtriya by caste but was without a child. Therefore, he married six times earlier. His first wife committed suicide. The second had gone mad who was a prisoner inside his huge mansion. His third wife ran away with another man. The fourth went away to her parents' house and never returned. The fifth was mute and could not narrate her ordeal in the mansion. The sixth died mysteriously. None of these women could give him a child. Therefore, he married Savitri. Savitri's parents were poor. So, they married her off to Jaidev. Besides, marrying several women at a time was a part of Kshatriya tradition. So, Savitri's parents found nothing wrong in marrying their young daughter to a man who had married several times before.

Savitri is pregnant and gives birth to a male child. Jaidev should have been happy, but he is not because the father of the child is young relative of his who often visited the mansion The news breaks out and everyone comes to know the truth. Everybody comes to know that Jaidev is impotent and it was no fault of the women who deserted him one by one. The secret comes out finally and has deeply hurt the man. His honour is damaged and he decides to take revenge against the woman. Savitri was once beautiful and her young profile made her extremely attractive. This had made her old and senile husband envious and jealous of her. He orders his servants to cut her breasts, nose and make her entire face ugly. They obey the order and the beautiful Savitri is humiliated publicly.

Savitri decides to take revenge, she disappears and manages to come in the darkness of night with deformed appearance. Her appearance resembles to that of an evil spirit, a female-ghost or vampire. She somehow gathers strength and courage and manages to cut the noses of those men who were involved in her humiliation. She spares women, but men are targeted in large numbers. A kind of terror breaks out and everywhere men are spotted with their noses covered with hands. People believe that here is 'pesuk' operating, and it is bent on destroying men in general. Savitri's son is with her husband, but is neglected and often falls ill. The child dies of some unknown disease. This sends Savitri in wilderness and her operation begins with additional momentum. Almost all of Jaidev's relatives are attacked. The existence of female evil spirit, 'pesuk', is confirmed. Jaidev himself is bewildered and panicked to the bones. He lives protected by powerful men who always walk with him. The age-related ailments and a profound sense of guilt kills him one day. His funeral pyre is taken out into the graveyard under police protection, without any noise and in the darkness of night. The dead body of Jaidev is placed on the pyre-wood. The pesuk appeared which was quite visible in the glaring light of the fire. It was Savitri looking terribly ugly with short hair and breasts cut. There were no clothes on her once beautiful body, and, as the dead body burnt up, she threw herself upon the burning pyre, lay still on it, and, within no time she was burnt alive.

The story is presented in a mysterious way. The narrator is a freedom fighter who is hiding himself from the British police. He carries a pistol with him and decides to face the 'pesuk' boldly. He has heard about the 'pesuk' and wanted to see it himself. As he is on the way hiding himself in a dark night he notices the funeral procession, the dead body put on pyre – and 'pesuk' appeared in the light of the fire. The narrator immediately recognises the figure — the pesuk was no other than Savitri whom he recognises immediately even in that deformed appearance. He notices further Savitri jumping upon the pyre of Jaidev, her husband. She had performed 'sati', as was the custom among the high caste Hindu women – during those days.

The narrator unfolds this story to listeners who are young boys and girls, and whose curiosity is aroused every now and then. Readers also grow equally curious to know as the story progresses. The story has the form of a mystery or a spy tale. Baburao Bagul has accomplished it to the desired effect.

The story moves on various levels. It exposes the hypocrisy of rich landlords, who, in order to save personal honour ruin lives of others, particularly women, whom they find easy victims.

Jaidev marries six women to hide his sexual deformity, and, in the process, seven women are destroyed. The story also takes readers to the British raj when freedom fighters laid their lives for the sake of freedom. The narrator is a freedom fighter himself and is hiding himself from the British police. It is during this ordeal that he spots Savitri killing herself as 'sati' on her husband's funeral pyre. Savitri represents a Hindu women of those days when 'sati' was an approved custom among the high caste Hindus. Savitri is tormented by her husband, and is deeply humiliated. He has got her hair cut and her breast lacerated. Her womanhood itself is mutilated. Yet, the woman performs 'sati' and dies for the sake of her husband.

Bagul certainly does not approve such customs. He is only trying to present social reality in a manner which was prevalent during those days. The presentation technique is equally remarkable......

Oh yes, the heart of a woman is a complete marvel. It is unparalleled, unequalled. It makes life rich and beautiful, as the dawn adorns the sky, Savitri, for instance, made sacrifices to give her useless husband son. To ensure his happiness, she climbed on to the pyre and was reduced to ash. And that evil creature could not see her greatness. The evil, hypocritical zamindar, Jaidev... Kaka had wandered off to another topic. His powerful words had us enthralled but also confused. Sindhu's curiosity was further excited by his silence, and she asked,'What exactly did Jaidev, the zamindar do, Kaka.....'(104)

Bagul's technical excellence is further enhanced by naturalistic details which made the readers visualise the situation —

Her dark hair turned into the colour of mud. Its beautiful velvet texture had gone; it was not matted and tangled. Where on her rosy forehead there had once been a kumkum, there were dark bruises. Her hand had been branded, and the scar ran from her eyebrows to the top of her head. Her straight nose was broken, her upper lips writhed with anger, like several snake's tail. Rage contorted her face and made it ugly; it made my heart burn even as my mind was struggling desperately with what I had seen. Both her breasts had been cut off. The left one, either by an oversight, or because the milk had been flowing when it was cut off, had some small lumps

of flesh still dangling, and as they had dried there, they looked like worms clinging to her body. Her entire body had been devastated...... (109, 110)

"Pesuk", thus, is remarkable thematically and technically as well.

10. When I Hid My Caste

When I Hid My Caste describes the situation wherein a Dalit youth is caught between two minds whether to reveal his caste or to hide it from his high caste colleagues with whom he has to work. This a typical situation in India after Independence where educated young men and women among the Dalits got jobs in government sectors and had to leave their home town to join duties elsewhere. They were denied accommodation in the high caste localities because of their caste, therefore, they were compelled to hide castes and adopt other name temporarily. They were bitterly punished, humiliated and penalised after their real caste came to be known. This is what happened to Dr Ambedkar when he had concealed his caste in order to procure accommodation in Baroda, when he was appointed as a high ranking officer in Maharaja Sayaji Rao's princely state. He had to hide his caste, and was driven out by the Parsi when he came to know Dr Ambedkar's caste. Such incidents took place in larger numbers and several Ambedkarite youths had to experience the outcome of the situation.

The story narrates the plight of a young man belonging to the Mahar community in Maharashtra. He got a small job in the Indian Railway and was appointed at Udhna, a small village in Gujarat on the Railway line. The protagonist of the story is also the narrator. He narrates how he felt after he got the job which would close down the financial worries at home and which will help him live with dignity among his kinsfolk —

At first light, I got down at Udhna station and was walking to the engine shed. The joy of having a job had made my mind as frisky as spring, as brave as rain. This sense of well-being had left me with no fear of anyone. No man was a stranger. I had not a care in the world. I was sure that every word I spoke would bring victory, every step I took would bring springs of fresh water spurting from the ground. For I had spent night in the train, dreaming up a wonderworld of happiness... (pp. 116,117)

He finds himself among the Gujarati workers with whom he was supposed to work. One of them was called Ranchhod Tiwari, who welcomes him as he approached the gang. The narrator answered in chaste Gujarati assuring him that all is well and he had already joined the assignment. The narrator was well dressed with coat, dhoti, Kolhapuri chappals and a book of Mayakovsky's poems in hand. He appeared cultured and well-educated. But the inevitable question comes up — Ranchhod asked — "What is your caste?" The narrator gets bewildered a little, but controlling himself instantly starts talking about the country, the freedom struggle, the citizens responsibility, lofty aims of the nation etc, and adds on the end that he is a Mumbaikar who is proud of being one. This has impressed the listeners deeply and he is mistaken as a Brahmin who alone can speak such chaste language and show such deep respect towards the nation. Besides, there was a question of renting a room which would fetch considerable amount of money. So, why let such opportunity slip away? Ranchhod is convinced. The narrator continues his speech further — "We are the children of Bharat Mata; no one should bother about caste, or creed or gender. We are the citizens of a new nation recently freed from the foreign rule. In a new nation there are no Dheds, no Chamars, no poor, no rich, no Mahars, no Brahmins.... Oh I'm sorry, apologies Ranchhod, and asks further — "Will you take my room on rent?" I want an educated and well cultured man like you as a tenant. I'll prefer you over others who have approached earlier?" And he describes the location —

There is a well near it, full of sweet water. And mango trees around it. Every day, you'll see birds, birds of many colours. And you'll have birdsongs and nice time... (119)

The narrator feels all these people are so small that they all can be accommodated in his shirt pocket.

At that time something strange happened. Another worker from Mumbai called Kashinath Sakpal entered the scene. He declared himself as Mahar — a follower of Dr Ambedkar and is bent on destroying the caste system. He abuses Brahmins and other caste Hindus for practising untouchability. He finds nothing wrong about his caste and declares it his right to work here in the government undertaking. A disturbing scene follows. Someone complaints to Tiwari, the head of the sector, to remove Kashinath immediately. Otherwise, they will be polluted and everyone will leave the site. The narrator is disturbed at the thought of revelation of his caste, and, in fact, wants to leave. But the thought of poverty at home, and the innumerable needs and wants of his kinsfolk retained him somehow. One of the persons approached him seeing his disordered profile and assures him protection from the unruly Dhed, Kashinath, and declares further that there are thieves around and most of them are from the untouchable communities.

The narrator is sympathetic towards Kashinath the Mahar, who openly challenges the caste Hindus, and is ready to suffer. He often thinks of telling Kashinath that he is one of them — an Ambedkarite like him, but is restrained by his own helplessness. He does not reveal his identity at this juncture and goes on pretending to be somebody else. But unjust treatment to Kashinath continues and the two Tiwari brothers — Mataprasad and Ramsharan continue their superiority over others. They keep calling Kashinath "untouchable". This infuriates the narrator-protagonist further, and, now, he decides to speak up — unmindful of the consequences. He roars — "Why do you call him untouchable? Who is untouchable? Fire is untouchable. The sun is untouchable. Death is untouchable. The fire elements are untouchable. Do you mean human beings can also be untouchable? The narrator's angry words are noteworthy —

I am from Mumbai. I am a graduate of the University of the Revolution. The people whom Manu rejected, whom he would have consigned to the dust-heap, who brought this great country its freedom, were those from my city. I am one of those great worker-warriors. My hands are the wheels of Bharat's progress......

I am the artisan of the new joys of the common man. I am a warrior in the cause of humanity. I am willing to give my life for it. I have a name. I have a city: Mumbai.... I am a poet. (123)

The Tiwari brothers were taken aback, but the narrator calmed down quickly. He felt the need of his job, and the thought of poverty-stricken home returned to him. He now began to speak in chaste Hindi. Tiwari's were pleased to listen to his Sanskritised Hindi and praised his accents. The narrator appeases them further by recalling Tulsidas, Kabir, Nirala, Premchand — the stalwarts of Hindi language and literature. That pleases them further. Interesting situation continues. In the course of conversation, the narrator tells them he is educated only upto to non-matric and left education because of his love for poetry. This gave Tiwari's another chance to abuse the untouchables who are highly educated these days and have grabbed higher jobs. We, the high caste people should be more careful about education and obtain higher degrees so that the progress of the untouchables – *acchuts* can be checked.

Meanwhile, the question of letting the room to the narrator had remained unanswered. Ramsharan Tiwari, whose room is to be let out, invites the narrator for dinner. His wife Saraswati serves him with utmost care so that he does not remain hungry and is fully satisfied. After having eaten up fully the narrator falls asleep in a room separately assigned to the guest. What woke him up was a sudden blow falling from every direction. The room was full of people, of Tiwari caste mostly, who had come to know the caste of the narrator. His office records tell it explicitly. He was a Mahar by caste and was appointed in a reserved vacancy. They were all terribly angry with him not for deception as much, but for polluting their houses and having trespassed in a region of higher castes among the Hindus. They showered punches of fist, kicked him, a few lathis were also used to beat him. He would have been dead had Kashinath not arrived on the occasion. Kashinath flashed knife at hand and threatened to stab everyone if they further persist in their behaviour. Everyone got frightened and dispersed with fear and panic. Tiwari's wife Saraswati, alarmed by the unexpected occurring, fell at Kashinath's feet pleading him to spare her husband who was good enough to invite the guest for dinner. Kashinath leaves everyone unpunished and takes the narrator out who is half-dead with pain and humiliation — He asks the narrator — Why had he come to the rascal's house, who is bent upon killing you because you are from lower caste? He wants to report the matter to the police. The narrator refuses to do so and explains that it was *Manu* who had beaten him – not those ignorant people who are the victims of *Manusmruti* themselves.

Thus, the story is a bitter comment on the caste system which had created hatred and enmity among the fellow-citizens. It was this caste system which had enslaved India for centuries together. Dalit writers, inspired by the Ambedkarite Maxim are out to annihilate caste system and create a better society based on liberty, equality and fraternity.

Anguish and desperation mark almost all the characters that appear in Baburao Bagul's short stories. Almost all the characters in ***Prisoner of Darkness*** — including Deoram Deshmukh suffer from anxiety and desperation. Daulat who kills Deshmukh while protecting his mother, is the victim of the same trait of mind. Damu in ***Bohudu***, Deva Mahar in ***Dassehra Sacrifice***, Bapu, the wrestler in ***Monkey*** — all are caught into similar situations. Girija in ***Streetwalker*** is most desperate and wants to earn money by selling her body to the customers. Yamuna and Chanda in ***Competition,*** Savitri in ***Pesuk*** are victims of the similar circumstances. The Mahar protagonist in ***When I Hid My Caste***, is perhaps, the best example of how an individual can be desperate and anxious when he is likely to be driven out of the home, out on the street. The factor responsible for this precarious condition is caste. Baburao Bagul has effectively demonstrated the role caste plays in the life of Indian community.

Social Issues in "When I Hid My Caste"

Baburao Bagul's ***When I Hid My Caste*** contains other social issues than "caste". In fact, Bagul's entire writings bear influences of other thinkers than that of Dr Ambedkar. He was actively involved in the communist movement and wrote under the influence of Marxist ideology. Nevertheless, Ambedkarite thoughts prevail throughout his writings, and he emerges as one of the major Ambedkarite writers in Marathi.

Bagul's human understanding and social issues are so vast that all sorts of themes and subject-matter surface in his writings. He writes about Streetwalker, the prostitute, a gangster, Hindu festivals and the rituals associated with them, a scavenger revolting against the traditional professional, blind faith in non-human entities and then, caste, as in *When I Hid My Caste*. Ultimately all Dalit writings comes heavily down on caste, as it is the sole cause of sufferings of the Dalits in India. Bagul's short stories in *Death is Getting Cheaper* (Maran Swast Hot Aahe) depict Death and its various forms. How people, the Dalit living in slums, die of different factors. Some of them die of hunger, some others of fatal diseases, some others are murdered, yet others commit suicide. Bagul has seen and witnessed people dying and shared their agonies, anguish and desperation. His depiction of these people is, therefore, authentic and expose an ugly face of Indian social reality.

Suffering of women find central place in Bagul's short stories. **Streetwalker**, is for example, concentrated upon a prostitute named Girija whose son is sick away in her native place. His medical treatment needs money. Therefore, the poor woman decides to earn it by whichever means available. Her anguish and desperation is brought out well in the street of Bombay. The author reveals her inner mind and her physical movement at the same time. The irony of the situation is moving as it occurs at the end of the story. The customer she finally had, turned out to be a rogue, who satisfies his sexual desire and abandons the woman without paying her dues. She is weak and helpless. Readers can very well understand feelings and sentiments of the woman. Girija, the prostitute, is left to suffer in silence.

Women characters in Bagul's stories are really remarkable. Their characterisation appeals for the various reasons. Banoo in ***Prisoners of Darkness*** is yet another character whose anguish and desperation is equally moving. She is *murali,* and from untouchable community.

Therefore, the Deshmukhs will never accept her as one among them, even though she is living with them as the Senior Deshmukh's concubine, or a 'keep' as the popular phraseology would describe her. After his death, she is alone and helpless. Devram, the junior Desmukh, turns against her. In fact, he has an eye on her youthful charm even during his father's lifetime. Now that he is no more, he wants to rape her and kill as she is a blemish on the glorious Deshmukh family. She runs away to avoid his lecherous motives, also for fear of life as he appears as deadly as death itself. Her story is well known among the people, who watch her running in the street helplessly calling for help. No one comes forward to save her. Finally Daulat, her son whom she had abandoned long back, comes to her rescue. He relieves his mother from the clutches of Devram and kills him with a knife. The onlookers disperse on their own. Bagul's characters are astounding. These men and women always live under the shadow of death. Violence appears prominently in all the major Characters (African-Americans). It is effectively depicted in African – American writings. Richard Wright, for example, has a young boy in his novel ***Native Son*** who kills a white girl for fear of touching her when she is drunk, and chops her body into pieces in order to dispose it off. Similar situation can be located in other literary works of the African-American writers even today. Baburao Bagul's stories abound with such scenes and situations. He has seen and witnessed Dalit life from close quarters and, in fact, led this life himself. Therefore, it comes to his creative writing as naturally as leaves come to trees in spring making them beautiful and prosperous. Bagul's stories gain literary richness and beauty as he writes out of his personal experiences.

Ritualism, blind faith and superstitions abound in Bagul's stories. **Dasserha Sacrifice** elaborately delineates the traditional ritual of Dasserha festival and the customary killing of he-buffalo. The animal is reared and brought up well, by being fed regularly with nutritious grass etc; so that it becomes strong, powerful and uncontrollable. And the ritual of killing it by a Mahar — another important ingredient in the custom — the Mahar should be equally strong and powerful, capable of controlling the animal and killing it with a stroke of sword. Otherwise, the Mahar himself is likely to be annihilated for his failure. This is watched and witnessed by anxious onlookers, the people gathered to watch the scene. Bagul has brought out well in the story -

The whole crowd grew excited as they watched and like the pole star, their gazes were steady. Some of them felt heart pass over their bodies; for others, it was as if lightning had run over them; a thousand

hands were raised and losing all control, people began to shout; some had weapons in their hands; some had trumps of jowar and bajra; apta leaves began to wave and a spark appeared in every eye. (52)

Bagul brings out every detail of the customary ritual, almost projects the realistic picture of the scene. He also successfully points out the meaninglessness of such rituals and the waste of time, money and energy caused by these customary rituals.

Pesuk is yet another story which brings out blind faith and fear in the minds and hearts of the people in general. In fact, the story is about atrocities inflicted upon a woman by her husband, and the society in general. It further narrated how the woman takes revenge against them. The author had made effective use of popular psychology replete with unknown fear and anxiety. Savitri is the seventh wife of Jaidev, a rich landlord who kept on marrying in hope and expectation of a child which none of his previous women had begotten. He had great expectations from his new bride, Savitri, who is young and beautiful. Contrary to his expectations, Savitri conceives from a young man who is Jaidev's friend and acquaintance. Jaidev lacks manhood and is incapable of producing children. In other words, he is impotent. He is ashamed of accepting the truth and keeps on marrying women one after the another. He is jealous as well. Therefore, he penalises Savitri by cutting her nose and breasts, thus depriving her of beauty and charm, which he thinks, were responsible for her deviation from the marriage.

Bagul has brought out the insignificance of marriage as a social custom. Marriage cannot really keep two persons happy for long. Shelley, the nineteenth century English poet, had described marriage as a trap from which both the spouses are willing to escape if given chance. They are compelled to live together by social customs. This is what precisely happens in Bagul's short story. Jaidev thinks that his money and richness will make his wives happy. However, they abandon him one after another. Some of them die, others run away with other men. Savitri is humiliated, and her deep sense of humiliation turns her against her husband, who she knows is impotent. She is deformed and made ugly. She looks almost like a witch, or 'pesuk' as the popular term is, and appears in the darkness of night cutting noses of those who have been unjust to her. Her regular appearance in the dark raises an image of a she-devil causing panic and fear among the people around.

Savitri has a son born while she lived with Jaidev. He was in Jaidev's possession and was ill-treated. The child dies in due course of time.

This infuriates Savitri to a great deal. She decides to give momentum to her mission. Consequently, several men lose their noses at the hands of 'pesuk'. A deep sense of mystery prevails when a dead body is carried by four men and kept on pyre to be cremated. As the pyre catches fire and alighted, the 'pesuk' appears from nowhere causing the men flew away in panic covering their noses with hands. The 'pesuk' jumps on the burning pyre and burns itself to death. This was Savitri performing 'sati' on the pyre of her husband, Jaidev who had died of unknown disease. Baburao has hinted at yet another social custom of 'sati' among the Hindu women. The Hindu women burn themselves alive on the pyre of their husband in order to prove their loyalty towards the man, even if he is good-for-nothing – as Jaidev is. That has been a social custom in India prevalent for many centuries. The woman forgives the man despite his cruelty, tyranny and violence against her. Savitri has suffered much at the hands of her husband, who has gone to the extent of cutting her nose and breasts, thus making her look like a 'pesuk'. Yet, she spares him and his misdeeds and burns herself on his pyre. This reveals nobility, generosity and large-heartedness on the part of the woman.

Hardened gangsters also have a good heart inside their rough bodies. This has been proved in the story ***Gangster*** wherein a formidable rogue is transformed into a sensitive human being by a young woman's request for favour. These men are often victims of circumstances which compel them to be what they ultimately become. The blame lies not on their personal being, but on the society which is often insensitive and hostile towards them. This shows the nature of the relationship between individual and the society. This nature is determined by the social factors. Cruel ways of a society create hardened criminals. This has been proved time and again. This has also been a favourite theme of creative writers. The French novelist Victor Hugo has produced a classic novel called ***The Miserable*** on this theme. The protagonist in the novel is imprisoned for a petty crime. He is ill-treated inside the prison. This hardens him as a criminal. On release from the prison he commits all sorts of heinous crimes, and is ultimately 'cured' by kind of a treatment of a bishop and by a woman's love. Bagul's story ***Gangster*** goes almost on the similar line. The gangster who has procured money from a money-lender by force, is anxious to know whether — "she loves me, Does she love me?" This reveals the sensitive human being inside the hardened criminal. Michael Foucault, the twentieth century French poststructuralist thinker, has recommended that prisoners lives should be taken up for study which certainly, would benefit the seekers of knowledge and enlarge their human understanding. Bagul attempts falls into the Foucauldian post modernist approach to humanity.

Finally, Bagul comes down to 'caste', the essence of Dalit literary movement. This has been effectively shown through two short stories in the collection — ***When I Hid My Caste*** — ***Revolt*** and ***When I Hid My Caste*** — Revolt indicates the beginning of social transformation likely to spread out among all castes treated as untouchables. The scavenger, those who clean the streets and old fashioned toilets consisting of human waste — were the followers of Gandhi who called them 'Harijan', glorifying their profession. They did not fall into the Ambedkarite movement despite several efforts by the messiah. Consequently, their social condition remains the same as it was in the past. Bagul takes the Ambedkarite ideology and among these people and makes a young man called Jai, who revolts against the prevailing circumstances.

Jai's parents are old and incapable of physical exertion. They, however, have sent their only son to school. Education has its effect on the young mind of the protagonist. He refuses to clean the human waste and wants to apply for a respectable job which will bring him regular money and respect among the people. Jai's ailing father, however, needs immediate help and is suspicious about the job Jai has in mind. Therefore, he asks Jai to take up cleaner's job which is easily available. That would bring some relief to the grieved family. Besides, Jai has a young wife, tradition bound and docile, who thinks of her husband as a freak who refuses to take up easily available job and runs after the non-existing one. The young girl serves the old father-in-law in the hope that better days will come. Jai almost hates his wife because of her imbecile thoughts and behaviour. He, however, is compel to join the toilet cleaners by his old mother's repeated pleas. Jai is not made for that filthy profession. He cannot concentrate on it, and commits a breach causing havoc among the toilet cleaners. A big quarrel comes up. He hits the opponent and leaves the site.

Jai's revolt is symbolic. No young man from his community will carry on the filthy profession in future. The abrupt end of the story foresees the bright future for Jai and his brethren's. He has refused to be submissive and meek. He will search for new ways of life. That is certain.

Bagul's short stories can be compared with Mulk Raj Anand's famous novel ***Untouchable***, where the protagonist is helpless and looks for his salvation from others. Bagul's protagonist has stepped out to find his own redemption. 'Atta Deep Bhav' said Buddha, meaning thereby that 'be your own light'. Do not rely on others for your salvation. That is Dalit literature. Bagul stands for it firmly.

When I Hid My Caste is a famous short story narrating the troubles caused by caste Hindus to young educated Dalits, who search for accommodation in a civilised locality. All Indians are divided by castes' and all of them hate Dalits even though they are financially better off and better educated. This sounds like a general statement, but true nonetheless, hundreds of years ago, Dr Ambedkar was driven out of home by a Parsi in Baroda, because Dr Ambedkar was a Mahar. And he was better educated than all the Parsis put together. Similar situation prevails even now in Independent India. Baburao's story is set in Gujarat, at Udhna railway station, to be precise during 1960s. The protagonist of the story is a Mahar from Maharashtra who is appointed as class IV railway employee at Udhna. He has command over chaste Marathi and Sanskritised Hindi. He can quote from famous Hindi writers like Premchand, Kabir, Raidas etc. and cite stories from the great epics. He is misunderstood as a Marathi Brahmin by his work-mates who are from the Brahmin community from the North. Besides, he is well-behaved, soft spoken and appears sober. Everyone is impressed by his disposition. He is a total contrast to another Mahar employee called Kashinath Sakpal, who is aggressive, loud and protesting against everything. Kashinath is feared by all, but he is sympathetic towards the protagonist as he happens to be of his own caste-men. The two, however, never meet or talk.

The protagonist needs accommodation, a small room perhaps, to live in while he is in Udhna. One of the Tiwari brothers has a room vacant and is looking for a tenant. He finds the protagonist suitable for the purpose. He invites the protagonist for dinner. Mrs Tiwari, the young Brahmin woman, is pleased to have a guest who is so well behaved and well educated and who is going to hire the room as a tenant. This will fetch her an extra means of income. The Tiwari's ask him to rest in separate room after having meal. Something goes wrong. Someone from the railway office has checked the record and has come to know the caste of the protagonist. He is appointed in a reserved post meant for the erstwhile untouchables. The news comes to the Tiwaris, who are enraged and turn violent against the guest who had hidden his caste. He is beaten up badly, and is rescued by Kashinath Sapkal who appears on the scene all of a sudden.

Later on, the protagonist tells his friend that the Tiwaris, nor the Brahmins, but Manu has beaten him for being a Mahar.

Thus, Baburao Bagul's creative genius encompasses within its range all those who are helpless, poor and abandoned by the society. He makes his protagonist revolt against the prevailing circumstances; his protagonist never gives in because tolerance has its limitations. One must revolt and retaliate in order to retain one's dignity. That was the teaching of Dr Ambedkar, who believed in transformation of political rule if it proves to be ineffective or tyrannical. Baburao is a staunch believer in the Ambedkarite ideology whose sympathy as a creative writer always flow towards the oppressed and the underprivileged. Baburao has several other books to his credit, including a renowned novel ***Sud*** – and all his literary efforts lead towards creation of a better society to live in. That is the one of the objectives of Dalit literary movement as a whole.

Notes

1. Baburao Bagul, (Tr.) Jerry Pinto. *When I Hid My Caste.* New Delhi, Speaking Tiger, 2018. (p. 1)
2. *Ibid.* (p. 18)
3. *Ibid.* (p. 20)
4. *Ibid.* (p. 32)
5. *Ibid.* (p. 42, 43)
6. *Ibid.* (p. 34)
7. *Ibid.* (pp. 44, 45)
8. *Ibid.* (p. 46)
9. *Ibid.* (p. 50)
10. *Ibid.* (p. 51)
11. *Ibid.* (p. 61)
12. *Ibid.* (p. 62)
13. *Ibid.* (p. 63)
14. *Ibid.* (p. 68)
15. *Ibid.* (p. 75)
16. *Ibid.* (pp. 88, 89)
17. *Ibid.* (p. 89)
18. *Ibid.* (p. 92)
19. *Ibid.* (p. 100)
20. *Ibid.* (p. 103)
21. *Ibid.* (p. 104)
22. *Ibid.* (pp. 109, 110)
23. *Ibid.* (pp. 116, 117)
24. *Ibid.* (p. 119)
25. *Ibid.* (p. 123)
26. *Ibid.* (p. 52)

Chapter - III (C)

Thunderstorm - Dalit Stories

— Ratan Kumar Sambharia

Thunderstorm is a collection of short stories by Ratan Kumar Sambharia from the original Hindi. These stories are translated in English by Dr Mridul Bhasin, who herself is an acclaimed writer, communication professional and social worker. She has worked on a variety of subjects like folk art of Rajasthan, the living Tradition of Rajasthan, culture and literature. She works for *Muskan*, a trust which works for the welfare of humanity.

Thunderstorm contains fifteen stories in all. However, only ten of these stories are taken up for study as ten stories by other writers are also considered for the same. The choice of the stories is based upon the content and subject-matter suitable for the present study.

Thematic analysis of the ten stories by Ratan Kumar Sambharia follows:

1. Phulwa

Phulwa is about the social transformation that has taken place in the lives of Dalits — the erstwhile untouchables after Independence. This can be due to several factors — socio-economic policies adopted by the government, reservation to the backward communities in public sectors etc. The transformation did take place. Rameshwar, the village landlord, has come to the city to meet Pandit Mataprasad – who once was a revered Brahmin in his village. Rameshwar believes that Pandit Mataprasad will help his son to obtain some job in the city, as the glory he once enjoyed had disappeared. The hundred *bigha* land his father possessed was divided into his five brothers, and his own share was further divided among his four sons, leaving each one of them a mere mendicant. Rameshwar's own position is precarious because now there is neither land nor lordship his family once enjoyed. He was past his youth, and cherished the memories of the days that are now no more.

He finds it difficult to find Pandit Mataprasad's address, but can easily locate Phulwa's mansion—like house. Phulwa is a chamar woman from his village who has worked on his farm and was treated like any other untouchable woman. Her husband was a farm labourer as well and as a chamar, was humiliated many a time by none other than the Rameshwar himself —

Now the changing times make his head spin — **Rameshwar's head spun. No one knew Pandit Ji. But everyone knows Phulwa's son. The young man on the scooter dropped him off in front of an ornate and imposing mansion. Rameshwar was taken by surprise. Was this mansion Phulwa's? He knocked nervously. An old woman sitting on the veranda came over. Her body was running to fat, but there was a glow on the fair, wrinkled face. She wore glasses and a pristine white saree. Covering her head with a saree, she opened the gate.**

It was Phulwa. Neither she nor Rameshwar recognised each other. They both kept staring at each other, Phulwa adjusted her spectacles on her nose, but her brain still did not register his identity.

Rameshwar narrowed his eyes. Recognition finally dawned. "Phulwa?"

The voice alerted her. "Who, Rameshwar?"

"Haan, Bhabi" (3)

This change in their personalities indicate the changing times. How everything has turned topsy turvy? Rameshwar, who once treated Phulwa like filth, is sitting at her door like a beggar. Phulwa's joy knew no bound. The zamindar's son who once ruled the village vicinity, was at her door-step. Phulwa's mind instantly goes into the past. Memories flashback on the screen of her mind —

Phulwa's husband had been trying to restrain and tame an aggressive bullock that belonged to the zamindar. The rope had slipped from his hand momentarily and the bullock sensing the slack, had gored him in the stomach with his horns, Phulwa's husband had writhed in agony, falling around, bleeding to death. Phulwa had become a widow. Their son Radhamohan had been about ten years old then. Phulwa had inherited her husband's legacy of serfdom and

debt, just as moneylenders inherit the business from their forefathers and landowners inherit land. There were two mouths to feed now. She began cutting grass, filling water and feeding the cattle at the zamindar's house. (4)

She comes back to the present and realises that the same zamindar's son Rameshwar is standing before. However, she is not angry with him. On the contrary, she welcomes him with due respect and takes him inside the house. Phulwa was happy because she was showing him her son's huge bungalow, and things inside which would not be there in the homes of the landlords and zamindars in the villages.

The house was enough to accommodate an entire *baarat* of a marriage, about twelve rooms in all. The walls were nicely painted and beautiful paintings hung on the walls. Phulwa requests Rameshwar to sit down upon the sofa and he almost sinks down half in its softness. There was a huge dining table with about ten chairs placed around. Phulwa tells Rameshwar that they eat together at the table. Rameshwar feels as if someone is pinching him with a needle because he eats simply sitting on a spread-out old mat. There was an enormous refrigerator standing beside. Phulwa opens it up for the guest. It was stocked with vegetables, cold-water bottles, cold-drinks, mangoes, apples, oranges and what not. There were cubes containing ice-cubes. Phulwa explains the meaning and utility of everything to the village-chief, who appears bewildered at every explanation.

Phulwa calls her maid servant and asks her to bring a glass of water for the guest. Her maid-servant is a Rajput by caste, abandoned by her husband and employed by her son to help his wife in the household. A Rajput woman working as a servant in the house of a *dhed*, Rameshwar's head starts reeling, but he controls himself. Phulwa takes him further into another room where fans, coolers and Air-conditioned apparatus were placed. Rameshwar remembers Phulwa waiting in the burning sun and trying to find shelter under the shadow of trees. Now the same Phulwa was basking under the cool winds of the air-conditioned device. He grew envious of her. She takes him further in her son's bed-room. It was an enormous room with attached toilet and bathroom. The bathroom was as big as Rameshwar's living room itself. How long does her son stay here, in such a big bathroom, he wonders. And there were Indian toilets, western commodes to get relieved. Rameshwar recalls Phulwa and the woman in her community going away in the open to relieve themselves. Now the radical change! He shudders, half with envy and half with anger.

Phulwa's house and the luxuries therein are beyond Rameshwar's imagination. And he is not really comfortable inside the house, and in Phulwa's company. It's meal-time now, and Phulwa offers him meal which he declines with an excuse of aching tooth. Phulwa also wants to make arrangement of his overnight stay. But he wants to leave house as early as he can. He asks Phulwa where Pandit Mataprasad's house is. It was close by in the same locality. Phulwa directs him there, telling him that it's time for her son to return home. Therefore, she must stay to receive him. She further requests him to stay for a while till her son arrives. He is uncomfortable and leaves the house hurriedly. He reaches Pandit Mataprasad's house. This house was a total contrast to Phulwa's huge mansion —

They reached Pandit Mataprasad's house. Two charcoal drums served the makeshift gate. The gate was just a barrier. The latrine and the bathroom were just next to it. A gunnysack hung on the door of the latrine. The bathroom had muddy floor. There were just two rooms. Close by stood a garage. The kitchen, set up in the passageway, was equipped with a few odd utensils. Crouched over the gas stove, Pandit Mataprasad's granddaughter was making rotis. (14)

Pandit Mataprasad died three years ago and his widow Parvati had no means of livelihood as her husband's days of offering 'puja' were no more. People rarely call Brahmins for puja these days, the widow narrates her story to Rameshwar. And, there is no other source of income. Her son does some sort of odd jobs in order to run the house. Rameshwar eats whatever is served in dinner. He does not relish it, though. He is made to spend night in a room where a few cows and buffaloes and other animals were tied down. Next morning, he explains the purpose with which he had come to the city, and to Pandit Mataprasad's house. He implores the Pandit's widow to recommend his son's name to some influential officer for a job. She expressed her inability and suggest that he should request Phulwa's son for that purpose. Phulwa's son is the District Superintendent of Police (DSP) and is influential enough to find a job for Rameshwar's son.

The story ends with an ironic hint that Rameshwar's feet turned towards Phulwa's mansion once again.

The story registers the changes that have taken place in Indian social structure after Independence. There is no suggestion on how things changed to Phulwa's benefits, one can conclude with the belief that they were largely due to the socio-economic policies adopted by the government from time to time. One cannot help feeling that there should have been references to Dr Ambedkar's efforts to ameliorate the conditions of the erstwhile untouchables in free India.

2. The Goat's Two Kids

The Goat's Two Kids depicts conflicts between the rich and the poor and the ultimate victory of the poor with the help of workers' union. The story begins with a naturalistic description of the village morning which is noteworthy —

The freezing cold of January… An oppressive sky, the still earth and a heavy white sheet of fog, with an entire village covering under it, numb shivering people, enduring temperatures low enough to chill the head of a porcupine. People prayed for the fog to lift so they could get on with their work. But it swayed over them, fanning its hood like a cobra. Normally, the sun appeared by nine but today, the sun God was nowhere to be seen, as if he had completely forgotten to visit the village. The road was about fifty paces from the village. The vehicles passing along it had all switched on their dippers and slowed to a crawl. (19)

This was a village in Northern part of India, Rajasthan most probably wherein lived a poor man called Dalpat. His house was close to the *haveli* of Dan Singh – a rich and influential landlord in the village. Dalpat lived with his wife and earned his livelihood by working on the field of landlords or of some rich farmers. People in the village tend cattle, cow, goat, buffalo from which they obtain milk, wool, meat, etc. fetching them good amount of money, also enjoying these things themselves sometimes. Therefore, Dalpat's wife wanted to buy a goat at least, that would add to prestige of the family. It was difficult to save money to buy a goat, because that would cost a big amount beyond the reach of the farm labourers — Dalpat and his wife were. It was their son Sampat Singh's money order with which they could buy a goat, that adorned their courtyard. Dalpat's wife was proud of the goat and she would be happy to hear the goat bleating.

Dalpat had two son's Ram Singh was in army and Sampat Singh worked in a factory in Faridabad. They helped their parents occasionally, but by and large, Dalpat and his wife Dharmakali lived independently. Therefore, they did not interfere in anybody's business, nor were they interested in receiving advice from anybody. They lived happily together. In the course of time, Dharamkali's goat became pregnant. Her joy knew no bounds at the realisation that soon more goats will be around. It so happened. The goat had given birth to two beautiful kids — one male another female. A few days afterwards, the two little kids started walking and flinging themselves around. Dalpat and Dharmakali would watch them with pride and happiness.

Dalpat's mud-house was close enough to Dan Singh's haveli with a *chabutra* in front of the main gate. It was here on this *chabutra* that Dan Singh's son Dharmapal used to sit killing time. Everyone knew that he was a bit abnormal, and would behave violently at times. One day, when Dalpat and his wife were busy and unmindful of the goat kid's movement, the two little animals trespassed into Dan Singh's courtyard. Dharmapal watched the two little goat kids. He was amused initially and then he butchered them mercilessly. He came down with the dead animals and threw them out at Dalpat's door complaining that they keep coming over to his house at any time of the day. It was a big nuisance. Therefore, he killed them outright. Dalpat was shocked. So was his wife. When Dalpat went to Dan Singh with complaint showing him the damage his son had done, Dan Singh dismissed Dalpat telling him that he does not count *dhed* and *Bhed* as living beings. He asked Dalpat to go back immediately. The helpless Daulat has no other alternative but to return home, crestfallen.

Dalpat's best friend Sharmchand came to visit him. He narrated what had happened to the two little kids of goats. Sharmchand advised him to report the matter to police. Dalpat was unwilling because he had never been to the police station before, besides, Dan Singh, he knew was powerful enough to influence the authority. Sharmchand could convince him with great difficulties. Finally, the two went to the town where the police station was situated. They carried the dead bodies of the two goat kids. Sharmchand explained the matter to the police and, with prints of Dalpat's thumb on it, he submitted a letter of complaint. The police officer, however, dismissed their complaint and asked them to leave the premises immediately. In fact, the two were driven out of the police station.

Sharmchand knew how to handle the situation. He immediately contacted Ramdulare, who was a relative and leader of the *Kamgar* Union. Ramdulare rushed to help the two. He marched to the police station with his union colleagues and demanded the action against the culprit. The in-charge of the police station did not budge a little. Ramdulare decided to see the Superintendent of Police. He did, and explained the matter to him. The DSP immediately ordered the police station in-charge to arrest

Dan Singh and report the action taken immediately. Consequently, Dan Singh is arrested and brought to the police station. Further, legal action was initiated against him.

The story is full of action. The goat delivering two kids, Dan Singh's son killing them, Dalpat's ineffective imploration to Dan Singh. Sharmchand taking Dalpat to the Police station, Ramdulare's Kamgar Union, his visit to District Superintendent of Police, and the final arrest of Dan Singh. The story, however, brings out perfect characterisation of the village folk. Dharamkali, for example, is brought alive through such description:

Dharamkali was a petite woman with a delicate build. This palm-span of a woman still had the nimbleness of an unmarried girl and the arrogance of a married woman. She talked a lot about her past. Every time a girl was reluctant or unwilling to work, Dharamkali would bristle with irritation and say — "When I was your age, I could walk briskly from the well to my home carrying a child, two pitchers tucked into the curve of my waist, and a bucket on my head....

When the girls heard her boast, they would either look away and laugh, or quietly disperse, inserting the corner of their dupattas in their mouth to stifle their giggles.... (p. 26)

Here is the Superintendent of Police who decides to take action against Dan Singh for the atrocity committed against Dalpat....

The Superintendent of Police had himself grown up playing with bat and ball of penury and poverty. However, hard work, honesty and devotion to duty had been his followers. Self-respect was his mainstay. When he heard the woeful tale of some poor man, his downtrodden conscience was sometimes roused by pity. This complaint was definitely noteworthy. (p. 33)

In this manner, the story sets out to delineate the condition in which the poor are exploited and how they have to struggle a great deal to obtain justice.

3. Terms and Conditions

Terms and Conditions is about the avenging spirit shown by an oppressed man in retaliation to injustice and atrocity inflicted upon him and his daughter by an upper caste man's son. The condition he puts forward to spare the high-caste man is bold indeed, and amazing at the same time.

Jasveer Singh is a fifty years old man who is the chief of the village. Presently, he is worried and anxious and waiting for Panaram whom he has called for in the *haveli*. His servant Birju was sent to bring Panaram home. Since no one has arrived as yet. Jasveer, is worried and looks depressed. At last Birju arrives. But he is alone and tells Jasveer that Pania, that is Panaram has refused to come. He is old, weak and unable even to walk. Birju wanted to bring him in rikshaw, but he did not budge. This worries Jasveer further. He was the village chief, but was never popular among the village folk. The author writes about him:

He had never regarded his fellow men as human beings. He wore safari suits and his gaunt face sported a sparse beard and moustache. All day long, he would chew tobacco and spit out the juice. At night, it was alcohol and hunger that took him over. Setting a chair down outside his *haveli*, he would instal himself in it, his cane resting beside him. He would stop passers-by and so that he could pile chores and errands upon them, abuse them at will or whack them with his cane for no good reason. That was his pastime……(58)

What happened to Pania and his family was shocking. Everyone in the village, including Jasveer's elder brother, had gone to console him. Pania was on hunger strike demanding action against Jasveer and his son who was involved in the heinous crime. Jasveer is so mean and cynic that he suspects his elder brother's sincerity and thinks that he has gone to console Pania to derive something out of the situation to use against him. He has developed tremendous ego which was further fattened by his legacy of fame and the years of uninterrupted authority he had enjoyed as the village headman. As the story reveals he has let his son free to do whatever he wants to — even rape Pania's daughter because she is poor and helpless. This is precisely what has happened in the present context. It is against this crime that Pania is agitating. The crime is so heinous and inhuman that it attracts severe legal action, besides tarnishing fame and prestige of Jasveer which he somehow could manage to sustain. That is the reason why he is so disturbed. He wants to meet Pania in person and tempt him into some kind of compensation — maybe a few hundred rupees or even a few acres of land out of the vast number of acres that the labourers are tilling for him. Therefore, he anxiously waits for him. Panaram, a poor labourer in the village was all without means or support. He must have made every effort to seek justice. But authorities in India are always against the poor and helpless. No one seems to have come to his help. Having failed at every front he decides to fight his own battle. He goes on indefinite hunger strike squatting in the middle of the village.

No one really is in a position to help him out. People come to see him, speak a few words of consolation and turn away. Even the Government authorities seem to be insensitive towards his case. He finally comes down to the *haveli* and confronts Jasveer.

Jasveer is full of regrets and asked Pania to forgive his son who is the only heir to his unaccountable property. He tells him further that his son's uncontrollable nasty behaviour has already damaged his prestige. He clarifies his position thus:

Forced into this stance by the prevailing circumstances and his own helplessness, he placed a pacifying hand on Panaram's grimy shoulder and stared at the tears caught in the folds of his wrinkles. Then putting on a wounded expression he said, Pania, there was a time when people would feel obliged to acknowledge even this chair of mine in greeting if I happened to be away. Now even if I am there and cough to register my presence, they pass me by, their faces averted and spit on the ground in contempt once they've moved away. To tell the truth, I actually sense their spittle hitting my face. The whole village has lost faith in me, Pania.... (60, 61)

Jasveer begs and pleads before Pania to forget the mishap. He tries to appease Pania's anger and alleviate his distress and inner turmoil. But Pania is unmoved. Jasveer tells Pania further that his authority in the village is unchallenged due to the support he receives from Pania's caste people. These people, he tells further, are loyal, generous and large hearted. Why, then Pania has become so cross and narrow minded. Even this does not have any impact on the stubborn Pania. He tells him further, to get his daughter married off to some suitable boy. He will pay for all the expenses incurred in marriage. Pania looks determined and, refusing his offer of money, and threatens Jasveer that if justice is denied to him, he will consume poison along with his family and commit suicide before everybody in the village. This frightens Jasveer further, he implores and pleads before Pania to take whatever he likes from his huge estate — a few thousand rupees perhaps, or a few acres of land. Pania is firm and still. He declares that he can forget the event and close it down on one condition. This lifts up Jasveer's spirit. He is so overjoyed that his blood pressure shoots up with emotions. **"Tell me, tell me your condition,"** he implores passionately. Pania tells him calmly — **"I want your daughter to spend a night with my son."**

Jasveer is deeply hurt. Pania had challenged his sense of honour. His daughter in the arms of an untouchable boy. The thought itself sent him into wilderness. He lifts the gun lying nearby and kills Panaram, and, caught into the whirlwind of uncontrollable emotions, receives massive heart attack. He falls down, dead.

The story is all about "honour". Honour of a poor Dalit which can be violated by anybody without paying anything for it and the honour of rich which needs to be sustained at any cost. Panaram a poor Dalit, is conscious about his honour, and wants avenge its violation. The author makes it clear:

> **Panaram's mind was in turmoil. Life was not just about inhalation and exhalation of breath, he thought. It was tied to man's honour, his reputation. Shorn of those, a man was no more than a corpse. The one responsible for murdering honour he mused, must suffer for it. Let me just press the nerve that will cause him pain too.** (63, 64)

4. The Old Woman

The Old Woman is an interesting story of a 80 years old woman in a village who stays alone and loves her only daughter Sarita who is away in a town.

It is a summer day. Everyone is distraught by heat and sweat, more so the old woman, because of her age and weakness. Her name is Chunni, but is better known as the old woman in the entire village. She is so frail that she appears as if she might fall down with a small gust of wind. She knows that her days are over and the Yamraj might knock at her door any moment. Yet, she wants to live for the sake of her daughter who is married off in a rich family and keeps enquiring about her on and off.

As she is about to lie down and seek relief from the blistering heat, the postman calls her from outside — **"Telegram for you, old woman."** She springs up like a young girl and comes to the door. The postman hands the telegram over to her and goes away. She, of course, is unable to read the telegram, though she realises that the only person who can send her an urgent message is — Sarita, her daughter But what message? What's written in telegram? She wonders and decides to go out and get hold of someone who could read out to her. The entire village makes fun of her for living alone and leading a destitute life, while her daughter is rich and well off. She avoids them all. The only person who gets along well is the school master Khyal Chand, who feels pity and sympathy for the woman's miserable condition. The old woman walks out in the heat of the sun. Most of the doors are closed because people are resting inside the burning hours. She reaches to Master Khyal Chand's house and knocks the door. The man, who is already disturbed by the heat in the climate, is further annoyed by the knock. "Who is there?" he almost shouts from within. The old woman's trembling voice compels him to open the door. He has taken off his clothes except *dhoti* covering the legs upto the waist. His chest is covered with grey hair and his large face is adorned by an abundant moustache. Sambharia, the author has a remarkable style of portraying characters — he has already presented a vivid picture of the old woman – now the portrait of master Khyal Chand is note-worthy:

Just shy of fifty-six, Master Khyal Chand had salt and pepper hair sprouting around the bald patch. He was short and heavily built and the flesh on his entire body jiggled when he walked. His clothes were a reflection of the culture he respected and lived by: he always wore a dhoti and kurta. He carried a cane in his hand all the time and was never seen without it, whether in school or outside it. That is why the children had teasingly nicknamed him "the bull that canes". So obsessed was he with money that he would keep calculating the interest he could earn from his investment in an attempt to improve his financial status. He was worried about his yet-to-be-married-off daughters than a patient suffering from blood pressure would be about his state of health. (84, 85)

He was shocked to see the old woman standing at his thresholds – **"Do you want to die in this heat, old woman?"** he asked indignantly. The old woman explained to him the reason of her coming in the parching sun. The master reads out the telegram to the old woman. It was from her daughter Sarita, who will come to see her mother on Wednesday. The old woman is extremely happy, but alarmed at the same time because that day was Wednesday itself and its almost time for the bus to arrive at the bus stand. **"Oh God"**, she exclaims **"How can my daughter travel from the bus stand which is at least two kilometres away from my house? She is married to a rich young man who has a government job and earns a great deal. I must arrange some vehicle to take her home?"** She rushes to Babu Khan, who plies horse-driven tonga from the bus stand to the village. Babu Khan had just arrived home after his day's work and was about to enter the house when the old woman called at him. She explains the situation and requests him to take her to the bus stand so that she can bring her daughter home. She is a rich woman, and to walk upto the village on foot is below her dignity. Babu Khan dismisses her request as his horse is tired and he himself is hungry. It's time for him to rest and give the same to his tired horse whom he loves very much. But the old woman implores him passionately and is ready to give him double the amount he would otherwise charge for a journey from the bus stand to the village. Babu Khan is amused. He is not a greedy man, but the double amount of the usual charge makes him think about the offer. He agrees not out of pure greed, but more so out to help the old woman and bring her daughter home. That would not take more than an hour or so, he thinks and the tonga is driven towards the bus stand. When the two reach the bus stand, they learn that the bus has already arrived and the passengers went away to their homes. The old woman's daughter was nowhere to be seen. She looks for her all around, walks a few yards here and there, and is dejected to find her nowhere. Babu Khan consoles her by telling that there could be some reason for her absence and wants to take her back home. The old woman sits in the tonga unwillingly and muses a great deal as to why her daughter has not arrived. The tonga finally stops at the old woman's hut-like house. A well-clad woman with a suitcase is standing beside a white car near her hut. The woman in her late thirties is Sarita, the old woman's rich daughter, who has forgotten to mention in the telegram the mode of her journey. She has come in car with her husband.

The story is remarkable for descriptive pictures of the scenes and portraits of human beings. The old woman's anxiety and love for her daughter is well brought out. This description of the old woman, for example:

The old woman's back was so bent, she looked like a four-legged beast. Clad in a ghagri and a blouse, she draped her lugri over her silver white head. Her feet were shod in tiny slippers that had seen better days. Her body was as delicate as a draught of air. The sun was a ball of fire floating over her head. But if one is resolute, one can defeat the most hostile conditions imposed by nature. The old woman now walked across the hot sand in her worn-out slippers like an agile performer treading on burning coals. (84)

There are several such descriptions that make the story a realistic piece of art.

5. Thunderstorm

Thunderstorm narrates an experience of Dalit Sikh in a village at the border of Punjab, Haryana and Rajasthan. The story brings out the caste differences among Sikh community Ramdasi chamar, the followers of Saint Ramdas, or Raidas, are supposed to be inferior to the pure Sikh who follow Guru Granth. The story begins with Daryav's Singh and his young wife Sheran sitting in their small house with their six month old child when, all of a sudden, heavy knocks fall upon their door. Parmesh Singh and his son Bakhtiyar enter the house. They both look disturbed, and ask Daryav if his dying father has told him anything. Daryav remembers his father saying — **"I spit on your money. To hell with it. To hell with the money."** When his old father Dilbagh was on his deathbed he had noticed a big spider trying to attract an insect, helpless as it was. The insect runs away from the spider's net, yet the spider somehow gets it inside. Then, there the life-taking struggle to get out of the trap.

Daryav does not relate all this to Parmesh and his son, who appear very rude and authoritative in approach. Even Sheran is annoyed at their behaviour. They behave as if they are the masters even in Daryav's house, and unmindful of Sheran's presence, babble irrelevantly. Daryav's old father was working in Parmesh Singh's *haveli*. He seemed to have witnessed a scene — a murder inside the *haveli* — but died before Parmesh and Bakhtiyar could be punished for the crime. The two, however, are terribly frightened, and wanted to know if he had narrated the scene to Daryav. They have a different plan to operate and save themselves from imprisonment, or even death sentence. They have come in a jeep and ask Daryav to accompany them to a farmhouse — an old house they own outside of the village. Daryav is unwilling to leave the house, to leave his young wife and infant alone in the darkness of night. They somehow succeed in pursuing him and the three start their journey through darkness. Parmesh has a huge bag, and clutch it to his chest, indicating that something precious is inside it. The jeep runs with tremendous speed, tearing darkness apart. Bhaktiyar is tense and he abuses Daryav for enquiring about the hurry. Daryav curses himself for leaving the house even though barely three days have passed since his father died. He is unable to understand what plan Parmesh and Bakhtiyar have in mind. They finally reach the old house where a police inspector is anxiously waiting for them. The policeman has a pistol placed on a small table. His eyes inquiringly look at both Parmesh and Bakhtiyar. Parmesh rushes to the inspector with the bag. He opens it up showing bundles of currency notes. They must amount at least ten lakhs. Now, the operation of the plan. The police Inspector asks Daryav to hold the pistol and aim it outside. Daryav smells something wrong. In the meantime, the conversion among the other three reveal that Bakhtiyar has killed his step brother Karanhool who demanded his share in Parmesh Singh's property. Parmesh Singh is equally opposed to his demand. Therefore, they got rid of him by murdering the man outright. Daryav's father, who was a servant at Parmesh's haveli, must have watched the act. But he died soon after. Now, the charge of murder is to be placed on Daryav, drag him to the police station and get him imprisoned. Bakhtiyar has an eye on Daryav's young wife too. A sudden realisation dawns upon Daryav, and, without wasting time, he shoots the inspector with the pistol in his hand.

The story exposes how the rich in society inflict atrocities upon the low caste poor people. But Daryav, the poor man, awakens to reality and saves himself from the clutches of the rich and powerful.

The story is remarkable for vivid pictures of scenes and situations, and of realistic characterisation — A symbolic situation depicting helpless insect being caught by a spider in its web is noteworthy:

Dilbagh, Daryav's father, is sick and frail. His days are numbered, and he is about to breathe his last. It is at this time that the dying man visualises the trap that lies ahead for his son:

His sunken, upturned eyes had remained fixed on the ceiling, where a spider's web hung between the iron ring and the joint in the wall. An insect had been inching towards the web, when the spider seized it and dragged it closer. The insect had torn itself free and moved ahead. It was obvious that the spider was playing a game to trap the insect, which was making every effort to evade it. (112)

Ratan Kumar Sambharia's observation and skilful presentation of the outer surrounding is attractive and convincing:

The moon was about to set. The stars glittered in the sky like sequins embroidered on a wedded woman's veil. The night was not so dark as to make it impossible to spot another human being through the gloom. Nor was it so dark as to obscure the gleam of an eye. The moment of semi-gloom, marking the merging of night into day, was unique to the month of Kartik that began some time in October. There was a slight nip in the air. Every suckling baby in the village slept soundly as the night stood sentinel, resounding with its many echoes. 'Whoo-whoo' came the hoot of an owl perched on the branch of a neem tree. The terrifying call reverberating in the silence. (117)

6. The Farmland

The Farmland is about an old man called Ker Singh who owns two hundred square yards of land and decides to grow different types of crops — gram, barley, wheat, spinach, coriander, fenugreek etc. on it. He would sell the product and thus earn livelihood. He is happy doing so and loves his farmland because he has inherited it from his father who is now no more.

The towns, these days, have expanded in every direction. The town Ker Singh lives in has come up to his farmland. There are buildings surrounding it and roads have been constructed to reach these buildings. Ker Singh's farmland, thus, falls exactly in the middle of the town. Everyone has an eye on the piece of land; the builders, contractors, middlemen — all want to buy it and earn money out of the construction thereupon. The old man, however, is of firm opinion that selling land would fetch money just once, which will trickle away out of his pocket like sand trickling away out of the fist. On the other hand, farming on it will give him annual income besides fresh vegetables for himself and for the customers. He is emotionally attached to the farmland. He works on it, and knows every bit of farming from weeding to hoeing to reaping the harvest. He has built up a little hut there and lives alone. He has lost his wife long back whose memories come forth at times and make him nostalgic. He has a son who is away on some government project with his wife and children. The old man lives alone and is happy.

Several people have approached Ker Singh asking the price of land; he has sent everyone back chiding them for troubling a man who wants to live peacefully and who enjoyed being a farmer:

At seventy-four, Ker Singh took it lightly. He would toil on the parcels of land he was cultivating, digging the soil and watering the crops himself. He would prepare his meals himself. As night descended, he would lie down to rest on the rope-string bed in the cottage. As the hours passed, the old man would be lost in memories of the past. Today, the past and the present stood like two poles in his life. Mapping the sky, the moon and the stars, the old man would curl up, like a bird resting, wings folded, in its nest, and drift into slumber on the bed's rope string that had sagged with the years. (129, 130)

Once Ker Singh fell ill and several of his relatives came to see him. They all advised the old Ker Singh that he should go to live with his son, as living alone at this age could be disastrous. They suggested he can come down to the other side of the farm and live with them. Ker Singh, however, declined their suggestions and made up his mind not to budge. The people, those who longed for a piece of land that belonged to Ker Singh, would not let him live in peace. One day, after having recuperated from the illness, he walked towards the weekly market to sell vegetables reaped from his own farmland. Somebody placed his hand upon Ker Singh's shoulder and asked — **"How much do you want for the plot of yours?"** Ker Singh was irritated and wanted to slap the man on his cheek, but somehow controlled himself and sent him away scolding.

One of Ker Singh's acquaintances included an advocate, who visited him occasionally. The two got on well with each other. The advocate would tell him stories about the court cases wherein the poor and the innocents are trapped and robbed of their belongings. He had helped several poor men by providing them legal assistance and had won cases for them, he would relate his generosity and large heartedness to Ker Singh. The old man trusted the advocate totally. He has produced some papers on one of such delightful occasions, and obtained Ker Singh's signature, maybe as witness or something in a poor man's case which the advocate was standing for in the court of law. Ker Singh happily obliged him.

A few days later, while he was resting his tired limbs on the rope string inside his house a police van appeared on the farm. Ker Singh was alarmed and astonished. The men who alighted from the van began to measure the land. "Who are you and what are you doing?" Ker Singh enquired with the men. "Why", one of them explained, "measuring the plot before further works began on it" Meaning? Ker Singh was bewildered and annoyed. "Meaning what?" the man replied, "I am the one who has purchased the land you sold. Now, move away and let me do my work."

Ker Singh sank down with sorrow and disbelief. "No, this is not true, I have never sold my farmland. This is not true, this cannot be true" he cried. The man came forward and unfolded the paper which carried Ker Singh's signature. It was a proper legal document showing the selling of Ker Singh's farm land with a certain amount of money.

From that day onwards Ker Singh was compelled to live in a small house that was left to his disposal. He regularly goes to his advocate friend's house and knocks his door. The door never opens and he comes back like a child who has lost his parents in a crowded *mela*.

The story, thus, depicts the pathetic condition of an old man who is deceived by his trusted friend. It raises the question of greed and deception and its impact on a lonely old man's life. The pathos in the story comes out clearly towards the end:

As his breathing steadied, the old man sat down on the bed. He felt something crackle under the mattress. He folded it over and discovered a ten-rupee work stamp paper with something handwritten on it. He noted the two signatures, verified by notary

public. He was stunned. Ker Singh was known in the colony as a bold hearty fellow. He thought himself to be arrogant. But now his fearful eyes did not dare need what was written on the papers. Words kept forming in his mind and slipping away.

In times of crisis, a person's courage comes in handy. The old man held the stems of his spectacles to keep them steady and read carefully through the entire document, word by word.

It was clear that a conspiracy had been hatched.

His hand now felt the plastic bag. The amount — five thousand rupees — was written right there on the paper. He began to sweat. He shook his head, overcome by rage, self-derision and shame. I am an old man, he mused, all alone in the world. Come cremate me without ceremony. The lawyer's face loomed large in his imagination like tiger's head terrifying and deadly. It was evident that while he was ill, the lawyer had extracted every morsel of information from him. The police officer who had come to measure his plot had verified it. Heaven and earth seemed to swirl around the old man in vertiginous motion. (141)

7. The Buffalo

Ratan Kumar Sambharia's stories indicate that he is deeply influenced by Premchand, the great Hindi novelist and short story writer of the last century. Like Premchand, Sambharia is more interested in miseries and fortunes of individual character than the social issues that are responsible for their plight. His characters are poor, and their hard work and determination steer out of the situation and are happy and victorious towards the end. ***The Buffalo*** narrates the story of a poor, twenty five year old man called *Mangla,* who is weak and leads a miserable life. He is an orphan with no close relatives, except Samjhi, whom he calls Bhabi and visits her on and off. Mangla's social status is described by the author thus:

An orphan, he had no siblings to speak to either. A dead tree, standing in the wilderness, as it were; a lapse of nature, falling short in rank and physical stature, devoid of both self-awareness and self-confidence. Endless worries and a sense of hopelessness lay in wait for him; desperation was his bedmate. A couple of thatchless roofs were all he had to call his own. Hunger growled in his belly; penury ruled at home. His was a life that hung in balance, tossed between the devil and the deep sea. He neither had work at hand nor enjoyed

respect from his peers. Eyebrows were raised in disdain when he went to pick up his dues. Mangla and work? It seemed laughable to mention both in the same breath. He could pick up neither a spade nor a loaded *tasla.* He was incapable of cutting the grain stalks ready for harvest. Nor was he able to carry anything as heavy as ten kilos. (65)

It is this character Mangla around whom the entire story revolves. One day, he visits Samjhi Bhabi who gives him a surprising offer. She tells Mangla that her parents are looking for a suitable boy for her younger sister Sonwa, and she has suggested Mangla's name who would make a good match for the girl. If Mangla agrees, Samjhi tells him further, she will give him a calf – a two year old buffalo – which will grow up into a good buffalo within a couple of years. That will fetch him fortune, with milk and all — and the two – Mangla and Sonwa – will live happily together. For Mangla, it was no less than a dream – a dream, if it comes true, will change his life into paradise. He agrees and takes the calf to his house. The calf, in fact, is very weak. It was scrawny, all skin and bones. Her hairy hide was infested with ticks. Fleas clung to her every part. The calf, obviously, was a victim of malnutrition and neglect. Mangla was a bit unhappy initially, but he soon swung into clime. He started taking care of the animal. He gave the animal regular bath with plenty of water, got green grass to feed it, took it out for walk, and did away with all the ticks and fleas. The animal looked beautiful within a couple of months. It grew strong as well. Now Mangla drowned himself in dreams of his would-be-bride Sonwa. He had not seen her, but could imagine his future wife – short enough to reach upto his shoulders, fair complexioned, curly hair, loaded with ornament – looking almost like Lakshmi. A kind of new energy took hold of him. His laziness for which he was reprimanded several times earlier, had disappeared. He worked hard and ate enough to build up strength. And he took proper care of the animal which now was big enough for mating. The buffalo (now no more calf) adored his lonely house. But Samjhi Bhabi had not approached him with Sonwa's news. He himself did. Samjhi told him that his sister is coming with other relatives for the fair in the village due next month. He can meet the girl personally and further programmes will follow. Mangla's dreams grow day by day. He longs to see Sonwa in person and waits for the day when fair – that is *mela* is due. On the day of mela, Mangla gets up early, takes bath, wears new clothes and heads towards the fair. He locates Samjhi Bhabhi and other women in the fair, but cannot make out Sonwa – who should be younger among the elderly women. All the women dressed up brightly are of Samjhi's age. Who among them is Sonwa? He wonders. He learnt later on from Samjhi that Sonwa had developed fever last night. Therefore, she could not come to the fair. Mangla is dejected and prays for Sonwa's rapid recovery.

Mangla is transformed totally. His habits have improved, his daily life has come on the right track. He is totally dedicated to the Buffalo who is pregnant and is likely to deliver the baby soon. The buffalo has grown strong and is fond of her owner. The two often spend time together. Mangla takes her to the jungle for grazing, takes her to the river for drinking water, scrubs her hide and washes her regularly. After due time the buffalo delivers the baby – a calf as beautiful as its mother. Mangla is very happy. He distributed jaggery among his neighbours and gave a tray of sweets to Samjhi as well. He planned milking the buffalo and selling the milk to make money for himself and for Sonwa – his bride-to-be.

One day, when he was alone with the buffalo patting her back and talking to her in some kind of language understood by those two alone – the village chief, a zamindar with executive authority – popularly known as the *lambardar* came with his men and wanted to take the buffalo away. He was known for his terror-tactics and a tyrant who tortured people for no fault of theirs. The buffalo was sitting down in resting position and did not seem to be disturbed at all by the commotion caused by the *lambardar* and his men. Mangla was pleading to him to spare his buffalo and himself as he was a poor man without any other source of income. The *lambardar* made up a story and told Mangla that his father had borrowed ten thousand rupees from him but failed to repay the debt before he died. Therefore, he must take away the buffalo as compensation for the amount he spent on his father's illness. Without waiting for Mangla's response, he asked his men to untie the buffalo from the peg and take it away. His men tried to raise the animal from its sitting position, shouting at her, beating with sticks and trying to drag it with the rope. The animal, however, did not move. The *lambardar* yelled at them — his men, cursed them for their inability to accomplish the job. The men collected dried grass and set it afire. They put the burning grass over the buffalo's back. The animal stood up suddenly and, mad with anger, advanced towards the *lambardar* who was standing close-by with a gun in his hand. The animal pushed the man against the wall and taking him on the horns, hurled him away into the gutter. His men ran away with fear and panic.

The end here – it shows a poor man's inner working of the mind. Mangla, who was supposed to be good for nothing, improves his worth in the eyes of others, because of a woman's image he holds before his eyes and dreams of her. Credit goes to Samjhi who, considering Mangla a worthless man, gives him the calf which has become a sort of burden to her and tempts him into marriage. This calf brings about remarkable change in his life. His love for his buffalo saves him from being destroyed at the hands of *lambardar*, who is frightened away and will never return to him again. The situation in which Mangla is caught and how intimidating the *Lambardar* could be, is brought out through these words:

The Lambardar was well aware that Mangla's father had repaid his loan and closed his account with his employer. Yet, he had no qualms about cutting his son's throat. How would thieves and dacoits survive unless they were unscrupulous? The Lambardar had an eye on Mangla's beautiful robust buffalo. She was one in a million. She should adorn his pen, not Mangla's. When the cattle fair was held, an exhibition would be organised. The buffalo would fetch him a prize. He would earn both money and honour. The most significant point to bear in mind was that the puny Mangla had neither patron nor protector. If things went out of hand now, the Lambardar could toss five hundred rupees or even a thousand to Mangla to settle the matters. Whatever happened, the Lambardar was bent on appropriating the buffalo and tethering it in his own pen. (80)

The buffalo itself thwarts his plan and saves Mangla from further discomfiture.

8. A Chance Meeting

A Chance Meeting is an interesting story of a couple who were separated out of misunderstanding and unite after a long lapse of time – in old age. The woman was pregnant when her husband had abandoned her. Now, in old age, they looked set apart, because they live in different social conditions. The woman is rich while the man is poor. The contrast is well brought out by the author:

The woman was about sixty. She was tall and dark. Her wrinkles somehow made her eyes look sunken. Her cheeks hollow. She wore a ghagra and kameez and had wrapped herself in her lugdi. She wore gold earrings, a rose-ring also made of gold, silver bangles and silver anklets. Just as a mirror reflects the refined tastes of those living in an aristocratic home; so, too, does an individual's personality reveal how she has been brought up. And this woman's face bore a mark of good breeding. One's personality mirrors the stature of

one's home. And this rural women's face had the polish of good breeding. (36)

And the man:

The man was about sixty-five. From the tattered turban he wore, shreds of torn fabric stuck out like the wild growth of hair on some unkempt ascetic's head. His shirt and dhoti had been patched and mended in many places. Gold earrings adorned his lobes. They were his only valuables. With age, his earlobes, too, had worn him. A tug or two would have been enough to tear the earrings off. His footwear was worn to shreds. One of his shoes was fastened to his foot with a string to prevent it from slipping off. But for a couple of molars and one front tooth, his gums were bare. His jaws were in constant motion, like that of an old ox chewing the cud. (37, 38)

The two once lived together as man and woman under the same roof. As destiny would have it, the woman had conceived from her husband before he deserted her. There were rumours that she remarried and is living happily with her second husband. But those were rumours only. In reality, she stayed with her parents, gave birth to a male child and brought him up with loving care. The boy grew up, finely educated, he now is called Khet Singh, loves his mother and has deep regard for her. He knows well enough that she had faced numerous hardships while bringing him up, sacrificed a great deal for the sake of his education. His wife Shyama, is also full of respect for her mother-in-law. They have a daughter named Kalavati whose marriage ceremony is arranged. The girl was to be married off the next day.

The two meet in a bus accidentally, by chance. Otherwise, both of them had forgotten each other. Their journey together for a few hours is interestingly drawn by the author —

The woman was startled. Despite her efforts to keep herself from uttering the word "Baba", her lips parted, as if of their volition, and she heard herself say — "Baba, which village are you from?"

The old man puffed on his bidi. His weak eyes blinked.

"Retpur."

"Retpur?"

Giving her clothes a tug here and there, the woman spruced herself up a bit. Her manner grew alert. "Your name?" she asked with keen interest.

'Ramdayal', the old man's demeanour remained unchanged.

"And, what caste do you belong to?"

'I am from Balai – the weaver community – old woman, he replied in the same composed manner.

The woman heaved a prolonged sigh. (37)

The old woman gradually recognises the man — the same man who drove her out from his house barely twenty days after her marriage. The reason. She was dark complexioned — not even dark – only *saanwali* - brown, so to say. After that she faced innumerable hardships. People cast aspersions on her, and suspected her character. She faced it all – alone. The same man was sitting before her. Right in front of her. The woman inside melts down. She feels pity for the man, who is old and in utter poverty. He needs support. She takes him with her against his will. He is unable to understand why the woman is being so kind to him. As they alight the bus, she buys a good pair of shoes for him, a new turban and dhoti, a new shirt as well. She takes him to her house. Everyone at home is surprised to see this old man accompanied by her. Shyama finds it difficult to accept him, while her husband Khet Singh follows his mother's instructions and advice. Next day, after Kalavati's marriage ceremony is accomplished, she takes him on the dais, on the platform where the bride and bridegroom are seated, and she declares his identity.

The story is devoid of 'Dalit' sensibility and is focused upon two individual's sentiments.It makes a good reading, though.

9. Lathi

Lathi depicts misunderstanding between two individuals – a Muslim family – Chand Mohammad and his wife Salma. The story does not narrate any episode, really, except in the past the memories cause turmoil in the heart of the spouses. They have a seven year old son, Deen, who is also under tremendous pressure because of his parents stupid apprehension.

The story narrates a petty incident that occurs at the residence of Chand Mohammad's Hindu neighbour — Harman Singh, an old man simply known as Harman Chacha. The two families are neighbours and their houses are adjoining to each other. The relationship between the two families, in fact, is cordial. Chand Mohammad and Harman Chacha have helped each other several times in the past. Harman Chacha's wife has also interacted with Salma many times. There was no major cause of hostility between the two families except one —Harman Chacha was annoyed with Chand Mohammad's cow who had urinated in front of his gate. This happened several times. Therefore, Harman Chacha had warned Chand Mohammad against this nuisance. But cow is an animal and follows the same thing again and again without reasoning. Chand Mohammad had begged Harman Chacha's pardon for his cow's mischief. The matter seemed to have settled there. Nothing more of it.

Recently, however, policies in India have poisoned the minds of the people against each other. Demolition of Babri Mosque in Ayodhya and the bloody riots that broke out everywhere in India had set the two communities — the Hindus and the Muslims — against each other. Chand Mohammad's was the only Muslim family residing happily among the Hindus. The family participated in all the Hindu festivals, and invited Hindu friends on the occasion of Eid and other festivals of its religion. Recent occurings on the national level – elsewhere – not in their locality — had created a feeling of insecurity. Chand Mohammad's wife — Salma in particular, had grown sceptic by the rumours that repeatedly fell upon her ears. Chand Mohammad was away all the while on account of his work, Salma with her son stayed alone at home. She groomed all sorts of misunderstandings about the people at large. Her husband, however, tried to expel all her doubts and assured their safety. He was particularly convinced of Harman Chacha's secular beliefs and his behaviour towards his family:

Like a cloud gathering overhead, certain memories began to take shape in his mind. Every time a dozen people gathered in the village courtyard, they would begin talking about the communal riots of 1947 that had created a rift between Hindus and the Muslims. Harman Chacha would then put his arm around Chand affectionately and narrate the incidents of those days. He would describe how a wall of distrust and hatred had risen between the members of both communities and how they had been at each other's throat. With murder and mayhem taking over, it had been each man for himself, everyone fleeing for his life. Harman would relate how he had stood up to armed rioters from his own community and saved the lives of both Chand's father and grandfather – Raj and Taj Mohammad. He had persuaded the two men to stay on in their village with their families, with assurances of protection against possible communal violence targeting Muslims. (181, 182)

Chand Mohammad, therefore, had no fear of anyone attacking his family because they are the Muslims. His wife, however, has developed mistrust against Harman Chacha today because Harman Chacha was seen carrying two big lathis and beating the ground with them. This one act of Harman Chacha sends the Muslim family into wilderness. Salma fears that her neighbour is going to attack her family with the lathis. She asks her husband to get ready for defence, and call for some assistance from somewhere if possible. They are tense with fear because the noise of beating the ground with lathis keeps coming on and off. They are awake the whole night. Next morning Harman Chacha's voice is heard. He is coming towards Chand's house calling:

"Hey Chand, there is a snake that has crept into my house. We were all after it the whole night. But could not locate it. There is a possibility of it creeping into your house. So, take this lathi and use it for driving the snake out of house." So, saying Harman Chacha hands the lathi over to Chand Mohammad and returns.

The story is a bitter comment on the recent political climate in India that has made the two communities suspicious of each other. They lived harmoniously after Independence. Recently, however, the relationship between the two communities has gone sore. There are passages in the story that depict the causes of distrust:

It's complicated, Salma, Chand Mohammad went on, from the time the matter of Babri Mosque came up, ten years back, a rift has grown between the two communities. Political leaders with vested interests are bent on destroying the harmony there had existed all along between Hindus and Muslims. The evils of communalism have now tainted our village. Of the homes in the twenty - odd villages spread over this area, ours is the only Muslim one. There was a time when Harman Chacha was so poor, he had to worry about where his next meal was coming from. But now that he has earned some money, and came up in the world, he is singing praises of religion... (184)

This precisely is the cause of hysteria among the Muslims in India. The man who was busy looking for 'next meal', has started singing religious songs, has joined the chorus of majoritarianism. The Muslims, who are a minority community feel insecure and intimidated.

The story has brought about the elements of social realism in an effective manner. It has made an effective use of snake as a symbol of the poisonous factor that has psychologically separated the two communities.

10. Bes

Bes, in local Rajasthan language means attire — dress worn by the people of a particular community. Here, Bes refers to the dress worn by the high-caste Rajput woman in Rajasthan. The story delineates the caste superiority of the Rajputs who once ruled the entire region. The Rajputs were so powerful that even dacoits would not dare touch their women in their critical time. They would rather help them out of the situation and prove their loyalty towards the ruling clan.

Agani, a young girl from tribal community in Rajasthan, has gone out to buy some essentials as required for her engagement ceremony. She is an educated girl who does not stick to the tribal tradition, but wants to look like Rajputani by wearing the dress the high-caste women do. Her mother Hugana had reprimanded her for imitating the high caste women, and had asked to remain within the limitations of their tribal ethos. But Agani never listened to her mother's advice and disregarded the tradition, at least the tradition of dressing up like a tribal woman covering face and leaving breasts uncovered to be scanned by the high caste onlookers.

It so happened that Agani, dressed up like a Rajputani, was travelling in a bus to Udaipur whereabout her muddy house is situated. She is bold enough to travel alone and return home safe. She had done it several times before. Agani is very happy because her marriage is finalised with an educated man of her community, and the engagement ceremony is going to take place tomorrow. The bus making way through unaccountable potholes, stops suddenly and unexpectedly, with a big jolt to the passengers inside. The driver and conductor get down to check what is wrong, and announce after sometimes that the bus is unable to move forward as a major breakdown has occurred. They further announced that the passengers can take another bus from across the road. Some people decided to wait till the bus gets repaired, others moved away walking up to nearby villages. Agani is in two minds, unable to decide what to do. It is already around eight o'clock. Her mother must be anxiously waiting for her arrival. She finally decides to move out of the bus and take another form other side of the road. She goes out and stands on the platform waiting for the bus to arrive. She is alone and feels insecure in the darkness of night. The bus stop is away from the nearby localities, and it does not seemed to be in use. Solitary vehicles pass by her with speed. Nobody bothers to look at her. Its ten o'clock now. It seems to be an infinite wait. There is no sign of any bus arriving. Two drunk men appear through darkness. They are dead drunk, unable even to walk. They call each other. Harji and Marji and speak the tribal language which is well understood by Agani. They have realised the girl's loneliness, and would certainly take undue advantage of her position. They babble in the inebriated state looking at her closely, obviously with vile intention. The girl is terribly frightened. She sits down trying to cover herself with clothes as much as possible. They watch her closely and are taken aback because the girl, lonely though she is, is from a Rajput clan. She does not look like an ordinary woman, but from an educated family, probably a Rajputani. Their intoxication drops down and they slip away in the darkness of night.

The night passes on. The wild beasts step out in search of food. The surrounding area was filled with trees and bushes and animals like Jackals, and foxes abound among them. Two jackals come forward and notice the lonely girl. They straight away march towards her. Agani shoos them away with hands, crying – "go away, go away…." The animals do not budge. They keep on moving towards the girl. While she tries to ward her off from the wild beasts. It is at this time that a hunter arrives at the spot. He realises the situation in which the lonely girl is caught and immediately fires in the sky with gun. The animals run away. The girl breathes a sigh of relief. She finds some sort of comfort with herself as there is a man, who has protected her from the wild beasts. But, she soon realises, here is another beast walking on two legs. The hunter now was approaching her, obviously with ill intention. Agani is frightened once again, and starts praying to God asking him to come to her rescue in this horrible condition. The hunter comes close to her, is in fact, aroused by her beautiful well curved body that shines in the moonlight. He comes closer to her. Agani's position becomes hopeless. Who will save her now, that the saviour himself has turned out to be an enemy. The hunter watches her closely and is alarmed within. Agani's *bes* reveals that she is a Rajputani — not an ordinary helpless tribal woman. Maybe, he muses, her family members or her husband have gone for some business nearby and are likely to return soon. He asks her about her family members but Agani does not answer as she was scared that if speaks with her tribal accent, he will come to know that she is not a Rajputani but a tribal woman. When he does not get an answer, he is sure that she is a Rajputani and he cannot dare touch a Rajput girl. He fears the consequences and withdraws. He kicks the motorbike and speeds up the vehicle.

It is morning now. People have started moving out of their houses. Agani, who had lost all hopes, is enlightened now with rays of the rising sun. The essentials she has brought for the engagement ceremony are safe, and she herself is completely secure, untouched, unravished. She, however, felt terribly hungry and moves out to find some shop or hotel on the roadside. She finds one. She also learns that a bus to Udaipur is due shortly. She eats hurriedly as a bus to Udaipur was approaching fast.

The story makes interesting reading as usual. Ratna Kumar Sambharia had a knack of bringing his characters fully alive with complete details about their inner and outer personalities. Agani's position as a young girl trapped in formidable circumstances is brought out with vivid description —

People from these parts were not unfamiliar with the evil deeds of passing truck drivers. They were known to prey on women travelling alone on these roads at unearthly hours and they would force them into their vehicles. The following days, the women would be tossed out– dead, half-dead, conscious or unconscious. If she hid in the jungle to escape her tormentors, wild animals would attack and devour her, not even leaving a trace of her bones. There were so many predators – hunters of birds or beasts, on the one hand, and thieves on the other. Agani found herself trapped between the devil and the deep sea. She could expect no mercy from one, no compassion from the other. Oh, Mother! What on earth would she do now? (224)

Like the rest of his characters, Sambharia presents Agani as bold and courageous. She is alone in the darkness of night fighting men and animals — and though she loses hope, at times, is never disheartened. She is a prototype of a modern girl — leaving aside tradition and adopts ways of the world. She neglects her mother's advice to dress like a tribal girl, even though she has not gone to school and obtained degree, Agani, on the other hand, does what she likes. She is capable of keeping her spirit high even in the face of disasters that surround her in the darkness of night. The title of the story – ***Bes*** – is really appropriate and contains the gist of the story fully well. The story points out how Rajputs in Rajasthan are powerful. Everyone fears them, even thieves and dacoits run away at the mention of their caste. In fact, Agani, is saved by the attire she puts on. She, in her tribal dress up, would have been ruined totally. Rajput woman needs to be protected, at any cost —

The moon had begun to set. The night too, was fading fast. The hunter went back to his motorbike and sat there like a sentinel, guarding the woman against anticipated dangers. Some wild animals might snatch her. A trucker could abduct her. Somebody might try molesting her. Let her husband return, he mused, I will teach him a lesson for a lifetime. (234)

Thus, the story is a remarkable example of Ratan Kumar Sambharia's art of social realism.

Sambharia's stories are less concerned with caste factor, but his characters are equally tortured by anguish and desperation. They are poor and helpless, but struggle stoically against the circumstance. Phulwa has overcome poverty of earlier days and is well settled presently. Other characters like Dalpat in ***The Goat's Two Little Kids***, Panaram in ***Terms and Condition***. ***The Old Woman***, the old man who is deceived by his best friend, suffers but is victorious towards the end. Yet the traits of agony and desperation mark their personalities. ***The Buffalo, Lathi*** are also replete with characters who suffer from anxiety and desperation as they are uncertain about their future. ***Bes*** also has Agani, the young girl who spent the whole night in darkness, torn within with agony and desperation.

Ratan Kumar Sambharia's Concept of "Dalitness"

Ten Dalit stories by Ratan Kumar Sambharia that are chosen for study deal with the poor and the helpless in society. Almost all this characters — the protagonists of his tales — are the ones who have uplifted themselves up from the ground under their feet. This ground is often shaky, almost hostile and even detrimental. They are poor, helpless and belong to that class of society which can be termed as underprivileged. Their struggle, however, is not against the caste-system, or it seems to be less so than against class — that social group which the Marxist would term as "have-nots". Ratan Kumar Sambharia does not seem to have derived anything from the Ambedkarite ideology because there is no grain of revolt or protest, not even a mild sense of anger against the establishment. Nevertheless, these characters are shown struggling against the odds and are often victorious in the end.

Phulwa is one of the best-known stories of Sambharia. Phulwa belongs to the erstwhile untouchable community who, now, has made up to the influential lot among the rich. Her son is a big police officer, holding the rank of Superintendent of Police or so and is said to have powerful impact on the government administration. The author, however, does not give details of how this social transformation has taken place. Is it because of Phulwa's personal struggle and commitment to her family? Or is it because of the Government policy of reservation for backward classes in public services? Does Phulwa owe a sense of obligation to any social thinker, a reformer or at least a leader? Nothing comes out clearly. And she has no memories of the past which is revealed through the author's narration. The whole story is narrated through plain realism offering details of the house and its inner content — the sofa, the table, the refrigerator, kitchen, big dining room etc. Then comes Pandit Mata Prasad's old dilapidated house – with its lack of space, stinking bed-room etc. This plain realism, is, of course, much used technique of fiction writing —both in English and in Indian languages. Premchand in Hindi, is, perhaps the most renowned writer of this style. Therefore, Sambharia's fiction writing has certain weightage, certain importance in the realm of Hindi short story. ***The Goat's Two Kids*** registers the victory of the poor – Dalpat, whose animals were killed by Dan Singh's demented son Dharampal just because they had trespassed in their neighbouring house. Dan Singh is a rich landlord for whom 'dhed and bhed' have no significance. Therefore, he does not listen to Dalpat's complaint and sends him away without compensation. Even police fail to give him justice. It is because of Ramdulare, a union leader, who comes his assistance and Dan Singh's son is arrested for crime. ***Terms and Conditions*** offers a strange kind of justice to Panaram, a poor man whose daughter is raped by Jasveer Singh's son. As revenge and retaliation, Panaram demands that Jasveer Singh's daughter should spend a night with his son. Consequently, he is killed by the rich Jasveer who himself gets heart attack and dies.

This is not poetic justice. This is neither the Dalit concept of retaliation. As in the case of earlier story, Panaram should have left the matter to the law, which of course, is always indifferent in the case of the poor sympathy and the downtrodden. But, that, at least, would have won sympathy of the readers. This, again, does not mean that the Dalits should always be the loser. Panaram's demand however, cannot be justified. This is another type of atrocity inflicted upon Jasveer's daughter whose sense of dignity and honour is as important as that of Panaram's daughter, who unfortunately, is humiliated. A Dalit who is guided and directed by the constitution which treats everyone equal. He honours other women as much as his own. The movement of Dalit literature, or, in fact, the entire Dalit movement, wants to destroy injustice, and, at the same time, is keen in recreating a better society based on equality, liberty and brotherhood. A Dalit wants a new world, a better place to live in where egalitarian values prevail. Panaram's Terms and Condition to forgive Jasveer Singh's son, therefore, are barbaric. They do not fit into the Dalit concept of justice. What the author is upto, perhaps, is to reveal the intensity of anger, a deep sense of retaliation accumulated in the heart and mind of Panaram, who, otherwise, have no means to avenge. ***The Old woman*** is an excellent portrayal of a old village women whose love and concern for her daughter is noteworthy. The story, again like in 'Phulwa', shows social transformation. The old woman, who lives in hut-like muddy house, has a daughter who travels in a car. A new Dalit is born. It is hoped and expected that this new Dalit will take everyone along with him and march towards a new horizon.

Thunderstorm is written in narrative description style and brings out caste-differences among the Sikhs in Punjab. Daryav Singh, a Ramdasi Sikh is trapped into a murderous game by Parmesh Singh and his son Bakhtiyar. Daryav, however, is able to turn the tables against the duo. He realises, on spur of the movement, that his life is in danger and must act swiftly. He does. He saves himself and his young wife, who was marked as the next victim after her husband's departure from the world. Sambharia's protagonist always wins – is able to steer himself out of the hostile circumstances. He is Dalits only by caste and possesses all the virtues of adorable heroes. ***Bes*** is another short story in which a Dalit girl is able to overcome all odds that come on her way. Agani, as the girl is named, dresses up like a Rajputani, and saves herself from two drunkards of her own community and a hunter, who, otherwise, would have molested her and ruined her reputation. Ratna Kumar writes mostly about imaginary situations — the old man and woman meeting by chance after a long lapse of time and realise that they are spouse as in — ***"A Chance of Meeting***" a buffalo saving its master's honour by attacking the lambardar as in "The Buffalo" etc. The sentiments that lie at the background of these, offer a beautiful combination of realism marked with artistic elements.

Ratan Kumar's concept of Dalitness, so to say, differs from those of other two authors chosen for this study. B. Rangrao and Baburao Bagul uphold Dalitness as a revolutionary ideology which works out not only for salvation of an individual, but also for social transformation. Dr Ambedkar is a source of inspiration for these two writers in Maharashtra, for Ratan Kumar Sambharia, Dr Ambedkar appears just as a name, or at the most, a leader of the untouchables who quarrelled with Gandhi for their rights. Sambharia has attempted a biographical sketch of Dr Ambedkar, the Ambedkarite ideology, however, is missing in his writings. His stories bear deep influence of Munshi Premchand, a remarkable Hindi writer of the last century. Ratan Kumar's protagonists, though born as Dalits, strive for personal salvation, and have no sense of social obligation. They are individuals rather than representatives of their community. Thus, Ratan Kumar Sambharia's concept of 'Dalitness' is loose and diluted and lacks the ideological core that appears prominently in the stories of B. Rangrao and Baburao Bagul.

Notes

1. Ratan Kumar Sambharia. *Thunderstorm.* Hachette India, 10 Dec. 2015. (p. 3)
2. Ratan Kumar Sambharia. *Thunderstorm.* Hachette India, 10 Dec. 2015. (p. 4)
3. Ratan Kumar Sambharia. *Thunderstorm.* Hachette India, 10 Dec. 2015. (p. 14)
4. *Ibid.* (p. 19)
5. *Ibid.* (p. 26)
6. *Ibid.* (p. 33)
7. *Ibid.* (p. 58)
8. *Ibid.* (pp. 60, 61)
9. *Ibid.* (pp. 63, 64)
10. *Ibid.* (pp. 84, 85)
11. *Ibid.* (p. 84)
12. *Ibid.* (p. 112)
13. *Ibid.* (pp. 129, 130)
14. *Ibid.* (p. 141)
15. *Ibid.* (p. 65)
16. *Ibid.* (p. 80)
17. *Ibid.* (p. 36)
18. *Ibid.* (pp. 37, 38)
19. *Ibid.* (p. 37)
20. *Ibid.* (pp. 181, 182)
21. *Ibid.* (p. 184)
22. *Ibid.* (p. 224)
23. *Ibid.* (p. 234)

Chapter - IV

Interviews with the Authors

As a part of this study, interviews with the writers chosen for the study is necessary. Of the three writers I have chosen, Baburao Bagul is no more. I could not contact Ratan Kumar Sambharia despite my repeated efforts. B. Rangrao, who resides in Mumbai, was kind enough to spare time and respond positively to my request for interview:

Here is the content of the interview, I had with B. Rangrao, the Indian English short-story writer:

AN INTERVIEW WITH B. RANGRAO

I had an opportunity to interview B. Rangrao, one of the authors of my study, and to interact with him on the various issues related to my subject. He is a renowned Dalit writer writing in Marathi as well as in English. A Collection of his short stories ***Desperate Men and Women: Ten Dalit Short Stories From India*** is one of the books undertaken for study. He was kind enough to respond to my questions positively, and thus, help me formulate a thesis.

The content of the interview taken place at his residence in Mumbai on 10th October, 2022 — is as follows:

Me : Good Afternoon, Sir. I am Swati Chandorkar working on Dalit short stories in Three Indian Languages your book.

— ***Desperate Men and Women: Ten Dalit Short StoriesFrom India*** is one of the books I have chosen for study.

BR : Oh, really. That's wonderful. Who are the other writers?

Me : Baburao Bagul in Marathi and Ratan Kumar Sambharia in Hindi.

BR : Why have you chosen these writers? Any particular reason?

Me : There are similarities between your short stories and those of Baburao Bagul. Ratan Kumar is also a famous Dalit writer in Hindi who writes about Dalit issues.

BR : Okay. Have you studied the background against which Dalit literary movement has arisen?

Me : Yes. To some extent.

BR : Good. Now tell me what are your queries and questions.

Me : I have read your books. I am also acquainted with your background. I would like to know a few more things which will help me further in my study.

BR : Please go ahead.

Me : You come from a poor family and from a community which once was considered as untouchable. How did you manage to come out of those circumstances and reach upto this status of a writer?

BR : I could manage to come out of those circumstances but could not reach upto my desired status. I am a small writer who has been writing continuously for almost forty years now, but have not achieved any recognition, except, perhaps, a few awards here and there, and a few readers.

Me : That's your modesty. Your short stories in English are read by a vast majority of readers because, they are perhaps, pioneering effort increative writing in Indian English by a Dalit writer.

BR: That's true. Writers like Bama has written ***Karakku*** – a biography in English, Meena Kandaswami – I don't know whether she belongs to Dalit community or not — has published books in English. Mine is also a small attempt to express Dalit sensibility through creative acts like writing short stories.

Me : You have also published poems in English.

BR : There is a book called ***The Moon at the Window*** containing some forty poems or so.

Me : Do these poems also belong to Dalit genre as the short stories do?

BR : Not really. Some of them are about Nature some express frustration in love. A few poems are also about the city of Mumbai – Bombay as it was called during those days.

Me : Okay. Tell me why have you chosen to write about Dalit issues? Or Dalit sensibility as you put it?

BR : Chosen? Where is the question of choice? A writer writes out of personal experiences. Personal sufferings are moulded into art. A man who suffers and the artist who creates — is how T. S. Eliot has described the process of poetic creation.

Me : Do you mean to say that you have suffered a great deal and that suffering is resulted into creative writing?

BR : Precisely.

Me : Tell me something about what you have suffered from? What has inspired (or compelled) you to be a writer?

BR : There is a saga of my suffering — I was born and brought up in a very poor family. My parents were farm labourers who could not afford to send their children to school. But those were the days when the entire Mahar community in Maharashtra was inspired by Dr B. R. Ambedkar's teachings. One of the maxims Dr Ambedkar had put forward to his disciples was — 'Educate, unite and agitate'. He insisted on education for the untouchable boys and girls. Consequently, I was enrolled to school along with my siblings. There was never enough food to eat, never proper clothes to wear, yet my schooling continued and never interrupted. My native place had school upto VIII standard. I did matriculation from a school in another village which was ten kilometres away from home. So, we used to walk up and down daily from home to school and back.

Me : There were scholarships for Scheduled Castes and Tribes form the Central Government.

BR : Yes. But those scholarships came for higher education. I received those scholarship from the central government for college education. I completed BA and MA in English language and literature from Amravati – the district place some 40 km away from my village.

Me : How were you drawn into writing?

BR : Well, I studied Hindi and English language and literature, and philosophy for BA. For postgraduate study I had taken English literature. These subjects were good enough for any sensitive student to get into writing itself, instead of only studying.

Me : Who were your inspiration for writing, I mean, how did you start writing?

BR : I believe, any young man or woman begins writing — and they start writing poems first – after falling in love. So it happened to me. Initially, I wrote love poems expressing disappointment in love. In due course of time, I was inevitably drawn towards the Ambedkarite movement, participated in morchas, bhajans, jalasas, plays etc. propagating the philosophy and social messages of Dr Ambedkar. I even started lecturing to the masses on the occasion of Ambedkar Jayanti, Dhamma Chakra Pravartan Din, on 6th December, the day Dr Ambedkar passed away etc. This compelled me to write down the Ambedkarite songs, speeches and present them in gatherings.

Me : How could you manage this all with your study and other responsibilities.

BR : That was a movement and each one of us committed to it. The sense of responsibility and the sense of commitment went hand in hand.

Me : Were those days of poverty and want over yet?

BR : Yes, Yes. I was appointed as lecturer in English immediately after I passed MA. That was in the Government college in Amravati — the institution from where I had completed my postgraduate studies. I was placed Second in order of merit from the entire University. So, the offer came almost running to me.

Me : How were your earlier love poems transformed into Dalit poetry and Dalit literature as a whole?

BR : Again, those were the days when the movement of Dalit literature was in full swing. *Asmitadarsh*, a Marathi journal dedicated to Dalit literary movement, edited by Gangadhar Pantawane, published our poems from time to time. *Asmitadarsh* rejected love poems, or any article on other than the Ambedkarite topic. Besides, we had developed a profound sense of social obligation. I was an active member of Dalit Panther, the militant Dalit organisation founded by Namdeo Dhasal, Raja Dhale, J. V. Pawar and others. We retaliated against social injustice by striking back. Dalit Panther had created a kind of terror among the caste-Hindus and a sense of security among the Dalit masses.... My love poems disappeared in the course of time, my priorities as a writer turned out to be social issues.

Me : When was your first book published? And how was it received by the readers in general?

BR : My first book of poems was published in 1979. It was a collection of Dalit poems and was titled as ***Oedipus***. It was published with the help of Maharashtra Sahitya Sanskriti Mandal which had paid the cost of publication.

Me : Tell me about your further journey as a writer and social thinker.

BR : Well, after having taught in Vidarbha Mahavidyalaya, Amravati for almost sixteen years, I was transferred to Mumbai. Generally, people are unwilling to leave their native town and go to a metropolis city like Mumbai where everyone is lost in the crowd. But I had decided to go to Mumbai. Joined Elphinstone College in 1986. Lived alone for one complete year, brought my family after an accommodation at Government colony, Bandra, was offered to me. Gradually settled down in Mumbai.

Me : But you were Professor at the University of Mumbai?

BR : Yes, that is also an interesting story. I left the state government job and joined the University initially as a Reader in English in 1991, then as Professor of English in 1995. I had completed my Research Study (Ph.D.) in 1991 itself under the supervision of Vilas Sarang, who was a renowned writer in Marathi and in English. I worked with such literary giants like Nissim Ezekiel, B. R. Patankar at the University and had an opportunity to interact with Gieve Patel, Adil Jussawala, Shashi Deshpande, Eijaj Ahmad and several European and American scholars who visited the University on and off for academic purposes. I was the Head of the University Department of English and stayed in Germany as DAAD Professor at OttO Von Guericke University, Magdeburg, Germany.

Me : That was a big achievement and a long journey from where you began....

BR : Yes, that was. And a painful journey as well, because Elphinstone college and Mumbai University during those days were reputed centres of higher education. Most of the teachers were Parsi ladies and other Westernised persons. A Head of English Department of Bombay University looked down upon the Indian English teachers for their native accents and is said to have yelled out — "my dog speaks better English than that you Indians do!" I worked with such people considering these as opportunities to improve myself. However, I never surrendered to their inhuman approaches and asserted myself whenever necessary.

Me : What about your image as a writer?

BR : Indian writings for those colleagues of mine was a product of lesser breed, and Dalit literature was filth. I had given one of my novels to a lady teacher who was a Maharashtrian Brahmin. She returned the book the next day telling me that she does not read such books. "Does not read such books", I wondered, "Was it about a taboo subject? Or about non-existing issues?" But I did not say anything and accepted the returned book.

Me : I would like to know how you progressed as a Dalit writer and thinker.

BR : A writer must acquaint himself with the works of other writers. He must know what is happening around the world, must study the various literary trends and tendencies. I had this advantage of knowing the world literature being a University teacher of English language and literature. So, I had read almost all the major African-American writers like Ralph Ellison, Richard Wright, James Baldwin, Nobel Laureate Toni Morrison, Alice Walker, Gloria Naylor, Maya Angelou, Le Roi Jones, Malcolm X… acquainted myself with the Marxist literary theory, and studied the various critical trends – modernist, postmodernist. This was enough to formulate a literary theory of my own. I brought it all into my writings, published poems, fiction, plays criticism….

Me : Did you face the problem of publication because big and famous publication houses generally do not publish Dalit literature. They prefer to publish what is mainstream and popular.

BR : That is very true. And I experienced it all. Therefore, I did not run after big publication houses, and published my books whichever publisher agreed on my conditions. Nevertheless, one of my books of poems is published by Pras Prakashan of Ashok Shahane, which was a big and prestigious name during those days. I have myself published a few of my books.

Me : How do you see the status of Dalit literary movement today? Are the writers in other languages doing justice to the Ambedkarite ideology which is at the core of Marathi Dalit literature?

BR : That is a good question. The movement of Dalit literature has spread out in other regions of the nation. It is powerful in the Hindi belt and in Gujarat. But, unfortunately, the Ambedkarite ideology, as you put it, is missing. Dr Ambedkar had asked to repudiate and renounce the Hindu religious practices, because they are meaningless and obstruct your thinking capacity. A total revolt is what Dr Ambedkar had visualised. Marathi Dalit writers — almost all of them — fulfil his dream. They renounced Hindu religious practices because Hinduism had enslaved them perpetually. They embraced Buddha's Dhamma which teaches rational approach to life. Their literature, therefore, is more rational, subtle and appealing to human sentiments.

Me : Do you mean other Dalits should also quit Hinduism and follow Buddhism as Dr Ambedkar and his followers did?

BR : That's what Dr Ambedkar had in mind.

Me : But that would hurt the sentiments of the Hindus.

BR : High caste Hindus. Those who want to keep their religious authority unchallenged and intact. The so-called low-caste Hindus should realise this.... But let's leave this topic and discuss literature.

Me : How do you see the future of Dalit literary movement in India?

BR : With the spread of education and democratic values, Dalits are awakened everywhere in India. They have started asserting their identity. They have started producing their own arts and literature. Therefore, I can see the movement of Dalit literature widening and raising itself up to the artistic level. I see the future of Dalit literature bright as long as democracy in our country is sustained and constitutional rights of every individual are upheld.

Me : What are your plans for the future?

BR: There are no plans as such. I'll keep on writing as long as I can, and will contribute, in whichever form I can, to the development of Dalit literature on the national level. That's all I can say at this moment?

Me : Thank you, Sir. Thank you so much for sparing time and responding positively to my queries.

Chapter - V

Conclusion

The movement of Dalit literature began in Maharashtra during 1960s. It was in full swing for almost four decades. However, its origin goes back to early decades of the last century when Gopal Buwa Valangkar, Kisan Faguji Bansode and a few others wrote in praise of Dr Ambedkar, criticising unjust Hindu tradition and the miserable plight of the untouchables. Some thinkers and critics trace the Dalit literary tradition even to the Middle Ages when saint-poets like Chokha Mela and his wife complained against the miseries and the wretchedness to the God Vitthala of Pandharpur through their poems. This argument is not acceptable to the present-day generation of Dalit writers because, they believe, saint poets showed social disparity and injustice, through their poems, but never revolted against them or did nothing that could bring social change. The Bhakti movement had spread out in all the regions from South to North, from East to West — it shows emotional turmoil, but because of the lack of political support, it remained confined merely to God, and religion – and to literature. As the saint poets wrote in regional language, the Sanskritised literary canons did not recognise its relevance. It was only in the last century that poets like Kabir, Tukaram, Namdeo, Janabai and others received recognition.

The movement of Dalit literature was an outcome of Dr Babasaheb Ambedkar's ceaseless efforts to awaken the oppressed classes. Dr. Ambedkar fought single-handedly for their rights, while the Indian National Congress Party of those days struggled for political freedom. Dr Ambedkar pointed out to the Congress and other so-called patriots that social slavery that exists in India for centuries together needs to be abolished first, because it flourished during the native rule and no efforts were made to abolish it. Therefore, the fate of the oppressed classes — the untouchable community — needs to be attended to first; political freedom will follow. Dr Ambedkar was a scholar-politician with higher degrees from the USA and UK and had studied deeply subjects like law, religion, sociology, economics, human anthropology, politics and humanities. He, however, was not an armchair scholar, but an activist who utilised his knowledge and scholarship for the betterment of his community, and wiped out the stigma that Indian society bore for centuries together. He was a lone crusader fighting for the cause of the people at large. Dr. Ambedkar held prestigious posts in the British legislation. He was a member of Mumbai legislative council, labour minister and a member of several bodies constituted by the British Government to rule the nation. This was not because of his scholarship or caste, but because of the political weightage he carried through the political parties he had founded and contested for those positions. The Labour Party, later re-named as The Scheduled Castes Federation was powerful next only to the Congress. Therefore, he could easily have access into the British legislation from where he could wield influence to enact laws to improve the plight of the untouchables.

Dr. Ambedkar did not fight for political freedom because political freedom alone does not make a nation free. 'Nation' does not consist of freedom of a privileged few, but freedom of one and all, despite caste, creed or gender. Unfortunately, the leaders of the Congress party and other leaders never realised this and never bothered about the social slavery of the untouchables and other under-privileged people including Hindu women. Dr Ambedkar wanted these unfortunate people to breathe in free air which they never did before. Indian political freedom did not assure that; therefore, he continuously pleaded for the case of the oppressed classes with the British Government and fought for their rights single-handedly. This was the main cause of differences between Dr Ambedkar and Gandhi. In a meeting between the two, Gandhi had suggested that Dr Ambedkar should fight for his motherland. Dr Ambedkar retaliated by telling Gandhi that he has no motherland. How can he call India his motherland where his forefathers and innumerable others are treated worse than animals. Where they are compelled to lead the life of sub-humans. After having initiated the battle for freedom for the untouchables, Dr Ambedkar inculcated in them a sense of dignity and self-respect. He repeatedly asked them to educate, organise and agitate against injustice, particularly against the caste system that was responsible for their misery and wretchedness.

Dr. Ambedkar was not a social reformer with goody- goody approach toward the social issues that had plagued the society for centuries together. He was a social revolutionary who wanted to transform the Indian society into a better place to live in. He had described the Indian social structure as a dilapidated building which requires not just a whitewash, but total restructuring. He further compared it with a multi-storied building without lift or staircase where people on one story live without any contact with the people living on another. They live segregated and they die in the similar condition. How can such people be citizens of the same country? How can India be a nation if the people are unaware of each other's sentiments? A nation divided by the caste system will remain internally divided; therefore, annihilation of castes is essential. Dr Ambedkar wrote down his speech called ***Annihilation of Castes*** in 1936 which he was to deliver at an annual conference of Jat-Pat Todak Mandal of Lahore. The speech could not be delivered because of the differences between Dr Ambedkar and the organising committee. Dr Ambedkar published the undelivered speech which became an authoritative document on the Indian caste system and its ill-effects on the national life. Dr Ambedkar held 'caste' as the sole factor responsible for the misery and wretchedness of the untouchables. It was 'caste' which made them utterly poor and incapable of earning respectable livelihood. It was 'caste' which deprived them of education and pushed them into perpetual darkness of ignorance. It was 'caste' which compelled them to live in dehumanised social conditions. And finally, it was 'caste' which divided the country and threw it away into political slavery.

Annihilation of Caste produced the famous controversy between Gandhi and Ambedkar. Gandhi opposed several points raised by Dr. Ambedkar in his speech, while Dr Ambedkar retaliated by explaining them further convincingly. Dr Ambedkar also researched into the Indian history and produced such remarkable books like ***Who were the Shudras? How they came to be called the Fourth Varna?***, ***What Congress and Gandhi have done to the Untouchables? Revolutions and Counter Revolutions*** and several others in which he explains how caste had played a pivotal role in destroying the lives of the oppressed classes. Caste, unfortunately, was and continues to be, a major supporting pillar of Hinduism. It is an off-shoot of the Varna system on which the entire Hindu culture is based. Therefore, Dr Ambedkar thought and suggested, the Hindus should mend their ways of life, should learn to respect the Shudras and treat them as equals. The notion of untouchability must be done away with, because it divides the Hindus themselves. The so-called untouchables should be allowed to live with dignity, they should be allowed to come up on a par with other Hindus. This will inculcate in them a sense of belonging and of citizenship of the nation. That will create unity and oneness among the Indians. Dr Ambedkar points out that the notion of "Unity in diversity" is a mere myth — a lie, because that neglects the social truth and approves of the sense of superiority among the high caste Hindus. Dr Ambedkar made several efforts to bring the oppressed communities on a par with the caste-Hindus. The Mahad Satyagraha of 1927, burning of *Manusmriti* publically, the movement of temple-entry to the untouchables are some of the examples of his sincere efforts to unite the Hindus who were segregated in the name of castes. When his efforts did not come off and the Hindu authorities refused to respond to his pleas, he decided to quit Hinduism. Consequently, he embraced Buddhism along with his followers in 1956, a few months prior to his sad demise in December, the same year.

Dr. Ambedkar was a practical strategist who in order to awaken the oppressed classes intellectually and spiritually, insisted upon their education. Later in life, he established People's Education Society, which began educational institutions first in Aurangabad, then in Mumbai for young men and women from the Depressed classes. He had also initiated journals and periodicals — *Mooknayak* (1920), *Janata* (1930), and *Bahishkrit Bharat* (1927) which were meant to offer political knowledge and develop reading habits among those who never went to school. This produced miraculous results. Dr Ambedkar's followers not only raced ahead in education, but also produced their own literature. Dalit literature, as it came to be called.

Today, Dalit literature is a national phenomenon. However, as we understand it today, has its beginning in Maharashtra during 1960s. Those were the days when the entire nation was beaming with political activities. The government had initiated nationalisation of the banks, and the ceiling Act of surplus land raised hopes of the poor. The *Bhoodan* movement had spread out everywhere in the nation; In Maharashtra the movement of landless labourers under the leadership of Dadasaheb Gaikwad had stirred the region. The movement of Little magazine led by such writers like Bhalchandra Nemade, Raja Dhale, Ashok Shahane, Chandrakant Khot and others had given new direction to Marathi literature. Elsewhere in the world, the decade 1960s has also left remarkable imprints. It was the decade when the man had landed on the moon. The murder of John F. Kennedy, the US president, and that of Martin Luther King (Jr.) occurred during this decade itself. Malcolm X, the militant Black activist and the writer was put to death by a white man in America during this decade. The global literature had become 'universal', encompassing within its range all human tendencies. African-American literature, Women's literature, literature in the African continents, literature of the working classes based on the Marxist ideology, Dalit literature in India, subaltern literature — all these literary movements had opened up new vistas and new avenues upon the literary horizon. Old literary canons were challenged, new aesthetics was initiated and it was accepted, though grudgingly, by one and all. Culture itself assumed altogether new form. Literature, music, dance, paintings, architect, sculpture, movies etc. formulated a new world which never existed before. A general voice of dissent against the old culture and the canonical norms was heard everywhere. Classicism came to be looked upon as discriminatory and was discarded for its policy of 'the Best and the Rest'. Modernism, which was an extension and supporter of classicism, was no better because both of these tendencies discarded the "low and the rustic". They were elite trends maintaining their superiority to the masses. Contemporary social reality however, discarded these claims and demanded its recognition and reflection in arts and literature. It was for this reason that Classicism and Modernism were old and outdated. A new phase had begun. This phase was called Postmodernism.

Indian Dalit literature is a product of post-modern situation. Spread of education and democratic values created awareness among the masses. Dr Ambedkar's message **'educate, unite and agitate'** had its effect on his followers. The Mahars in Maharashtra explored history and found out how Hindu mythology and history had been unjust to them, how they have been neglected throughout literary history. Like Dr B. R. Ambedkar, his followers in Maharashtra also came to realise that the country as a whole had been cruel to them. Mother India treated them like unwanted children. They revolted. They developed extreme sentiments against Mother India herself. Tryambak Sapkale, a prominent Dalit poet in Marathi, expressed his sense of revolt in the following words:

O, Mother India —

You abandoned me

after cutting the umbilical cord,

You never gave me love and affection.

If in the flow of Time,

Instead of Karna, I approached your bed

Like Oedipus —

Do not blame me in that event.

Indian history and culture, the epics and mythology, the Vedas and Puranas — everyone treated the Shudras like animals. The Four Varna system had compartmentalised the people into four groups which were not allowed to interact with each other. Purush Sukta in the Vedas stated firmly that the Brahmins were born out of the mouth, the Kshtriya were born out of arms, the Vaishya were born out of thighs, and the Shudras, the fourth Varna, out of feet of the Mahapurush — that is God. Then, there is a conflict between the Aryans and non-Aryans. The defeated non-Aryans were pushed back towards the South, and were rendered into *Dasas*, and were compelled to lead the life of beasts. These *Dasas* or the slaves, were considered as untouchable in the course of time. This social history comes down to our own times, where a large number of people in India are still considered as untouchable. Dr Ambedkar fought for the human rights and dignity of these people, and was successful, to a considerable extent, to free them from the social thraldom. The Indian constitution has abolished untouchability and made provision to penalise them who practise it. Yet, there are innumerable instances when the erst-while untouchables are ill-treated at the hands of caste-Hindus. Political freedom brought little cheers to these people — now known as Scheduled Castes and Tribes — and they continue to suffer despite the constitutional provision meant to protect them.

Dalit literature is a voice of protest against social injustice and violation of constitutional norms. It brings out the unknown social reality, neglected by the mainstream writers in all the major languages, and exposes double- dealing of the caste-Hindus in social behaviour. Dalit literature not only delineates the unsavoury social reality, but also protest against it. This protest often assumes the form of revolt, particularly in Maharashtra where the legacy of Dr B. R. Ambedkar looms large. Marathi Dalit poets like Namdeo Dhasal are famous for revolutionary spirit in style as well as in subject-matter. Dhasal's collection of poems ***Golpeetha*** is often considered as one among the best in contemporary poetic expression. Several critics found it worthy of the Nobel Prize neglected by the Establishment. Yet, ***Golpeetha*** remains as the best loved and read book of the time, though in Marathi. Its translation by Dilip Chitre, somehow, failed to reach out to the global readers.

The term 'Dalit' literary means 'the downtrodden', the one who has been oppressed by the tradition, the one who has no role to play in the national scenario, because he is untouchable and devoid of human values. The Dalit is made so by the tradition itself, and no one has made efforts to raise him up to the human level. The stories of Eklavya and Shambuka attest to the truth that their communities were castigated and tortured if they tried to enlighten themselves. Karna in ***Mahabharata*** is a victim of caste-system. These mythological characters are the protagonists of Dalit literary texts. Dalit, in canonical literature, appeared as an object of pity or hatred. The Marathi Brahmin saint-poet Eknath is said to have poured handful of water to an untouchable boy from distance because he felt pity on him. Other writers like Mate, Sane Guruji are known for their sympathetic approach towards the cause of the oppressed. Yet, no one among the caste-Hindus came forward to lift them up socially and spiritually. It was Dr Ambedkar, solely and predominantly, who appeared like an angel trying to raise them up like a father caring for his children. No wonder, then, that Dr Ambedkar was called "Babasaheb" by the oppressed and the downtrodden communities.

The term Dalit came to mean different to different authors. Baburao Bagul, for example explains the meaning to the term — **as the one who raises the voice of protest and revolts against all sorts of injustice — social, religious, economic or political.** Other thinkers in Maharashtra, however, do not approve of the term and want to do away with it. They want to replace it with the term 'Ambedkarite', due to the efforts made by the man to awaken them spiritually and offering them a social platform which they never had before. The term 'Ambedkarite' also denotes the democratic values envisaged by Dr Ambedkar and his dreams of the Indian society based on liberty, equality and fraternity wherein everyone will lead the life of self-respect and dignity.

The movement of Dalit literature, with its beginning in Maharashtra, was also inspired by Buddha and his teachings which believed in human dignity and welfare of every individual, when the Hindu authority failed to listen to the pleas of Dr Ambedkar to treat the untouchables as equals, he quit the Hindu fold and embraced Buddhism. This was the revival of Buddhism in India which seemed to have disappeared in the course of history. Buddha taught compassion towards every living being. He believed in the immense potentialities of every individual despite caste, creed, race or gender. Buddhism is not religion in the conventional meaning of the word, rather, a way of life whereupon every one walks peacefully and with self-dignity. Buddha had revolted against the Vedic religion of his times because it propagated violence (sacrifice) discriminate (four Varnas) and hatred amongst the human beings.

Dr Ambedkar followed Buddha and got himself converted onto the path of Buddha. Thousands of his followers did the likewise.

Dalit writers in Maharashtra are immensely influenced by the teachings of Buddha. They also sought inspiration from Jyotiba Phule, the nineteenth century social thinker and revolutionary. Phule had received English education in the missionary school and was well acquainted with the works of the western thinkers like Thomas Penn, J. S. Mill, Berkeley and others. He came from the Mali (gardener) community and knew the pangs of social neglect by the high caste Brahmins. Therefore, he decided to fight for the rights of the oppressed. He wrote books on social conditions of the time dealing with issues like farmers' plight, miseries of the untouchables, etc. He is credited to have opened school for the untouchable children. His wife Savitribai Phule, inspired by her husband, undertook the task of educating girls – something unique and revolutionary during those days. Savitribai, thus, is considered as the first female teacher teaching the girls and inculcating in them a sense of dignity and self-respect. Jyotiba and his wife Savitribai — both are source of inspiration and idols to contemporary Dalit writers.

The most prominent and the immediate inspiration and encouragement came from Dr Ambedkar. Marathi Dalit literature is replete with the Ambedkarite sense of social transformation, an urge to create something new and to bring about cultural change through literary creativity. Poetry as a literary genre is prolific and always challenging the canonical norms. It refuses to be judged by the old Brahmanical standards and demands independent inquiry into the Dalit literary texts. The first generation of Dalit poets after independence include Namdeo Dhasal, Keshav Meshram, Daya Pawar, Trayambak Sapkale, Waman Nimbalkar, Yashwant Manohar, Arjun Dangle, J. V. Pawar, Prahlad Chandwankar. These poets came from the Mahar community which was included among the untouchables in Maharashtra. They were the first generation of educated Mahars who, after the *Mahaparinirvana* of their beloved leader, Dr B. R. Ambedkar, had grown more militant and more aware of their rights in independent India. They were also the ones who had experienced the pangs of untouchability, suffered from discriminatory social modes and lived in utter poverty. Their poetry, therefore, has the authenticity of poetic urge and direct appeal to the readers. Most of them had even worked with Dr Ambedkar and had participated in the *Satyagrahas* he had organised. Therefore, their dedication and commitment towards the Dalit cause is unquestionable. Their poetry reflects all this and created a new chapter in the history of Marathi poetry.

The movement of Dalit literature in Marathi was enhanced and carried forward by Gangadhar Pantawane, who edited a journal *Asmitadarsh*, and offered scope for Dalit writings. The journal was established by the efforts of Dr M. N. Wankhade, a learned scholar and professor of English, and was taken over by Pantawane after his death in 1972. Dr Pantawane himself was a University Professor and taught Marathi language and literature for nearly thirty years. His scholarly research and study of Dalit movement as a whole added lustre to his academic personality.

Second generation of Marathi Dalit poet was slightly fortunate as it treaded upon the fertile land created by the first generation of Dalit poets. These men and women were educated, most of them had received university education, and were articulate when it came to give expression through speeches. These men and women revealed awareness about social trends in global literature, in African-American literature, in particular. The Dalit women poets were also acquainted with women's literary movement and often adopted feminist stand, never forgetting the stigma of untouchability their forefathers carried upon their existence. These women Dalit poets — Heera Bansode, Jyoti Lanjewar, Surekha Bhagat, Pradnya Daya Pawar — wrote remarakable poems revealing dual victimisation of being Dalit and a woman at the same time.

Second generation of Marathi Dalit poets include Damodhar More, Baban Chahande, E. M. Narnaware, Ram Dotonde, B. Rangrao, W. Kapoor, Prakash Kharat (Mumbai), Prakash Kharat (Nagpur), Bhimsen Dethe, Yuvraj Sontakke and others. Most of these poets are well-educated and know the art of poetry. Their work is marked with controlled artefact and profound sense of nostalgia striking back to memory. Their personal life seems to be comfortable, but memories of the miserable past and the knowledge of the historical injustice make them sad and rebellious at the same time. A shoe-makers profession that his forefathers' followed was always dirty and humiliating. This makes Ram Dotonde nostalgic and sad; but he desires to write down new history with the same instruments which mended shoes of the upper caste people (*When Rapi became pen*). There are extraordinary and revolutionary thoughts like "Spitting on the sun", "Exploring the ocean", bringing the heaven down on the earth" etc. This reveals an extensive range of optimism and a keen desire to ameliorate the existing social condition.

Third generation of Marathi Dalit poets are young men and women in their late forties and in early fifties. Their grievances are not as much against the caste though it continues to exert its influence, as perhaps against the existing socio-political hypocrisy. They become truly Ambedkarite desirous to see the Indian constitution is honoured and properly implemented by those who rule the nation. They also show their discomfort at administrative lapses which fail to bring the government policies down to the last man. These young men and women are angry and want to bring social change through democratic norms.

Marathi Dalit short story is another rich literary genre practised by these writers from the early days itself. Short story, in fact, is innate to human kind, particularly to the Dalits who entertained themselves by narrating real or imaginary tales. In India, short stories have existed from ancient times. ***Kathasaritsagar, Vetal Panchishi*** are some of the famous collections of entertaining short stories. Elsewhere in the world — ***Arabian Nights, Aesop's Tales*** have caught attention of the readers and listeners since antiquity. Dalit writers inherited this art of tale-telling and have written remarkable short stories — Baburao Bagul's two collection of short stories — ***When I Hid My Caste and Death is Getting Cheaper*** are landmarks in Indian literature. Bagul is often compared with two giants of Marathi short-story — G. A. Kulkarni and Gangadhar Gadgil — who are the exponents of avant-garde literary trends in Marathi. Baburao Bagul, however, is little concerned with technicalities; his main concern is with the lives of those who live in dehumanised social conditions. Baburao's voice is as powerful and resounding while narrating a tale as that of Maxim Gorky or even Charles Dickens who projects the miserable working conditions in factories where poor David Copperfield is compelled to work. Other remarkable short story writers are Waman Ohal, Yogiraj Waghmare, Sukhram Hiwrale, Amitav Bandhu Mahau and others.

B. Rangrao, who has made a remarkable contribution to Marathi Dalit poetry and novel, has also equally remarkable collection of short-stories in Indian English. The book ***Desperate Men and Women: Ten Dalit Short Stories From India*** was well received by the readers of Indian English and was discussed extensively in a literary event organised in London in 2015.

Dalit Novel in Marathi is comparatively less significant because not many novels are written till day. However, those that are available are indicative of the writers' commitment to a profound understanding of the oppressed community. Baburao Bagul's ***Sud*** narrates the story of a Dalit woman whose life is ruined by the uppercaste people, and who, retaliates by being one of them in a strange manner. Keshav Mesharam's ***Pokharan*** is another remarkable novel wherein the entire history of the Dalit past is excavated. Bhimsen Dethe's ***Eskot***, Ashok Whatkar's ***MelelaPani***, Namdeo Dhasal's ***HadkiHadavala*** deal with the life of the oppressed and its impact on the existing social ethos. B. Rangrao is yet another writer who has written three novels that read like a novel sequence. ***Soma***, ***Timirangan*** and ***Eka Amurtachi Gost*** are about the same protagonist — namely Soma – whose experiences as a Dalit young boy to a matured Dalit adult are delineated effectively. The last novel — ***Eka Amrutachi Gost***, is in fact, a postmodernist piece of writing which flouts all traditional norms of fiction-writing, is set to open up new avenues for Marathi novel. It goes beyond the tradition and modernity and explores a new universe. The novel narrated the story of a girl student researching into the history of Mahars in Maharashtra, she interviews a Mahar Professor at a University as a part of her research technique, and the professor unfolds his seven generations going back to the seventeenth century when his ancestors fought for Swaraj with Shivaji, the great, and contributed to the foundation of Maratha rule in Maharashtra. Several historical characters come alive in the course of narration, Shivaji Maharaj, Sambhaji, Tara Rani, Bajirao Peshwa and Mastani, Jyotiba Phule, the Shastris of Chiplun, Dr Ambedkar and several others. The story ends with the narrator's miserable plight in the contemporary world of dirty politics.

The novel is remarkable for its postmodernist technique which combines extracts from the ***Sanskrit epics***, ***Bhagvadgeeta, Arabian Nights, Panchtantra,*** songs from popular Hindi movies, nursery rhymes etc. The combination of all these factors makes the novel a delightful reading experience. The novel had won the Shobhnath Yadav Rashtriya Samman Award in 2015.

Dalit Theatre in Marathi is a rich experience. It continues to be a movement even today. Playwrights like Premchand Gajvi with his ***Sambodhi*** group stages Dalit performances every now and then. Gajvi's plays — ***Gothbhar Pani***, ***Tanmajori***, ***Kirwant, Gandhi and Ambedkar*** etc. are invaluable contribution to the Dalit theatre in Marathi. Datta Bhagat is another important playwright in the present context. His plays ***Wata-Palwata*** was performed at a national theatre in New Delhi. The movement of Dalit theatre included plays like ***Thamba Ramrajya Yet Ahe*** by Prakash Tribuwan, ***Bamanwada*** by Ramesh Chavan, ***Naukrichya Jalat*** by Prabhakar Ganveer, ***Manuskiche Band*** by Gangadhar Pantawane etc. Recently, popular performances of ***Shivaji Underground via Bhimnagar Mohalla*** by Rajkumar Tagade have contributed a great deal to the success of Dalit Theatre in Marathi. Professor Rustam Achalkamb of Aurangabad has made a specialised study of Dalit theatre whose conclusions and observations on the subject are noteworthy.

Dalit Autobiography in Marathi has made the movement more vocal and articulate as these autobiographies speak loudly about the discrimination and injustice inflicted upon these individuals by the society. They are the authentic documents of the Indian social structure in which certain individuals and communities were at the receiving end. It began with ***Balut***, an autobiography by a Dalit poet Daya Pawar which exposed his personal agony and wretchedness. Several autobiographies followed — ***Aathwaniche Pakshi*** by P. E. Sonkamble, ***Mukkam Post***, ***Devache Gothne*** by Mahdhav Kandvilkar, ***Fanjar*** by Nanasaheb Zodge, ***Taral-Antral*** by Shankarrao Kharat, ***Gawki*** by Rustam Achalkamb, ***De Dan SuteGirhan*** by R. K. Tribhuwan, ***Abhran*** by Parth Polke, ***Katyawarchi Pot*** by Uttam Bandu Tupe, ***Akkarmashi*** by Sharan Kumar Limbale, etc. Besides these autobiographies by writers belonging to nomadic tribes like ***Uparya*** by Laxman Mane, ***Uchlya*** by Laxman Gaiwad, ***Kolhatyacha Por*** by Kishor Shantabai Kale have also made impact upon the Marathi Dalit autobiography. However, these autobiographies fall slightly out of the concept 'Dalit', because the communities these writers belong to were never parts of the Hindu fold which had smothered and killed the ati-shudra and the untouchables mentally and spiritually. Nevertheless, their presence does matter because they explore yet another ugly facet of Indian social reality.

Dalit women in Maharashtra have also came forward to narrate their experiences being 'woman' and 'Dalit' simultaneously. They have produced a new literary genre reaching upto African-American women's aesthetic heights and narrative authenticity. Shantabai Kamble's ***Mazya Jalmachi Chittarkatha*** (Picturesque Story of My Life) was the first to create sensation in the Marathi literary world, for it narrates the pathetic story of woman's life who was Mahar (untouchable) and female in the male dominated society. The book was praised by critics and average readers. It was followed by ***Jinha Amcha*** by Baby Kamble, ***Mitleli Kawada*** by Mukta Saurwagaud, ***Antasphot*** by Kumud Pawade, ***I want of Destroy Myself*** by Malika Amar Sheikh. The autobiography of Namdeo Dhasal's wife Malika Amar Sheikh was an eye-opener to the Dalit readers, because it had exposed the inner working of the Dalit Panther, the militant organisation of the Dalit youths, which was said to be struggling to restore the human rights to the oppressed communities. Malika criticised her husband, Namdeo Dhasal, who was considered as the leading light of the Dalit literary movement, for his insensitive approach towards his wife and inhuman treatment meted out to her. She also exposed the ideological contradiction within the movement as a whole. The Dalit youths who were fighting for social justice are devoid of human values. They treat their wives like slaves etc. The book, however, was charged of being popular and cheap sensationalism.

Marathi Dalit literary movement, thus, was a turning point in the history of Indian literature. It was a creative expression of those who were dumb and incapable of uttering grievances because of social restriction and traditional denial. The canonical literary artist could never reach out to the Dalit sentiments because he lived within the ivory tower of his own limited experiences. He wrote either of mythological characters like Radha and Krishna, or of imaginary stories like Kalidas's ***Meghdoot***. The social reformers never took such drastic steps like challenging the logic behind irrational social practices like untouchability and remained confined to superficial issues like Sati, widow remarriage etc. while a large number of under privileged people lived in social thraldom. It was Dr Ambedkar who fought against the entire system and created social awareness and the sense of dignity and self-respect among the oppressed communities. It was his insistence on education for the Dalit which ultimately resulted into literary movement, initially in Maharashtra, and later, in other parts of the nation.

Anguish and desperation are the traits of mind caused by extreme anxiety and helplessness. Anguish is extreme pain or misery indicating mental or physical torture. It can be agony that wreaths a person within. Desperation shows despair and hopelessness when a person is in distress or in extreme misery. These traits of mind — the psychological condition — has its roots in social and economic factors often related with poverty and social insecurity. This is an evitable outcome of untouchability in India where innumerable individuals and social groups were doomed to mental torture and physical devastation. Similar situation existed in the United States of America before slavery was constitutionally terminated. The Negros, as they were called during those days, the African-Americans of contemporary US, were tortured and compelled to lead lives of misery and wretchedness. When the free Negros began to write, they wrote mostly about their experiences as slaves, working on plantations and singing to themselves songs of sorrows and sufferings. These songs known as *blues* — form a part of Black culture in America. They are also important parts of the Jazz orchestra being performed everywhere in the world. In black literature, or literature of the blacks in America, better known as African-American literature today — alienation, anger, violence, protest, desperation, anguish, anxiety, deprivation —all prevail in abundance. Comparison between the African-American literature and Dalit literature in India always form an important aspect of literary discussions. The socio-economic condition of the blacks in America and those of the Dalits in India are more or less similar. The psychological set up of the two communities resemble to a large extent. Literature of the two communities, therefore, became a favourite topic of comparative study of literature in the academic circles of India and the US. The Indian Dalits are terribly angry with the religious authority for neglect and indifference — the Hindu code of conduct which does not allow the untouchables to breathe in free air; similarly, the blacks in America expressed their disapproval towards the Christian generosity which turns a blind eye towards racial atrocities against the blacks. Several militant black writers like Le Roi Jones, Malcolm X and others had repudiated Christianity and embraced Islam in protest and retaliation almost in the same manner in which Dr Ambedkar and his followers had quit Hinduism and embraced Buddha Dhamma. Comparative study of the two literary movements, therefore, is relevant and fruitful academically. The present study, however is concerned with and concentrates upon the movement of Dalit literature, and short story as a genre practised by three major Dalit writers.

B. Rangrao's ***Desperate Men and Women: Ten Dalit Short Stories from India*** is all about anguish and desperation of the Dalit community so effectively revealed through every short story in the book. The Dalit movement in Maharashtra, under leadership of Dr B. R. Ambedkar was so powerful and effective that it changed the original facet of the Marathi culture. The erstwhile Mahar, now the Buddhist, grew militant and aggressive and fought for their constitutional rights. Each one of them was well educated and aware of the constitutional provision laid down for the upliftment of the Scheduled Castes. They, therefore, fought bravely and achieved what was their due. This is reflected in their writings. Marathi Dalit literature is a manifestation of this militancy, and enlightenment simultaneously, something which is missing in Dalit literature in other Indian languages, even in Hindi and Gujarati which claim loyalty and affinity towards the Ambedkarite ideology. This, however, does not belittle creative efforts of the writers in these languages. They are effective and praiseworthy, nonetheless.

The short stories in ***Desperate Men and Women*** are a realistic presentation of the plight of the Dalits in India. The stories are set in different regions, yet, as the writer rightly points out — the nature of suffering of the untouchables has no agreeable difference. They toil and labour to build up the nation, and the nation neglects them wherever they are. The nature of suffering is the same – resulting out of religious tyranny and discriminatory arrogance. Poverty and perpetual want make them docile, meek, anxious and desperate. Some of them assert themselves over the situation and make a way out, some others perish. Rakhma in ***Childbirth***, for example, delivers a baby against all odds. She knows what a mother needs to do while the baby tumbles out into the world. There are no doctors, no nurses, no attendants — not even the traditional *dai* who attends childbirths in villages — the woman delivers the baby all alone, cuts the umbilical cord and goes out in search of food. The poor woman has nothing to eat. The writer has commented on irony of the situation — **"God has created hunger, but the creator has failed to produce means to pacify it."** She returns home with a handful of groundnuts, but collapses in a desperate attempt to reach towards her newborn child. Similar desperation is indicated in the case of Satya in ***Death of a Rich Man***, who falls down trying to catch hold of coins hurled across the dead body, and is trodden upon by the men in procession. Lakhan in ***Farewell*** defies the command of the village chief and takes his father's funeral procession through the same lane as his dead father would have liked. He is excommunicated. He takes on the punishment and leaves the village with a heavy heart. Lakhan's anguish, anxiety and desperation are written large on every page of the story. ***When the Sun God Refused to Set*** is perhaps, one of the best short stories in Indian languages. It reveals the psychological disturbance of an old man who has spent his entire life raising his children after the death of his wife when they were young. Love for his son and the memories of his wife who would have been happy to see her son comfortably settled, excite him to the extent of walking into his son's bedroom when he is alone with his wife. Dementia caused by socio-economic conditions which itself is the result of "graded social inequality" is effectively drawn by the author. Raghoba, as the old man is called, suffers from anxiety, anguish and desperation which are the result of social conditions prevailing in his life.

Revolt and rebellion are important traits of the Dalit movement. The erst-while untouchables have flouted social norms and are articulate in their social behaviour. In literature, this revolt is explicit, particularly in Marathi Dalit literature. Rangrao, who is an Ambedkarite social thinker and progressive writer, depicts revolutionary characters through his writings. This is true about the stories in ***Desperate Men and Women.*** Lakhan disregards the unjust command of the village chief, Baiju in

And Quiet Flowed The Purnamai is drawn into physical relationship with a high caste woman though he knows the repercussions. Wasudeo, the ex-soldier in ***Loneliness of An Ex-soldier*** initiates revolutionary activities in his native place drawing young boys into his scheme. The unnamed scavenger takes a mad woman home and places her comfortably against his parents' desire. Bhutya the graveyard keeper, buries his mother's dead body in a graveyard meant exclusively for the high caste men and women. Kulatha in ***Kulatha Rangan*** is an epitome of revolt and suffering who refuses to be concubine of a man who raped her and she leaves the village. She comes out into the darkness of night when Rangan drives her out of her house. Kulatha's stoicism and readiness to suffer for no fault of her raises her up to an adorable character. Her innocence, gullibility and readiness to face disastrous social situations are brought out remarkably well.

B. Rangrao's short stories, thus, are landmark of Dalit creative sensibility. These stories depict social discrimination and its effects on individual characters who suffer from anxiety, anger and desperation. In the words of a critic —

Due to the use of irony and subtle humour, the somewhat poetic descriptions and detailed picturisation, the reminiscing and commentary, the stories make Rangrao an author who should have found place in the critical discourse in English on Dalit literature. There are aberrations like stilted and unidiomatic use of language, but they are not obstructions to an enjoyable reading experience and the poignancy of stories touch an emotional nerve....

— (Shoma Sen in a paper presented in a literary meet held in London, 2015)

Baburao Bagul's ***When I Hid My Caste*** is a remarkable collection of short stories in Marathi. The stories are translated in English by Jerry Pinto who had brought out subtleties of the original tales and their literary significance. Bagul is considered as a literary stalwart in Marathi and is highly esteemed for his creative genius.

The stories in ***When I Hid My Caste*** were highly praised for a profound sense of social obligation on the part of the author, and his deep insight into issues like caste, poverty, prostitution, superstitions and meaningless religious rituals. Like rest of the Dalit writings, his short stories are also replete with psychological tension and disturbances exposing anxiety, anguish and desperation as major trait of the characters' personalities. Protest, anger, violence, distrust pervades his world, as the characters are driven mad by outer surroundings. Each of the short stories has something unique to show. In ***Prisoners of Darkness*** Deoram Deshmukh wants to take revenge against Banoo, his father's concubine who has come to stay in Deshmukh *wada*; now that his father is no more, he wants to kill her for maligning the Deshmukh clan. Banoo, who had loved and trusted Deoram's father while he was alive, now is wild with fear and runs out in the street yelling for help from the onlookers. Daulat, Banoo's son, who is terribly angry with his mother for her misdemeanour, comes forward to help her and kills Deoram Deshmukh. Violence pervades the story – so is anguish, anxiety and desperation. Damu Mahar in ***Bohada*** rebels against the village tradition and wants to play Narsimha instead of being a mute spectator. He does it with perfect skill and agility. The villagers cheer up Damu and praise his performance. As a result, the ***Bohada*** tradition was terminated by the village chief. Patil's envy and anger towards the well-meaning Damu Mahar, not because he is an accomplished performer, but because he is a Mahar by caste who proved his superiority, has what pinched the village-chief. Caste-prejudices, and a sense of caste honour is effectively depicted in the story. ***Streetwalker*** is a story of a prostitute Girija who is desperate to earn money enough to treat her sick son who is away in her native place. Desperation and anguish come out fully well towards the end of the story when the customer, after having satisfied his sexual urge, pushes Girija away and turns back without paying her dues. ***Gangster*** narrates the anxiety of a man who is feared by all because of his inhuman, beastly behaviour, but is keen to help out a woman who has requested him to help her out of financial need **"Does she love me?",** he keeps on repeating to himself and is taken aback at the realisation that the woman has no such feelings towards him; only a humane request as there is no one else who could come to her rescue. Anguish and desperation mark the story ***Competition*** between two poor women Yamuna and Chandra. Each one of them is anxious and desperate to win over the other in competition to sell bananas and earn more money. Yamuna, a woman from lower caste, ultimately accepts defeat and allow Chandra, the competitor, to go ahead with her business:

Chandra is my daughter-in-law. She is the daughter of the ruling class and the daughter-in-law of royalty. Am I supposed to make a prostitute of her with my own hands? No, good sirs, that is never going to happen. I am going to the village....as long as my hands work, I will try to make my son's world a better one. And if I die... I will go quietly... (88)

Pesuk, a tale narrated in an interesting style, depicts the plight of a woman, who is out to take revenge on her in-laws and her husband because they have tortured her mentally and physically — have cut off her nose and breasts — as she has a child from other man than her husband. She is her husband's seventh wife, the previous six have either been murdered or abandoned because the man did not have children from any one of them. In fact, he is impotent who had blamed his wives for his personal physical inability. Savitri, the protagonist in the story knows this and decides to have a child from other man. She is brutally punished. Now, she is out to penalise those who are responsible for her misery. She appears in the darkness of night and attacks those men trying to cut off their noses. When her husband dies, she frightens away the men in the funeral procession and jumps on her husband's burning pyre performing *sati.* The woman is appropriately called Savitri — the one who dies for the sake of her husband, even though he is impotent and tyrant. Her anguish and desperation is explicit throughout the narration. ***When I Hid My Caste*** is a popular short story of Baburao Bagul because of its caste implications. The Mahar protagonist, who has secured a job in the Indian Railways, has to hide his caste in order to get accommodation. He does not want to stay with his caste people as the local habits there do not suit this educated youth. He hires a house with a Brahmin family which appreciates his manners and cultured behaviour. The young man, however, is always anxious as to what will happen when his real caste becomes known. His anguish and desperation do not allow him to rest in peace. He is always tense and lost in nightmarish thinking. The inevitable happens. His caste is revealed and exposed through an event. Everybody is taken aghast. A Mahar staying with a Brahmin family! Everyone is stunned and everyone is angry bent on punishing the young man for his misadventure and misbehaviour. Luckily, he is saved by another Mahar youth who is ill-famous for rowdyism and unruly behaviour.

The story offers a bitter comment on the caste system which divides men from each other. It is 'caste' which operates everywhere and determines the fate of a man. It is the caste-system against which the entire Dalit sensibility revolts. Baburao Bagul has brought it out very effectively. His stories have an impact of a poem or a painting, vividly projecting the essence of the texts. His protagonists are dissatisfied with the tradition and revolt against it as in the case of Jai in ***Revolt***. Jai's revolt is beyond the onlookers' understanding because "they were all murdered long ago by Manu". Shanta Gokhale who wrote Introduction to ***When I Hid My Caste***, has this comment to offer:

Shankarrao Kharat and Annabhau Sathe, the other big names in the early Dalit fiction, were ten years older than Bagul. Some of their work had made a deep impact on readers. But it was nothing as compared to the veritable storm that Bagul's "Jevha Mi Jaat Chorli Hoti" created when it appeared in 1963. He knocked readers off their feet by the sheer elemental force of his stories. But more importantly, he liberated younger Dalit writers from the shackles of literary Marathi. They were now free to write in their own tongues......

Ratan Kumar Sambharia's ***Thunderstorm***, a collection of short stories in Hindi, offers yet another interesting reading of a less privileged community's sentiments. Sambharia is not an Ambedkarite, in a sense B. Rangrao and Baburao Bagul are — his characters do not revolt against the tradition, or rather, their quarrel, as in the case of Daryav in ***Thunderstorm***, is not for social cause, but for personal sense of justice and honour. His characters are equally anxious and desperate but their anxiety, anguish and desperation is the result of 'poverty', not caste. Phulwa is from a low caste, and has suffered much at the hands of *zamindar* Rameshwar's father. Her son is now a big police officer and has laid down all luxuries at his mother's feet. She now is in a position to make *zamindar* bow down to her. But there is not a word describing who had done it, or how this transformation took place. In the case of other characters, however, Panaram in ***Terms and Conditions*** there are references to his 'low' caste and Panaram's sense of retaliation is equally amazing. He wants the Mukhia's daughter to spend night with his son, because his honour was killed when the Mukhia's son has raped his daughter. Other characters like Mangla in ***The Buffalo***, the unnamed Character in ***The Old Woman***, Ker Singh in ***The Farmland***, Agani, the young girl in ***Bes*** etc. suffer from anxiety, anguish and desperation. However, their sufferings remain confined to their personal beings. It never becomes communal — or of the community they belong to. Nevertheless, it can be argued that these characters are from the oppressed community, therefore their anguish and desperation could be associated with their community as a whole.

Ratan Kumar Sambharia is deeply influenced by Premchand, the twentieth century Hindi novelist and short story writer. Almost all his stories carry this impression. He writes mostly about the poor individual caught in the midst of an economic crisis. They are always hopeful of their salvation, and come up victorious in most of the cases. They are strugglers, but the ones whose struggle is never wasted. Their courage and stoicism make them really memorable.

One can see the difference between the two writers from Maharashtra— B. Rangrao and Baburao Bagul — and the one from the Hindi belt — Jaipur in Rajasthan, in this context — Ratan Kumar Sambharia lacks the revolutionary spirit as a writer, the Ambedkarite sense of social transformation. He depicts the individual characters suffering and struggling against the social and economic odds, but never revolt, or their revolt remains confined to their personal self. B. Rangrao and Baburao Bagul, on the contrary, reveal a profound sense of rebellion — Wasudeo, the Ex-soldier in ***Loneliness of An Ex-solider***, the graveyard keeper in ***Confessions of a Gravedigger***, even Lakhan in ***Farewell*** defy social customs knowingly and suffer. Bagul's characters like Damu Mahar in ***Bohada***, Savitri in ***Pesuk***, and the unnamed protagonist in ***When I Hid My Caste*** suffer because of their caste. 'Caste' plays a pivotal role in the lives of the characters of these two writers, while Sambharia's characters are driven more by economic compulsions than by caste factors. Ratan Kumar's literary approach is Gandhian, whereas B. Rangrao and Baburao Bagul are Ambedkarite in their approach to literature.

It can be concluded, therefore, that anguish and desperation are the major traits of personality of the Dalit characters depicted by the three writers in their short stories. These traits are the outcome of hostile social circumstances— casteism and untouchability, in particular and poverty, ignorance, illiteracy in general. The characters drawn by B. Rangrao and Baburao Bagul revolt against the hostile circumstances — they want to annihilate the caste-system in order to create a new world based on liberty, equality and fraternity — a better place to live in. They are the hard-core Ambedkarite striving for social transformation depicting similar characters in their literary creation. Ratan Kumar Sambharia, however, lacks this revolutionary spirit as his characters struggle for personal salvation — not for social transformation. The characters created by all the three writers are victims and plagued by such mental traits like anxiety, anguish and desperation. The writers reveal Dalit sensibility while creating these characters and are representatives of Dalit literary movement in India.

Anguish and desperation which mark the personalities of these characters are, obviously, the outcome of several social issues like untouchability, poverty, ignorance, social insecurity etc. All the three writers under study have depicted these social issues and their impact on personalities of their protagonists fairly well. Thus, anguish and desperation felt and experienced by the protagonists in these short stories are the inevitable outcome of the social issues which are often hostile and detrimental to these individual characters.

Notes

Sen, Shoma. "The Choice of Writing in English: Short Stories of B. Rangrao and Narendra Jadhav's Outcaste".

Baburao Bagul, and Jerry Pinto. **When I Hid My Caste**. New Delhi, Speaking Tiger, 2018. (p. 88)

Baburao Bagul, and Jerry Pinto. **When I Hid My Caste**. New Delhi, Speaking Tiger, 2018. (Introduction, viii)

Bibliography

Primary Sources:

- B. Rangrao, **Desperate Men and Women : Ten Dalit Short Stories from India**. Delhi, Kalpaz Publications ; New Delhi, 2013.
- Baburao Bagul, (Tr.) Jerry Pinto. **When I Hid My Caste**. New Delhi, Speaking Tiger, 2018.
- Ratan Kumar Sambharia. **Thunderstorm**. Hachette India, 10 Dec. 2015.

Secondary Sources:

- Abraham, Joshil K, and Judith Misrahi-Barak. **Dalit Literatures in India**. Routledge, 24 July 2015.
- Ambedkar, B R. **The Untouchables: Who Were They and Why They Became Untouchables?** Delhi, Kalpaz, New Delhi, India, 2017.
- Anand Teltumbde. **Dalits**. Routledge Chapman & Hall, 2019.
- Bhongle, Rangrao. **Saviour of the Nation: Dr B.R. Ambedkar and India Today.**
- Brueck, Laura R. **Writing Resistance.** Columbia University Press, 10 June 2014.
- Chandrakant Mhatre. **One Hundred Poems of Chokha Mela**. CreateSpace, 2015.
- Chinnaiah Jangam. **Dalits and the Making of Modern India**. New Delhi, Oxford University Press, 2017.
- **Dalit Sahitya Part 1** Sankalpana ani Swaroop (MA Part II).
- Dalit Short Story: A Study of Three Writers in India 297.
- Ingale, Dr Malti. **Baburao Bagul: Vyakti ani Vangmay**. Devyani Prakashan.
- Raj Kumar. **Dalit Literature and Criticism**. Hyderabad, Telangana, India, Orient Blackswan, 2019.
- Rāmacandra Kshīrasāgara. **Dalit Movement in India and Its Leaders, 1857-1956**. M.D. Publications Pvt. Ltd., 1994.
- Sarah Beth Hunt. **Hindi Dalit Literature and the Politics of Representation.** Routledge, 7 Aug. 2014.
- Śara akumār Limbāe. **Towards an Aesthetic of Dalit Literature**.
- Singh, Bijender. **Indian Dalit Literature**. Authors Press, 2015.
- Singhal, Deshraj. "Ratnakumar Sambhariya Ka Katha Sahitya_srijanKeVividhAayam." Handle.net, 2015, hdl.handle.net/10603/312506, http://hdl.handle.net/10603/312506.

- Snehlata. "Ratnakumar Sambhariya Ke Sahitya Mein Samajik Chetna." Handle.net, 2019, hdl.handle.net/10603/303803, http://hdl.handle.net/10603/303803.
- Yashica Dutt. **Coming out as Dalit**. Aleph Book Company, 2019.